SPLENDID POSEUR

"With Walt Whitman in Camden," by Horace Traubel

THIS IS THE PHOTOGRAPH JOAQUIN MILLER SENT TO
WALT WHITMAN FROM PARIS.

Splendid Poseur

JOAQUIN MILLER—AMERICAN POET

By

M. M. MARBERRY

THOMAS Y. CROWELL COMPANY

NEW YORK

Copyright 1953 by M. M. Marberry

Manufactured in the United States of America
by the Vail-Ballou Press, Inc., Binghamton, New York.

Library of Congress Catalog Card No. 53-8435

For

SIBYL AND STEWART HOLBROOK

Personal Acknowledgments

To William Poole and Lois Cole, of Thomas Y. Crowell Company: for editorial wisdom.

To Joseph S. Rambo, of Norristown, Pa.; John D. Morse and John Gardner, of New York; Lawrence A. Fitzgerald, of Chicago; Oland Russell, of Washington, D.C.; William Beale, of Boston; Eddy Shoaff, of Los Angeles; William Stegmeier, of Tamaqua, Pa., and Robert B. Marberry, of San Diego: for help in research, for advice and encouragement.

To many librarians, and particularly those of the New York Public Library—our always gracious and great public servants.

And, most of all, to Therese Pol: for her guidance, suggestions and labors over the manuscript.

Contents

Wagon Pointed West
1837-1854

I

"My cradle was a covered wagon, pointed West."

THIS was Joaquin Miller's proud poetic boast. Lyrically, the phrase has a splendid ring, but factually it is quite untrue. The covered wagon Joaquin Miller remembered so fondly came later, considerably later, when at the age of fourteen he rode West in one. The testimony of Joaquin's mother as to the exact location of his birth cannot be believed, either. By the time she had reached her nineties she suddenly conceived the notion that her then famous son had been born in a manger, but to Joaquin's credit it must be stated that he seldom claimed for himself such a hallowed place of birth. The fact of the matter is that Joaquin Miller, like most people of his day, was born at home, in bed.

Joaquin (the name he eventually adopted, pronounced wah'-keen) always was a little hazy when it came to the facts of his life. For example, he liked to recall that he was born, in that covered wagon, in Millersville, Indiana. This town, he said, had been named by a grateful frontier citizenry in honor of his father, an Indian scout so heroic that Daniel Boone jealously cursed his fame. Joaquin also remembered that he was born on November 10, either in the year 1841 or 1842 (the confusion came about, he explained, because his mother insisted it was 1842 while his father thought it was 1841), and was christened Cincinnatus Heine Miller.

Unfortunately, all of these basic facts as set down by Joaquin are what may be charitably described as extensions of the truth.

There is a Millersville in Indiana, but it was not named after his father. Joaquin was born some seventy miles distant, on a farm two and one-half miles outside Liberty, a hamlet in northeastern Indiana close by the Ohio state line.

Far from being an intrepid Indian scout, Joaquin's father was a prosaic schoolteacher and farmer, and a Quaker, to boot, who never in his life fired a gun. What is more, father Miller was in knee pants when Daniel Boone went to his grave.

Joaquin was born neither in 1841 nor in 1842. For many years the 1841 date was accepted, but recently students of his career decided that the date was 1839. Actually, Joaquin was born on September 8, 1837. That he had managed to subtract not two but four or five years from his age came to light a few years ago with the publication of his secret *California Diary* which had been suppressed for a quarter of a century after his death. There is a sound explanation for Joaquin's insistence on the birth years of 1841 or 1842, one that will be accepted sympathetically (though why he preferred the month of November to September we shall never know). Joaquin was thirty-three when he became a Poet. Reasoning that he was far too elderly to be received by public and critics as a new lyrical genius, he chopped five years off his age and said he was twenty-eight, for while a budding Poet in his twenties is a symbol of hope and promise, a struggling beginner in his thirties is not. Even as an old man,

Joaquin would casually subtract ten and even twenty years from his age.

Joaquin Miller may have fooled his biographers about his age (for after all there were no birth records kept in Indiana at the time, and when he explained that the family Bible containing the proper date had been lost, his word was taken), but it is doubtful if he fooled many of his friends. "That rascal is much older than I am," Ambrose Bierce, who was born in 1842, guessed correctly. But it is all the more puzzling that none of the chroniclers of Joaquin's life noticed the age of one of his brothers. If Joaquin actually had been born when he claimed, then his mother was a most unusual woman, capable of a prodigious feat, for she gave birth to another son five months before November 10, 1841, the date he gave most frequently for his own birth.

The baby born in 1837 was named Cincinnatus Hiner (not Heine) Miller. Joaquin said he was named Cincinnatus in honor of the Roman statesman, while in fact he received this name solely because his father was a native of Cincinnati, Ohio. Joaquin always asserted that his parents had bestowed on him the middle name of Heine because at his birth they astutely sensed that someday he would possess the lyrical gifts of the great German poet. In reality, Joaquin borrowed the *Heine* in signing his first two works; he owed the *Hiner* to an obscure doctor by that name who attended him at birth.

It is a matter of record, however, that Joaquin at no time in his life ever questioned the fact that his last name was Miller.

2

As far as can be ascertained, Joaquin was not, as he thought, a descendant of Pocahontas, but he *was* a fourth-generation son of American pioneers on both sides of his family. Joaquin said his grandfather, Colonel Robert Miller, died fighting in the Revolution. It could be that such a Colonel Miller was his great-grandfather; but we know that his grandfather, a man of Scotch descent, was killed during the War of 1812 in the massacre at Fort Meigs by Tecumseh's Indians, leaving a wife and fifteen children. One son, Hulings, born in 1811, was Joaquin Miller's father.

Joaquin's mother was born Margaret De Witt, the member of a fairly wealthy family of Dutch origin. Miss De Witt, who was known far and wide for owning six silk dresses—a sensational trousseau for a pioneer bride—was nineteen in 1835 when she married Hulings Miller. The De Witt family did not consider it a good match. Hulings had had a smattering of education at Miami University in Ohio, something unusual on the raw frontier, but he had no money and it was suspected that he would not prove a "good provider." The suspicions of the De Witts were correct; nevertheless Margaret and Hulings Miller were a happily married couple and raised five children. Joaquin was the next eldest. There were three brothers, John De Witt, George Melvin, James Henry Blair, and a sister, Ella.

After two futile years in Liberty, Hulings gave up his attempts to work the land with any prospect of success, and the sheriff took over the farm. (It undoubtedly would gratify Joaquin, if he could only know it, that today, more than a century after his birth, a Joaquin Miller road runs past the farm, and that a bronze tablet has been erected there to his memory.) Father Miller obtained a job as country schoolteacher in nearby Randolph county. He settled as a squatter and neighbors helped him erect his new home, a rough-hewn, one-room log cabin with a fireplace and a hard earthen floor.

There, near the banks of the Mississinewa River, Joaquin lived as a boy.

On the eve of his life, Joaquin recalled his earliest memory: Being in a wagon stalled in a swollen stream and Pap, as he always called his father, wading in water up to his waist, carrying his family to the shore one by one. There were other nostalgic scenes he remembered: Peering through the cabin window panes of greased paper and seeing a great bonfire, watching his mother and father dip colored candles by mixing dried berry juice with the hot tallow . . . His father coming home late at night, chased by wolves, while his mother frightened off the pack by brandishing a torch . . . Pap reading to him about the explorations of Captain Frémont, a man who was to become Joaquin's idol ("I never grew so fast in my life," Joaquin said, as when he listened to Frémont's feats) . . . His ecstatic delight when his teacher-father taught him to write with the old-fashioned goose quill of the frontier (Joaquin insisted on using a quill on into the twentieth century) . . . Memorizing Heine's "Du bist wie eine Blume" and "Die Lorelei," although this recollection is probably faulty, for in after years Joaquin knew no German.

And seventy years later, in a letter to an Indiana editor, the aged Joaquin would lovingly recall the golden memories of a carefree boy of six called "Nat"—shuffling down the old dusty corduroy road in moccasins, with pants rolled to the knees, pockets stuffed with doughnuts, armed with a bow and arrow, the points being fashioned from one of Pap's barrel hoops by Indians at the nearby Miami reservation, and fishing with Chief Shingle-ma-see (more correctly known as Meshingomesia), who showed him where the big fish lurked in the Mississinewa.

Above all Joaquin the boy remembered how hard his Pap

worked, scrabbling together every extra dime he could get by teaching at the Pipe Creek school, by selling maple sugar and chickens, and by working at a mill for fifty cents a night, all for the sake of saving a stake to take his family to Oregon Territory. Pap Miller's dream was to homestead there on the six hundred and forty acres of virgin soil, offered by Congress, that was theirs for the asking, providing they could get there. Pap Miller caught the "Oregon fever" as early as 1842, but ten years were to pass before he took his family across the great plains.

Father Miller as the best educated man in the settlement was elected Justice of the Peace—a suitably named post for a Quaker—which meant an increase in his income, for whenever he presided at weddings he was given a coonskin, or a bag of corn, or sometimes hard cash. The prestige of his office also enabled him to put aside a considerable sum of money. This happened when a pack of wolves attacked and destroyed all his sheep. Pap Miller was resigned to the loss, but an Indian trader friend, one Hugh McCulloch, pointed out to him that possibly the wolves were not wolves, but Indian dogs. Pap thought a long time and finally he remembered that they were indeed Indian dogs, and so the two presented this dastardly case of animal mayhem to Chief Meshingomesia.

It is not known what methods of persuasion were used, but eventually the Chief surrendered and gave Pap Miller a bag of gold coins in recompense for the damage done by the wild dogs of his Indians. This shrewd if unscrupulous deal enabled the Millers to pay their debts and move a little farther west, to Grant County in Indiana. We do not know whether McCulloch was rewarded for his services, but Hulings Miller got at least $200 on the transaction because that is the amount he paid, cash on the barrelhead, for a farm of one hundred and sixty acres.

Taking advantage of rising prices, Pap Miller sold sixty acres for $150 in 1848 and the remaining one hundred acres for $1,000 the following year, making a clear profit of $950 —one of the countless examples of American civilization forging ahead on the back of the Indians, for thanks to them the Millers now had enough money to get to Oregon. However, reports of the terrible Whitman massacre reached the Midwest and slowed down all emigration to the northwest territory.

In 1849 the whole nation, including the Millers, was electrified by the news from California. As Joaquin described it:

A tall dark man in buckskins came where Pap and I were splitting rails, and setting the butt of his long rifle heavily on the ground and throwing his right fist away toward the West with a sweep, shouted out: "Gold! Gold! Gold! Squire, they have found gold by the wagon load in Californy. The ground is full of gold in Californy, an' I'm goin' to Californy."

Pap Miller decided to leave early the following year for Oregon, where probably there was gold too, just as in Californy, but two more years were to pass before the trip got under way. It may be that Pap Miller tarried to add further to his savings, or perhaps the mother and father were ailing (for Joaquin tells us that he and his brothers harvested a crop of corn and drove it to the market because the parents were down with Indian ague, meaning malaria); in any event it was not until St. Patrick's Day, March 17, 1852, that the Millers pulled stakes and, like so many a pioneer family, faced West.

3

The Millers did not cross the plains on a shoestring, as had so many settlers before them. Theirs was a large party of nine people, fully equipped and accompanied by a herd of sixteen oxen and at least four horses. Pap Miller hired two teamsters to drive two covered wagons, each drawn by a yoke of eight oxen. Mother Miller and her small daughter rode in a carriage hitched to two horses, the father rode a saddle horse, and the boys took turns in sharing another horse.

The trip across Indiana and Illinois and on to the jumping-off place in Missouri, the tented city of St. Joseph, took two months. On May 15 the party crossed the Missouri, the river that Joaquin fifty years later would so aptly describe in the title of a poem as "Mad Molder of the Continent." Undoubtedly their hearts were buoyant as they started their trek, but a grueling march was ahead of them, for seven months were to pass before their wagons, traveling at two miles an hour, reached Oregon.

"The sundown seas were before us," Joaquin recorded, and he added, rather obscurely: "Civilization, such as we had known, and all sorts, lay before us." He made a point of mentioning that every member of the Miller expedition was fearless: "There could be no turning back. We were not of that material." Joaquin in later years liked to remember how he had courageously shepherded the family over the Wild West plains, bludgeoning his way through tribes of hostile Indians and personally shooting or riding down all Redmen in his path. This is doubtful, as he was only fourteen at the time (or nine, by his own age calculations); and yet he undoubtedly did have adventures rarely encountered by an American teen-age boy.

The Millers did not fight their way alone across the prairies. They were just another party of a huge caravan. The route headed northwest from St. Joseph to the Platte River, and there for the first time Joaquin saw some Plains Indians, mounted on mustangs. "Very decent, tall, fine fellows," he noted. The party followed the winding course of the Platte in what today is Nebraska, for they were now on the Oregon Trail.

The Oregon Trail was not particularly inspiring to the emigrant of 1852. Many covered wagons were returning, driven by survivors of the cholera epidemic which was raging at the time, and the sides of the rutted road were lined with bleached skeletons and graves—an ominous warning to the pioneers. The wagons inched along, making thirty miles in a good sixteen-hour day, following the Platte to Scotts Bluff and on to Fort Laramie, with rain and mud and dust and storms and cyclones slowing their pace. And yet this was the easy part of the journey, for ahead were the exhausting labors of ferrying across rivers, scaling mountains, braking down steep slopes, crossing the monotonous black lava plains, the sagebrush flats and pitiless deserts.

Leaving Laramie the caravan threaded its way through the foothills of the Rockies, passed Independence and Devil's Slide, then plodded alongside the Sweetwater River up to the threshold of South Pass. There, at the only gateway to California and Oregon open to heavy vehicles, one of the Miller wagons was sold. With additional oxen freed for the job, the remaining wagon was easily drawn over the summit. The Trail now led across the Green River and on to Sublett's

Cutoff. A turn slightly north, and the pioneer was on his way to Oregon, but the Millers decided to separate from the caravan and go southward to Salt Lake City, where Pap wanted to rest the animals and sell excess baggage.

Shortly afterwards there occurred what Joaquin always referred to as the Bloody Battle of Sublett's Cutoff. This is an engagement for which the reader will search in vain in the history books. The only information about this mysterious action stems from Joaquin alone, and he gave two versions—conflicting versions—of the fracas. The account as told to and recorded by his contemporaries was that Indians ambushed the Miller party. All seemed lost when, screaming encouragement to the defenders, the boy Joaquin snatched a rifle from his father's hands (Pap was a Quaker and refused to fire a gun, but evidently he had no scruples against carrying one) and got down to the business at hand. Joaquin fired three shots. The first pierced the forehead of the Chief, the second went smack dab through the eye of an Indian (the left eye), and the third surely hit its mark, the heart. Lo! the noble Redmen fled.

Joaquin's second version is a droll, and more believable, description of the supposed skirmish:

> I got behind a wagon with my gun and drew bead upon the nearest Indians, but as usual found there was no flint in the lock of my gun. The boys afterwards said that while I had no flint I had plenty of sand—that even the barrel of my gun was full of it.

The Millers continued on to Fort Bridger, crossed the uncharted Wasatch Mountains and rode into Salt Lake City, their journey more than half completed. Pap sold to Mormon traders eight of the oxen, two horses, the carriage and part of their equipment for a nice profit. It is quite possible that, during the stay in Salt Lake City, young Joaquin carefully observed Mormon habits and mores, for a quarter-century later he was to write a play about the people there, a play that was a tremendous success in every state of the Union except Utah.

The trek was resumed in mid-summer, the party heading north to Soda Springs in Idaho and going on to Fort Hall (the present Pocatello), at the headwaters of the Snake River. Joaquin has described a tense scene he witnessed there. An Indian Chief approached one Mr. Wagoner and asked the sales price of his beautiful white daughter. Wagoner jocosely replied that the price was ten spotted ponies such as the Chief was riding. The Chief soon returned leading the ten ponies. The horrified father declared that the "bargain" was a joke. The Chief and his retinue started brandishing their weapons. The Indian pointed out he had acted in good faith and the majority of the alarmed whites agreed. Pap Miller, as a one-time Justice of the Peace, was selected to marry the couple. And then, according to Joaquin, the terror-stricken daughter tried to throw herself from a cliff into the river. This conduct on the part of a bride-to-be for some reason displeased the Chief. He stalked off, scorning presents from white men who would not keep their word.

This dramatic interlude may well have happened in Joaquin's presence. It happened sometime, somewhere, as students of early Western history know only too well.

The Millers followed the sinuous Snake through a desolate country, devoid of game, filled with sunken canyons, lava flats, sagebrush and desert, making rafts to cross the seemingly innumerable streams, until they came to Fort Boise. But they stayed only overnight, for now, close to their goal, they were anxious to reach Oregon. They left the Snake and struck out cross-country, driving themselves relentlessly until at last, on September 26, 1852, they touched the soil of Oregon—"The Land of Man-Sized Men." They then pushed on to skirt the Blue Mountains and to reach the mighty Columbia River. From there it was an easy trip downstream to the military post of The Dalles. The distance from Fort Hall to The Dalles had been mastered in fast time—forty days.

The Miller pioneers were now confronted with the last leg of their journey—a short sixty miles to the mouth of the Willamette River. The routes numbered two and both were perilous. Pap Miller was undecided whether to attempt to float down the turbulent Columbia in a scow or raft, or to scale the steep Cascade Range.

It was then, as Joaquin later remembered, that luckily he was able to be of supreme assistance to his family, solely because of a casual friendship he made at The Dalles. This was a story he never forgot.

It seems that the young Joaquin met a thirty-year-old Army Captain at the post. This man took a wonderful fancy to Joaquin after he had patiently shown him how to bait a hook while fishing for salmon. The Captain was so grateful that he advised the Millers not to try the water route but to hire additional oxen to pull them over the Cascade Range. The kindly Captain insisted on loaning them the animals himself, and furthermore he furnished a military escort for the trip. It is not clear whether this escort was to ensure the return of the oxen, or merely to act as guides and guards.

This tale which Joaquin loved to tell at the slightest provocation always ended in a startling climax. "The Captain's name," Joaquin would intone impressively, "was Grant . . . Captain Grant . . . Captain U. S. Grant."

In 1876, twenty-four years after the chance meeting of these two kindred souls, Joaquin apparently encountered Grant for the second time, at a Presidential reception in the White House. As Joaquin remembered it:

> I took his hand and said, "I met you once, General." Quick as a flash he replied, "I remember you. It was in Oregon. You showed me how to put worms on my hook!"

This story, which Joaquin told so convincingly and so often, is an interesting anecdote, but its historical value is spoiled by an important fact. The emigrant Millers reached The Dalles around the first of October, 1852, while Army archives show that Grant at that time was sailing in the Pacific with his regiment, nearing the port of San Francisco.

4

The Millers and the oxen of "Captain U. S. Grant" reached the mountain pass of the Cascade Range. Below them spread the lush valley land of the Willamette, lying snug between the Cascades and the Coastal Range. Hardened by the journey, Joaquin had grown into a handsome lad just fifteen, with curly yellow hair. He stood nearly six feet, a brawny 170-pounder and broad-shouldered. Joaquin was an authentic pioneer, a real first son of Oregon, which was then a territory with 15,000 scattered inhabitants, a place wild and unsettled which would not acquire statehood until seven years later. Joaquin, who at a future date was to celebrate the arrival of the Millers in the Promised Land, wrote in rather unsteady meter and rhythm:

Full seven months and then
Mount Hood hung white and vast.
We left in March, our hopes proved true:
Three thousand miles to Oregon
Were ended in October, 1852.

Pap left his wife and children under the care of Reverend
E. E. Parish, a Methodist missionary who lived in the heart
of the fertile Willamette Valley. Had Miller Senior stayed
there, life would have been easier, but instead he filed for his
homestead land near Willamette Forks, in Lane County, getting a grant of three hundred and twenty, not six hundred
and forty acres. "The law had been meanly changed while
we were en route," Joaquin indignantly noted. We have
Joaquin's word for it that "My father had to build a fence to
keep the salmon off the pasture grass," and this may have been
so, but the three hundred and twenty acres he selected turned
out to be the worst farming land for miles around, and soon
he was forced to supplement his income by teaching school.
We may gather an idea as to the low value of this land from
the fact that a few years later Pap bought an adjoining three
hundred acres—for thirty-three cents an acre. The name
Oregon is believed to have been derived from an Indian word
meaning "a place of plenty," and so it was—in spots—but
Pap unfortunately picked the wrong spot.

"We were used to woods, and wanted to get near them"
—this was the reason Joaquin gave for his father's poor judgment. The farm was in a remote district outside Coburg. The
roads were straggly ruts, there were no bridges and few
ferries across the streams, and the nearest neighbors were
forty miles away. Yet these neighbors came to a cabin-raising.
Then the Millers set industriously to work. The land was
cleared, rails were split, an orchard and vineyard planted,

cloth was spun from flax and wool, butter was churned, there was the threshing and grinding of flour, until, as Mother Miller declared: "I tell you, boys, things are a-humming!" Poor land or not, Joaquin reveled in the picturesque setting of his new home. The cabin was set on a high and grassy hill —today it is called "Sunny Ridge"—while nearby the "swift, sweet river glistened under the great cedars and balm trees." The area abounded in grouse, quail and pheasant, while behind the cabin loomed the mountains with their giant firs and scrub pines, and it was here that Joaquin acquired his life-long love for trees.

In 1853, a year after he had arrived in Oregon, Joaquin met a man who was to influence his life, who was to send him out into the world. He was known as "Mountain Joe," a former Frémont guide who ran a packtrain all the way from Mexico to Oregon and so knew everyone and had all the latest news. "Mountain Joe" was Joseph de Bloney who claimed that he was descended from a prominent Swiss family who had sent him to study in Heidelberg, but that he had quit because he wanted to go West and fight the Indians. "He was a remarkable man in many ways, of good culture and family," wrote Joaquin, who was to introduce "Mountain Joe" into many of his books, "though a sad drunkard."

Farm life was monotonous, and Joaquin was overworked; so when "Mountain Joe" told him about the new gold fields opening in California, where gold dust was sprinkled around like snowflakes on Mount Hood, where a person could pry fat nuggets from the earth with his fingers, his imagination was fired. Joaquin decided to run away to California, never to return unless as a rich man who could shower presents on his family. But he kept postponing his departure. Then one day he and a boy named Will Willoughby were rolling boulders off a cliff and one of the rocks ran down a cow. Flight seemed the best solution. The getaway was made late at night. Pap Miller waited a day for his son, and then took off in pursuit on horseback. He overtook the two runaways at Jacksonville, Oregon. Joaquin refused to come home unless his Pap promised him that after working a year on the farm he would be permitted to leave. Father Miller agreed.

And, on October 23, 1854, shortly after his seventeenth birthday, he left the family farm, confident that both fame and fortune awaited him in the California gold fields.

CHAPTER TWO

California Myth-Maker
1854-1859

I

THERE are many stories concerning Joaquin Miller's first descent on California. Most of the accounts (which eventually grew into legends) were fostered by Joaquin himself, printed as gospel truth in his books, and in this guise made their way into serious scholarly studies as facts. Some of the stories were told in conversation with friends, who recorded and sometimes elaborated on them by the time they reached print. And, as has happened in similar instances in American history, other feats were later credited to him solely because he had become famous and at one time happened to live in the Shasta neighborhood in California. These manufactured yarns were accepted by Joaquin as an integral part of his life and times.

In Joaquin's lifetime some of his California exploits were received with a certain reserve and even with mild skepticism, but it was not proven until fairly recently that what Joaquin liked to call his five "decisive achievements" during his first visit to California were all inventions. The five fables were:

He was grievously wounded at the battle of Castle Crags when he fought so heroically against the Indians.

He traveled extensively to Nevada and Arizona and down into Mexico, and on these jaunts picked up the

Western lore that he later used to so enrich American literature.

He served under his beloved leader, General William Walker the Freebooter, in the Nicaraguan filibuster.

He established a Utopian Indian Republic on majestic Mount Shasta, monarch of the Sierra de Nevada range.

He had such pronounced sympathies for the down-trodden Indians that the whites branded him a renegade and ran him out of California.

Many people may have failed to doubt these mighty achievements because they were too preoccupied wondering about Joaquin's extreme youth. As an over-curious (and per-haps under-courteous) guest once remarked to him, "How could you at the age of twelve or thirteen accomplish these deeds?" Joaquin's reply, "I was old for my years," was re-garded as a lame and even evasive answer. It was more or less taken for granted that he lied about his age, but this seems to have had little bearing on the credibility of his tales. Some-times, when a person lies twice, one falsehood will be de-tected, while the other goes unnoticed; and this may have been the case here, though of course this is mere speculation.

Even if each of the five "achievements" were myths, Joa-quin did have enough genuine adventures as a teen-age boy in California to satisfy the most avid listener and reader, yet he seemed to be under a compulsion to dismiss his real experi-ences and build up the myths. For example, Joaquin was not in the battle of Castle Crags, as will be shown, but he did participate in other fights against the Indians and performed bravely—yet seldom could he be persuaded to discuss these actual experiences.

Thanks to the discovery of the diary he kept at the time, we know today more or less what Joaquin did do, and we know without question what he could *not* have done, during his three-year sojourn in California from November, 1854 to November, 1857. The existence of such a journal first was made known in 1912 when Joaquin's sister-in-law in Oregon sent a batch of dog-eared notebooks to Ina Coolbrith, a San Francisco writer and friend of Joaquin's, with the following letter: "The old manuscript goes to you by express today. Joaquin commanded me to burn it. If when you have looked it through, you think it should be burned, please order the cremation ceremony. One thing I am sure you will agree with me—it is not fitting that others should see it."

The predicament of the Miller family was this: the diary disclosed that, far from being the swaggering bravo who reveled in the derring-do that had been accepted for a half century as a *fait accompli*, Joaquin had been a homesick, insecure, immature youth who failed as a miner and, unable to bear up under the hardships of a white civilization, took an Indian woman, became a "squaw-man" and lived the easy life of an aborigine. Also, the diary on three occasions revealed his birthdate to be September 8, 1837, and not November 10, 1841 or 1842. The family rightly feared that such a publication might harm their darling's reputation, because the public would not forgive him for a wholesale stretching-of-the-truth.

In 1916 Joaquin's surviving brother wrote Ina Coolbrith asking for the return of the diary, as the Oregon Historical Society wished to examine it, but she refused. The journal later fell into the hands of a private collector, and it was not until 1936 that the manuscript, so ably edited by John S. Richards, was published in Seattle in a limited edition.

Joaquin's five "achievements" will be considered here individually. The one he related most often, in print and in conversation and in public lectures, concerned his splendid conduct in the battle of Castle Crags. The hostile Indians were intrenched in a seemingly impregnable position on a mountain peak, but, not dismayed, Joaquin unlimbered his rifle, checked his pistols, loosened his Bowie knife, stuffed his mouth full of extra bullets, and then courageously led the charge that was to carry the day and save white civilization from being destroyed by Indians.

But, according to Joaquin, he paid for his valor. "An arrow had struck the left side of my face, knocked out two teeth, and had forced its point through at the back of my neck," he wrote. From another account we learn that his faithful friend "Mountain Joe" "wrapped a blanket about me to catch stray arrows," a stratagem peculiar enough to intrigue any military man. Joaquin also reported, in a third version of the fight, that "Arrows were coming whiz, whistle, thud, right in our faces, too! I fell senseless."

His comrades-in-arms were quite worried. "If it touched his jugular vein he is done for, poor boy," one pal muttered, and Joaquin overheard the words before he swooned away.

"There was no surgeon," Joaquin continued in still another account. "The men tied up our wounds the best they could with saliva and tobacco-juice. My mind and energy both seemed to give way then. I have but a shadowy recollection of what passed during the next few months."

It is apparent today, now that his California diary has been unearthed, that Joaquin had an obsession about being wounded in the neck by an Indian arrow. The diary contains the draft of a letter he wrote to a school chum in Oregon. This letter, dated November 20, 1856, describes a fight he allegedly had had in 1855 with some Indians at Devil's

Castle after they had "stollen" his horse. There appeared the same turn of phrase: ". . . an arrow struck me fore on the left side and came out my neck." And, though his secret diary makes it clear that he was in perfect health at the time of the non-existent fight, the letter goes on—with Joaquin's supreme disregard for spelling and punctuation—to describe the gory details:

> it was an awful wound and I thought I would die   Ah it was a terrible thing   Ed   to lay there among the dead and dieing of both friends and enemys   What wild and dreadful thoughts crowded through my mind   But thank God I have recovered

Joaquin's attempt to impress a teen-age classmate is understandable. In later life he would declare that his reason for growing the beard that was to be his trademark was to hide the ugly scar on his neck from the wound received at Castle Crags—and yet he did not grow the beard until years later. At other times Joaquin explained that his poor handwriting was due to the poisoned arrow that had pierced his right wrist.

Now, there *was* a battle of Castle Crags and it was fought against the Modoc Indians on June 15, 1855. All residents of the area and all those who fought in the battle scoffed at the idea that Joaquin had been there, and there is no word in his diary to indicate that he knew such an engagement took place. Nonetheless, this was the start of the legend of Joaquin Miller the Indian Fighter.

As for the many excursions into Arizona and Mexico, when Joaquin supposedly sat by the camp fire and studied Latin and listened to the stories of vaqueros and outlaws ("Once when riding over the mountains of Durango, North

Mexico, I was overtaken by a band of robbers . . ." etc.),
the diary clearly shows that he did not leave the Shasta region in California except for a three-week visit to Oregon.

Joaquin's participation in the Nicaragua filibuster which
he so glorified in poetry and prose ("I loved the scenery and
hated the fighting.") was the result of his meeting Colonel
James Vaughn Thomas, the way Joaquin recalled it. Thomas,
an adventurer, whom Joaquin was to introduce into his books
under the sobriquet of "The Prince," is supposed to have persuaded him to join the expedition. One of Joaquin's more
cautious biographers once wrote: "He took less part in
Walker's campaigns than is generally supposed." This is true.
The *California Diary* shows that he did consider joining the
filibuster, provided he was paid enough, but, as the entry
reads:

> Fri. the 21st of December   Went to Horsetown 4 miles
> distant to learn what the chance was to enlist in the Ni-
> quaragua expedition   found terms not very flattering and
> did not enlist

Joaquin insisted all his life that he was wounded at Castle
Crags, but toward the end of his career he did concede that
he had never fought in the filibuster. "I told it so often I
finally believed it," he candidly admitted.

Joaquin as the founder of a Utopian Indian Republic was
a tale that never failed to arouse his listeners. The plan, Joaquin said, was to rescue the noble Red Man from the cor-
roding impact of white civilization. Mount Shasta was made
sacred to the Indians, and all others were barred, excepting
Joaquin. The tribes lived happily in their sanctuary in a communistic sort of way, with Joaquin officiating as the Great
White Father. What happened to the project was never ex-

plained. This is another instance where Joaquin's memory completely failed him. There is no mention of such a Utopia in the diary, and no one in the Shasta neighborhood ever heard of the scheme.

As for the fifth and last "achievement," here Joaquin deliberately sought to bring disrepute upon his own name. For reasons best known to himself, he insisted he had sided with the Indians after they had massacred the whites at Pit River, and as a result was branded a renegade and run out of the state. This is indeed a curious misrepresentation of the facts. Actually, he fought against the Indians, and with the whites after the Pit River massacre, as Army records show. Joaquin's distortion of this episode is hard to understand and can only be explained in terms of the personal guilt he felt toward the Indians. While later in life he posed as their protector, there was an interlude here that he was none too proud of, when, as will be told, he sired an Indian daughter and deserted her. Perhaps he preferred to appear as a traitor to his own race rather than to his own child, who must have been on his conscience—for Joaquin Miller did have a conscience.

2

All "achievements" aside, Joaquin invaded California as a boy just seventeen. On his way to the gold fields he paused at Klamath River in southern Oregon to cook for a party of miners, for he had no money, and because he insisted on eating his own food he came down with the scurvy. He crossed the California border into Siskiyou county, where he was treated and cured by a Dr. Ream of Yreka. He then went to Upper Soda Springs, in the midst of the Shasta mines, and secured another job as cook. It is to be presumed he was more careful there when it came to eating his own cooking.

The pay was $50 a month and the work exhausting. He rose at three o'clock every morning and was not through cleaning up the dishes until nine at night. "I cooked all winter for twenty-seven men," Joaquin remarked, "and every man was alive in the spring." He once called a miner from his bed at four o'clock in the morning. "I never get up until breakfast is ready," the man snarled. "But you must get up," the cook replied, "because you are sleeping on the tablecloth."

Joaquin the raw kid was not taken seriously. He was known in the settlement as "Crazy Miller," for even at the age of seventeen he showed signs of eccentricity, and it was suspected that he wrote poetry when no one was around the kitchen. Joaquin always remembered how lonely he was, and how every morning before he sliced the bacon he would cut a notch on the wooden table lest he forget what day of the month it was. But, because he was observant, there came the chance to graduate from cook to miner. Joaquin was to describe this incident in a number of ways; his humorous version is presented here. It seems that the youthful cook noticed a certain "Long Dan" (so nicknamed because his name was Daniel Long) emptying gold dust from his shoes into a chamois bag, and he informed on the man. In the diggings the automatic penalty for a "sluice robber" was death by hanging. "Long Dan" was forced to dig his own grave. The rope was slung and then, according to Joaquin, it was suggested that the thief be condemned to a worse fate: to eat one of Joaquin's dinners. Subsequently an even more hideous punishment was decreed: "Long Dan" was forced to marry "an extremely plain woman" in the camp—who undoubtedly was just that, her nickname being "Ugly Emma." The happy couple was sentenced to replace Joaquin as cook, leaving the jubilant boy free to gather gold.

That this was easier said than done is shown by the following diary entry, typical of many others revealing the depths of his discouragement:

Rested and enjoyed it too as never better, for it has been a hard week's work At work at sunrise in water up to my knees until twelve o'clock Then a little snack for dinner and at it until sundown as hard as you can hit into it, and this is life in land of gold It is worse than slavery in the South

The first two pages of Joaquin's *California Diary* are missing. The first entry we have shows, as do many others, a preoccupation with buying provisions:

Sat Made $3 bought 50 lbs of flour $3 75 one box of sardines 75 cts

Many of the entries consist of the same sad notation:

Made ooo

but others read:

made ½ oz . . . made $1\%_{16}$ oz . . . made $1 25 . . . Won $18 cards . . . made $\%_{16}$ oz . . .

all of which enabled Joaquin to go to nearby Jack Ass Flat and Horsetown, mining camps that were as wild as their names, to celebrate his luck. It was here, at the age of eighteen, that Joaquin developed a taste for whiskey—whiskey in quantities—a thirst that never was to desert him. Many accounts have recorded the amazement of his companions at the sight of Joaquin going energetically to work on a bottle of whiskey—or anything drinkable as long as it was "hard."

Joaquin set down whatever struck him as noteworthy in his new life, without regard for emphasis or selectivity, as a diarist should:

Fri the 9th   Went to Shasta City and saw A. Higgins executed for the crime of murder

Sa   Made $5.75 cts.   Bought one shirt $2   for writing materials $1   for candy 37 cts.   for straw for bed 50 cts   for one sack of flour $4.50 cts   beens $2   bacon $3.20 cts   yeast powder $1

Frid   No watter and did not work   lost at cards 50 cts   one box of Moffats pills at 75 cts   lost at cards $2.00 Bought one Colts revolver for $10.00   Number 35.4.81

Then, on December 6, 1855, there appears a long poem—the first that we know was written by Joaquin. It was proudly signed "Hiner Miller" and the first verse alone will be quoted here:

> Alone I sit in my cabbin today
> And all is quiet around
> Save the rain which falls on the canvas roof
> With a dull and monotinous sound

> By Hiner Miller of O.T.
> Squaw town, Shasta Co Cal

That the boy was discouraged and pathetically lonely is reflected in the somber, heart-searching entries made on Christmas Day, 1855 and New Year's Day, 1856:

Yes, Christmas eve of '55 has passed away and by me all most unnoticed save the loading and firing of my pistol thirty-six times and then the main spring broke and so I ceased firing

Yes the nineteenth Christmas eve has rolled over my head and as I sit in my cabbin today and look back over the past year I feel that I have not lived as I should have lived

Tuesday Jan. 1, 1856 Yes tis fifty-six another year of my life has passed away and where or in what point I have gained In none at all save in the knowledge of my weakness failty and irresolution One year ago I was on Humbug Creek, Ciskiyou County, California and on that day I took a review of the past year '54 and I said to myself if this coming year goes no more usefully spent than the past it will be a sin and a great sin but it is so it has been uselessly spent and what can I do but resolve to do better in this new year Yes, I will do better I will leave off my follies and try and be some one Yes, this is my resolve time alone will determine

Joaquin's gloom and doubts were to deepen, as is shown by the following entry, written in March, 1856:

Fri Sat Sun
It is now verging on to six months since I first landed in Shasta Co but how different are my feelings now to what they were then Then I thought I would pass the coming winter in working a claim and take out ounce after ounce of the shining metal And I fancied that the opening of Spring would find me seated on a splendid horse with a pocket full of gold and a joyous heart a bounding away for my Oregon home and bidding forever adieu to the miners and the miners life and laying down the pick & shovel to rust forever in the gulches of California but alas how different do I find my self from my bright anticipations
I have dug and tugged starved and economized the winter through and I could not this day raise the miserable sum of twenty-five dollars Yes here I find myself in this damned hole of Squaw town in poor health as I have been all winter without watter, no money to leave the place on and no prospect of making any

The homesick Joaquin again felt the urge to versify on April 6, 1856. The lonely boy penned a poem of eleven verses, three of which are quoted here:

> Oh how I wish I a gain was at home
> In the valley of the old Willamette
> And never again Id wish to roam
> Ile seal the assertion with damn it
>
> Ile not have to live on chile beans
> Short beef and rusty bacon
> Nor work in mud and mire and rain
> And be all the time a shaken
>
> So fare farewell all thoughts of home
> For as now I cannot go sir
> For Ive not made a penny yet
> I tell you it is so sir

Joaquin eventually was to make money, but not by mining, and in June, 1856 he gave up his golden dreams. A diary entry reveals his sense of doom:

> Mans a reaper full of woes
> cuts a caper & down he goes

but it can be inferred from his diary that there were two other reasons, apart from his inability to make a fortune, that impelled him to leave the mining town. Joaquin had a fight with a former partner and it is possible that gun-play might have followed if he had stayed. And, to use the colloquialism of the day, he "decamped," leaving behind unpaid debts.

His ex-partner's name was Volney Abbey, and trouble started between the two when Joaquin tacked a poem on a cabin wall for all the town to read:

Ye poets will open wide your eyes
  Excuse me for being gabby
For I write of the renown of a man in town
  By the name of Volney Abbey
Wise Dr Gates thus speaks and prates
  Though you know he is somewhat gabby
I've been bereft of some flour I left
  I believe by Volney Abbey

Volney did not relish being called a thief. The aftermath, as recorded by Joaquin, follows:

There I saw Volney Abbey my old partner who seemed greatly annoyed about some poetry that had been written about him. He accused me of being the author in such a way I could not well deny (For I was the author) . . . In a few minutes the pompous advance of Abbey was noticed. He carried a double barreled shotgun and was accompanied by Gates, J. and P. Mc. I then slipped off to my cabbin, loaded my riffle determined to meet him on equal footing but the men said I should not have my gun so I met him unarmed I told him I was the author of the piece that amazed him so badly After talking pretty rough with him some time while he made the air blue with curses I left him set him down in my mind as a notorious coward

The chances are the diarist gave the best of it to himself in this account, for it was Joaquin Miller, and not Volney Abbey, who fled. That night he stole away, saying good-bye to no one, leaving behind two unpaid notes of $25 and $15 and a personal debt of $3.30. "The notes that I gave to N. Walcott and S. Johns not paid up," he had noted earlier in his diary, "neither do I intend to for the claims were of no account I bought." Joaquin also felt his action was justified because he himself held notes of $75 for claims he had sold on Tadpole Creek and which he could not collect. He was in good financial shape and could have paid his debts, as the journal entry proves:

> I leave thee for Yreka with a pony and rigging worth $100　riffle worth $20 & $5.25 in pocket　Hurrah for little me

3

Joaquin started off for Yreka and his home in Oregon but he was sidetracked and more than a year would elapse (July, 1856 to November, 1857) before he got there. He stopped in Squaw Valley on the McCloud River where an Indian tribe lived. He liked their way of life and "went native," throwing away his clothes and wearing instead a soft doeskin suit and moccasins. He supplied the Indians with game, being a good shot (in his diary Joaquin claims he saw a three-year-old elk "standing a cross the river about 280 yards off" and then, bang, and the animal dropped dead), but most of the time he lolled about like a true brave while the women did all the work. At last he was happy, for as he noted in his journal:

> This is indeed a lovely day　my squaw is out digging roots　my dog is lying at my feet　my riffle is by my side my pipe is in my mouth

This lazy year in Joaquin's life, together with the fact that he took an Indian girl as a permanent bed companion, has been regarded variously. To those whose morals are on the severest level, it was a disreputable episode; to the more romantic-minded, it was a tender interlude with a beautiful dusky maiden—all Indian girls who figured in Joaquin's books were without exception beautiful dusky maidens. Joaquin was never ashamed of "going native," and in fact he made a reputation by writing about his halcyon squaw-man days. "Somehow I couldn't understand or get on with my fellow-man," he reminisced. "He seemed always to want to cheat me—to get my labor for nothing. I could appreciate and enter into the heart of an Indian."

In 1898, more than forty years after his year-long siesta with the Indians, Joaquin was traveling through the Shasta region with Harr Wagner, his business manager and close friend. "It was near here that I had my first carnal knowledge of women," Joaquin confided. The story of how he lost his virginity, and apparently lost it twice, was drolly told. Joaquin said he went with two young Indian girls to gather pine nuts. Apparently, the recognized procedure in gathering pine nuts, Indian fashion, was to chop down the trees and pick up the nuts, for that is what happened.

"After a while I grew tired and rested, placing the ax on the ground near me," Joaquin told Wagner. "One of the girls picked up the ax and ran behind some bushes. I followed her to get the ax. She placed it on the ground and lay flat on her back with the ax under her. In order to get the ax I attempted to turn her over . . . as Peter the Czar was accustomed to say, 'I had my will with her.' I then took the ax, chopped down several trees, rested, and the other Indian girl grabbed the ax and ran off into the bushes. I followed. The performance . . . was repeated."

It is not known whether one of these maidens was to become what Joaquin referred to in his diary as his *mahala* (sweetheart) and *pokona* (meaning *pocono*, wife), or sometimes more bluntly as "my squaw" or "my Indian woman." Joaquin said his *mahala* was named Paquita, the daughter of a Shasta Indian chief whom he alternately called Warrotetot,

Blackfoot and Black Beard in various books. J. H. Beadle, an early authority on the West who visited the McCloud settlement in 1876, said Joaquin's *pocono* (who by that time had been inherited by a white named Jim Brock) was a Digger, the member of a lowly tribe. "I should say a man must needs be very crazy to live with one of them," Beadle wrote sternly. "Their chief luxury is dried and tainted salmon and the sight and smell of most of them would turn the stomach of any other than a poet."

Joaquin regarded Paquita somewhat more romantically than did Beadle. "She was very pretty, not tall," he remembered later, "her breasts half curtained by her hair. I saw her bosom's wealth like wine, and all its wealth and worth seemed mine. I simply say that she was good and loved me with pure womanhood. When that is said, why what remains?"

The result of this "pure womanhood" friendship was a daughter, but while this aftermath is not mentioned or hinted at in the *California Diary*, Joaquin in later years never made any attempt to conceal or deny the fact. The child was named Cali-Shasta—Lily of Shasta. Although Joaquin deserted her soon after birth, he later found her and placed her in the home of a friend in San Francisco. Cali-Shasta was described by those who knew her as beautiful and talented.

Years later Joaquin was to declare that Paquita, his *pocono*, was killed by settlers in a raid on the Indian encampment, and that he was so disconsolate with grief that he reluctantly returned to civilization and became a white man again. Actually Paquita lived on half a century after her romance with Joaquin, to bathe in the reflected glory of a great poet who had been her man. When Paquita died in 1908 she was known as Mrs. Amanda Brock and, according to the San Francisco CALL, was "greatly honored and respected."

Paquita and her Indian companions liked and accepted Joaquin (who was known to them by the curious name of *Bo-Bo*, which indicated he had many foolish qualities), but when the warlike Modocs massacred a band of whites at Pit River, there was no question as to where his sympathies lay. Far from being the "renegade" he later claimed to have been, he volunteered and marched with the whites against the Modocs, and furthermore fought in the battle in which, as the diary says, fifteen of the two hundred Indians facing them were killed and eighteen taken prisoners.

This is another battle in which Joaquin asserted he was wounded, but he never specifically described the area of his injuries. Later he would write and talk much about his Indian wounds, but no one ever mentioned actually seeing the scars. In after years Joaquin occasionally would limp, attributing his affliction to arrow (not bullet) wounds received in the Modoc War. The sardonic Ambrose Bierce always guffawed when he thought about the "famous arrow wound" and he liked to complain that Joaquin "sometimes limps with the wrong leg."

There can be no question, however, but that Joaquin fought in the Modoc War. A quarter century later, when his status as Indian Fighter was being questioned and even ridiculed, he wrote to the Adjutant General's office and received in return a letter he always kept handy in his wallet. The letter certified that he had been one of the first volunteers, serving from March 16 to May 22, 1857, that he had furnished his own horse and weapons and that he did not ask for or receive the compensation he was entitled to. (And yet Joaquin was a man of contradictions; for at other times he claimed he was a renegade during the Modoc trouble.)

Joaquin's feelings toward the marauding Indians as recorded in his diary are considerably more hostile than the attitude he was to take later when he was writing about them. In one of his books he poignantly described the hanging of a Chief:

> The daughter of the leader was brought to him, just before the noose was drawn. He said not a word to her but with outstretched hand pointed to the North. She turned and walked northward, out over the hills, on out of sight, not turning her head. As she disappeared the rope was stretched.

In contrast, a few days after the decisive fight, when the defeated Indians were being run down, Joaquin made the laconic and callous entry in his journal:

> April the 13/57
> Took 5 squaws and one buck   hung the buck and freed the squaws

Joaquin had helped kill off one tribe of Indians, but this did not prevent him from returning in May to share again the easy life of his red friends in Squaw Valley. He stayed with them through the summer and on into the fall, when he left for his parents' home in Oregon. In the last diary entry made in California, dated November 4, he casually mentioned Paquita, "my little *mahala* who shed a tear at the idea of my departure." The daughter Cali-Shasta was too young to know or care that her father was abandoning her.

4

Returning to Coburg, Joaquin began to feel the gentle stirrings of a Poet. He decided he needed an education. He was twenty-one years old and, though his father was a part-time teacher, Joaquin had attended only a few elementary school grades. He now became a college graduate in one of the fastest times on record—in three months! What is more, he was valedictorian of his class.

His alma mater was Columbia College in Eugene, the forerunner of the University of Oregon, and Joaquin not only was the first graduate of the school but was close to the last. The college opened in December, 1858 and closed the following March. We know that Joaquin had the highest marks in his class, but we do not know what courses he took, as the school was so short-lived that none of its records survive. It is possible that Joaquin's Copperhead sympathies, which were to flare up in the Civil War just ahead and to cause him trouble, were implanted in him at Columbia. The college's President Ryan was a violent pro-slavery man, a persuasive hothead who is known to have influenced some of his students. Ryan one day in a pique shot a pro-Northern editor and was forced to flee the state. The editor lived, but Columbia College died.

Joaquin always said that the earliest verse of his to be published was the valedictory poem given at the Columbia College commencement. (Of course he never dreamed that the earlier rhymes he had scribbled as a boy-miner would, eighty years later, be unearthed and printed.) This poem was a rambling, lachrymose composition, with the general refrain:

> We are parting, brother, parting,
>   And this evening's sun will set
> On gay hearts with sorrow parting
> On bright eyes with weeping wet.

Joaquin recalled that after graduating from college he took another long trip into Mexico on horseback, where he had quite a number of thrilling adventures. This is a clear case of wishful thinking. He left Oregon, it is true, but he spent most of his time not as a free soul in Mexico but in a California jail, as an outlaw and then a fugitive from justice.

5

Joaquin's second descent on California brought him nothing but distress. It was a period in his life he preferred to forget—and as a matter of fact did forget, for he never talked about it. He was thrown in jail twice, the second time on a serious charge.

His troubles started when, soon after arriving in Siskiyou county, he happened to run into a half-crazed man named Sam Lockhart, whose brother had been killed in the Pit River massacre. Lockhart was determined to avenge the death, and when he heard that Joaquin had lived with a *mahala* he at once assumed the "renegade" had fought with the Indians against the whites. He secured a warrant and had Joaquin hauled before Judge Rosborough in Yreka. When Joaquin finally proved that he had been a member of the punitive expedition the charge (its exact nature is unknown) was dismissed; but the experience was a humiliating one, and he did not like to discuss it.

The second time Joaquin landed in prison he was in grave danger of being hung. Joaquin Miller holds one unrivaled distinction: he stands alone as the only bard in history known to have been indicted as a horse thief. Many writers have dismissed the episode as a harmless, childish prank. Not so. Stealing horses in 1859 on the frontier was considered as enormous a crime as kidnapping is today. Joaquin, by now grown up and approaching his twenty-second birthday, surely knew that the penalty he might be called on to pay might be worse than if he had committed murder. Murderers sometimes got off with light jail sentences; horse thieves usually were "swung."

Joaquin was working as a cowhand for Bill Hurst and Tom Bass, who owned a ranch near Millville in Shasta county. There are two explanations as to why he turned horse thief: either he had loaned the men money and they refused to pay it back, or the partners refused to give him his back wages. Whatever prompted him to act as he did, Joaquin stole a horse and away he ran. He was easily caught. Officers of the law reasoned that he would hide out with his *mahala* on the McCloud River. There he was found and taken into custody.

An indictment was returned by the Grand Jury on July 10, 1859 stating that: "Hiner Miller . . . stole one gelding horse of the Value of Eighty Dollars, one saddle of the Value of Fifteen Dollars and one bridle of the Value of Five . . ."

It is known that Joaquin escaped from jail, thus saving his life, or, at the very least, avoiding a prison sentence, and it is also known exactly how he escaped. But Joaquin's version of the jail-break, the one he reluctantly wrote about, differs radically from the facts. (Joaquin was loath to discuss the escape, because every time he did so he walked the tightrope; for at the same time he staunchly denied ever having been in jail in the first place.)

The account to be first presented here may be considered as the official, the authentic family version. It was written and published in 1941 by Juanita Joaquina Miller, Joaquin's daughter by a second marriage. And while it is true that the horse-stealing incident took place two decades before Miss Miller was born, and that this version was printed eighty-two years after the act itself, Miss Miller assured her readers that the words were identically those of her father Joaquin.

It seems that one night while in jail (where he found himself for some trivial reason) Joaquin heard the tremulous call of the night bird. He knew what that meant. He peered through the bars of his cell window and, sure enough, there was his faithful dusky Paquita, and behind her were two horses ready for the getaway. Then:

My Paquita was filing the rusty bar with two sharp little knives. The bars seemed to bend or break as she did so. It was almost dawn when we galloped toward the river. As we reached it we felt we were followed, so we took a leap—a fearful leap—not far, but sudden and ugly, with everything against us.

My horse and myself went far down the blue, cold river, but he rose bravely, and struck out fairly for the other side. Paquita was not so fortunate . . .

She was not forty feet away when discovered, and shots rained down upon her. I was out of reach and nearing the shore. Looking back, clinging to my horse's mane, I saw her wounded horse struggle on against the flood that swept about . . . Then, almost at my feet a little face was lifted as if rising from the water into mine. Her naked arms were reached out and holding on to the grassy bank but she could not draw her body from the water. I put my arms about her and with sudden and singular strength in my weakened state, I pulled her up to some dry rocks and sat down with the dying girl in my arms. She was bleeding from many wounds.

"Paquita!" I whispered, but she could not answer. It was the Fourth of July [*sic*], I remember. Tenderly at last I laid her down, gathered fallen branches and build a reedy pyre. I struck flint together, made a fire. I lighted more grass and tules around her. After awhile I gathered stones and made a circle around the embers. Saying a prayer for my dead, I rode slowly away, and almost fainting, dropped from my horse into the camp of Capt. Crook near Reading Adobe. Before I lost consciousness, I heard him say, as he recognized me, "Poor Boy veteran."

Joaquin wrote other versions of this dramatic moment ("This Indian maiden, pure as a vestal virgin, brave as was Lucretia, beautiful as any picture, lay dying in my arms . . ."), and all were sure-fire with the reading public. One cannot help but wonder what thoughts must have passed through the mind of Paquita, the pure vestal virgin who bore Joaquin's child, this Indian lady who lived peacefully on for a full half-century after her "death," when she read or was told about her romantic if somewhat premature demise.

As stated earlier, all of Joaquin's versions of the escape rather differ from the facts. Actually what happened was this: he was confined in a cell with a notorious badman, one Jack Marshall. The jail was flimsy and the two men easily sawed through the bars with a pocketknife. Then they fled to secluded Scott Valley and lived there in a cabin as out-laws.

There was an aftermath, however, that forced Joaquin out of the California he would return to so triumphantly at a much later date and that decreed that he spend his next ten years in Oregon. Marshall was uneasy in the hideout, and finally left, but Joaquin stayed on. Eventually word reached Sheriff Bradley as to his whereabouts, and the Sheriff and a deputy tracked him down to the cabin and called upon him to surrender. Desperate, determined not to be taken alive, Joaquin fired at the men, and he wounded the Sheriff in the knee. The officers returned to Deadwood to raise a posse, but by that time Joaquin had crossed the state line into Oregon.

No attempt seems to have been made to follow the fugitive once he reached Oregon. The indictment hung over Joaquin's head for the rest of his stay in the state, and indeed for the rest of his life, but that never seems to have worried him. He calmly denied any such thing had ever happened. Maybe to someone else named Miller. It was a common enough name. But not to Joaquin Miller, Poet.

In 1896 Harr Wagner visited Yreka and found that every saloon in town was exhibiting the one and only bullet that had struck Sheriff Bradley. When Wagner told this to his friend, Joaquin "after building up an elaborate denial of the crime" at last cried, "Anyhow, they were not horses, they were mules!"

CHAPTER THREE

Joaquin of All Trades
1860-1870

I

*T*HE next decade of Joaquin's life was marked with inde-
cision and restlessness. He knew by now what he
wanted to be—a Poet—but he could not support himself
by selling verse. Indeed, he could not even gain a small
reputation, for his lyrical efforts appeared in obscure weekly
newspapers and attracted no attention. Some of the more
solid citizens of Eugene began to think that the "Crazy Miller" sobriquet bestowed on him in California had been well
earned. So Joaquin, though he doggedly continued to write
poetry in private, took on a variety of jobs to make a living,
and, if he did not hold any one of them long, he was fairly
successful in all of them.

It is not known whether Joaquin studied law in his brief
three-month stint at Columbia College, but as soon as he returned to Oregon from California he was admitted to the bar.
His lack of legal education, and the fact that he was a fugitive
under indictment—a predicament which was rather vaguely
described as "some trouble" he had had in California—were
not held against him.

The competition was too spirited in Eugene, so lawyer
Joaquin went to Oro Fino, a small mining town in Idaho, and
nailed up his shingle—"C. H. Miller, Attorney and Counsel-

lor at Law and Solicitor in Chancery." He was hard-working and persistent in court, but he was lamentably ignorant in matters of law and could not build up a practice. He decided upon a more active life.

In October, 1861 Joaquin traveled to Walla Walla, Washington, and presented a letter of introduction to Isaac V. Mossman, the owner of a thriving pony express service from the mining regions of Montana and Idaho to Walla Walla. "He had one little pony and $5 in cash, but he could ride well and was a hustler," Mossman wrote in his reminiscences. "I had then eighteen head of good saddle horses, so I gave him an interest in the business."

Mossman gave Joaquin the route between Lewiston in Idaho to Florence City in Oregon and, when he became convinced that his new partner was a trustworthy courier, the longer and more important route between Oro Fino and Walla Walla. The winter of 1861–62 was the coldest ever remembered in the Northwest, with the snow piling so high that horses were immobilized. "I had walked all the way from Florence to Walla Walla on this crust, nearly two hundred miles as the trail ran, with nearly one hundred pounds of gold dust and letters on my back," Joaquin was to recall. There was the ever-present danger of being waylaid by Indians or road agents ("There came a rain of lead from the company of robbers lying in ambush," Joaquin remembered, and then he explained, with a minimum of detail, how he escaped), and there were the added hazards of the sudden snowfalls, the sub-zero drops in temperature, the bone-chilling Chinook wind, the encounters with mountain wolves, the streams to ford, the mountain passes to be crossed, and the risk of losing the trail.

There is no doubt that Joaquin was a hardy and courageous

pony express rider—a weakling could not have survived. But, if the work was hard, the pay was good and he saved a stake. When his express loads were light Joaquin would take newspapers into remote camps and sell them for $2.50 apiece, and occasionally the miners would reward him with a bonus, as, for instance, when the snow fell fifteen feet deep on Florence Mountain, penning hundreds in the town and Joaquin alone and on foot made his way to Lewiston and back with letters and vital supplies.

The partnership lasted until early in March, 1862 when Joaquin informed Mossman he wanted to quit. "So I paid him $600 over and above his profits, presented him with a fine horse, saddled and bridled," Mossman said. The senior partner had grown quite fond of Joaquin, the dependable pony express rider, but in after years his admiration faded. This was because Joaquin was to make the most of his brief career with the express service, at Mossman's expense, when he wrote about his experiences. The name of the company actually was Mossman's Express. Joaquin gradually came to remember it as Mossman's and Miller's, then as Miller's and Mossman's, and finally, more tersely and more grandly, as Miller's Express.

"I wish to say here, in justice to myself," Mossman sorrowfully wrote in 1901, "that in all of Joaquin Miller's writings he has never mentioned my name in connection with the express business, but has always taken the credit to himself of doing it all."

Mossman was irritated also by another flaw in his expartner's memory: Joaquin insisted that the grateful miners had renamed a town in his honor. Joaquin always had an obsessive fondness for associating place names with himself or his family. "He called Florence, Millersburg," Mossman snorted, "but no one of the old cradle-rockers of that day will recognize the place by that name."

2

Pap Miller was about to lose his Coburg farm through foreclosure, for the land he had selected was so barren that each year he lost money on the crops. Joaquin took his pony express profits (estimated at $3,000), paid off the mortgage and bought a house in Eugene, where he installed his father and mother.

Joaquin still had money left and, being literarily inclined, decided to invest it in a newspaper. Undoubtedly he would have perferred to have edited a poetry magazine, and if he had done so he would have saved himself much trouble, but there were no such publications in the West. Joaquin's father and brothers and almost all of his acquaintances were Republicans, staunch adherents of the Union cause, but he became a Democrat, the sort of Northern Democrat who sided with the Confederacy in the Civil War. He probably was influenced in his politics by the friendship and patronage of Senator Joe Lane of Oregon. Joe Lane had been defeated as candidate for Vice-President on the Breckinridge ticket of 1861—by the men named Lincoln and Hamlin—and the Senator helped him buy an interest in the Eugene DEMOCRATIC REGISTER. With Lane as silent partner and the boss, the weekly was fanatically "Reb," and Joaquin and his co-editor, one Tony Noltner, had no choice but to fall in with this trend.

Joaquin and Noltner were easy-going; they never locked the doors of the REGISTER office and usually were found in the saloon next door. They were liked personally, though their Copperhead sympathies were abhorred and their newspaper despised. No copies of the sheet survive today, so it is not known how seditious its editorial policy was. In 1913 a letter-writer to the New York TIMES was to remember Joaquin back in the distant days of the 1860's: "We called him 'Heiney.' To say the REGISTER was 'secesh' is to put it mildly." The military authorities thought so too, for the paper lasted only from March 15 until September 20, 1862 when it was summarily suppressed for spreading treasonable propaganda.

Joaquin's reputation was severely damaged, he was left with many enemies, and he barely escaped imprisonment. In later years, when he was taunted for having been a Copperhead and for failing to enlist in the Civil War as did his brother John and most of his contemporaries, Joaquin said he had not been so much pro-South as for the underdog, that he was influenced by his father's Quaker attitude toward war, and that anyway in 1861 he was but nineteen years old, too young to enlist. He was, of course, twenty-four.

3

During his pony express days, when Joaquin whiled away the long hours on the trail by reading the newspapers he was carrying, he had noticed the poems of Minnie Myrtle, known as "Sweet Singer of the Coquille." Minnie Myrtle was Miss Minnie Theresa Dyer, a resident of Port Orford in Oregon, whose father was Judge Dyer, and at a time when Joaquin was in his fumbling way trying to master the art of versification she already had a minor reputation as a poet.

Joaquin wrote to her, told her how much he admired her genius and confessed to his own poetic ambitions. This resulted in a correspondence (which has been lost), with Minnie Myrtle graciously criticizing sample stanzas he submit-

ted to her, exhorting him to follow the path that leads to pure estheticism, and finally advising him to buy a rhyming dictionary—a book Joaquin did not know existed. From then on, thanks to this invaluable technical device, his poetic problems were no longer quite so perplexing.

After the REGISTER was suppressed Joaquin could not find employment in Eugene, and so he decided to ride to Port Orford, a town of a few hundred, then as now, in Southern Oregon on the Pacific seaboard, to see what Minnie Myrtle was like in the flesh. The flesh was alluring, for on meeting Minnie Myrtle he found her a "handsome beauty" who was "tall, dark, and striking in every respect."

"I arrived on Thursday," said Joaquin. "On Sunday next we were married."

Joaquin literally overpowered Minnie Myrtle and, for that matter, her steady beau too, the man she intended to marry. The day after Joaquin arrived unannounced and uninvited at Port Orford this rival came to visit his fiancée. Joaquin was outraged. He drew his revolver and drove the bewildered young man from the house.

All this was done with a romantic flourish that might have been accepted by many a young lady as a tribute from an impetuous troubadour. It is known, however, that Minnie Myrtle resented not only the gesture but the entire whirlwind courtship conducted by Joaquin. In 1871, on a lecture platform, she publicly reproached Joaquin for "having driven my lover from my presence and separated us forever."

4

Joaquin and his quickly wooed-and-won bride rode back to Eugene on horseback. Because of his Southern sympathies Joaquin could not find a job, so the couple decided to try the big city, San Francisco. The Millers arrived there toward the end of 1862, but stayed only a few weeks. Joaquin had hoped to find work on a newspaper, but no one was interested in a small-time Oregon editor. Both Joaquin and Minnie Myrtle had also hoped to break into the tight literary circle of the town, but no one had heard of the "Sweet Singer of the Coquille" or of Cincinnatus Hiner Miller, and no one was sufficiently intrigued to find out what either of the visitors was like.

Yet, as Joaquin was to remember it, there was one compensation for the fruitless trip to San Francisco, and that was his warm and beautiful friendship with Adah Isaacs Menken. Miss Menken was the beauty who had captivated the theatregoing public with her "bad girl" reputation after her sensational appearance in "Mazeppa," one of the most popular of all plays in America, when she rode on the stage semi-nude, strapped to a horse.

It appears that a horse brought Joaquin and Miss Menken together. "When she asked that we ride and I teach her some Indian tricks she did not already know, Minnie was not in the least jealous," the brand-new bridegroom declared. "Miss Menken was rehearsing her 'Mazeppa' and found great relaxation in our rides out to the Cliffs on the shore of the Pacific . . . she would dismount, throw herself at full length, face downward, in the sand, and chant songs I could not understand." According to Joaquin, the friendship was not platonic. Years later, when he mentioned Adah Isaacs Menken to his daughter Juanita he confessed to their "dear delicious piracies of kisses upon love's seas"—but, being a gentleman, he would say no more.

Thirty years afterwards Joaquin described in the San Francisco CALL his friendship with Miss Menken, and his recollections, which were reprinted in a booklet, again were discreet when it came to their love affair.

"Little is known about her except lies," he tersely noted. Joaquin explained that, as a devotee of the theatre back in 1862, he was often backstage, and in this connection he told of a memorable scene he witnessed in Tom Maguire's Opera-House, where Miss Menken and the elder Junius Brutus Booth were rehearsing for the opening of "Mazeppa." Joaquin, who was onstage trying to help out, was holding Miss Menken's horse. "I was just down out of the saddle from a year's work as express rider," Joaquin wrote, emphasizing his fitness for the job. And then, suddenly, in a tantrum caused by overwork and tension, and possibly jealousy, Miss Menken chased the great Booth clear out of the theater. It was a clash between two artistic temperaments that Joaquin was never to forget.

"She seemed very happy, half wild all the way till we got down to the great beach beyond the Cliff House," Joaquin added. "But then, throwing herself from the saddle, she fell with her face almost in the Ocean and sobbed and cried as if her heart was broken." Joaquin always remembered Miss Menken walking around San Francisco in a yellow silk dress, a dress so unfashionable and plain that no other woman except the exquisite Adah could have worn it with impunity.

This, then, was the tumultuous meeting of two struggling souls, Joaquin Miller and Adah Isaacs Menken, who, though they did not know it, were each standing at the threshold of fame and/or notoriety. It is a fascinating story which would be of considerable historical interest if unfortunately it were not marred by many glaring inconsistencies which destroy our faith in Joaquin's faculties of total recall. To name but two:

Booth died in 1852, ten years before the alleged incident, and at a time incidentally when the fourteen-year-old Joaquin had not yet reached the West. And Miss Menken was not in San Francisco when Joaquin was there in 1862. Outside of that, it is a colorful, if over-imaginative, reminiscence, and it is quite true today, as Joaquin said years ago, that little is known of the actress "except lies."

Joaquin returned to Eugene and there his Copperhead friends at last came to his rescue. A successor to the suppressed REGISTER was started and named the DEMOCRATIC REVIEW. Joaquin was appointed editor. But sentiment for Lincoln's administration was mounting in Oregon (whose state motto was "The Union"). The paper could not establish any circulation, and Joaquin's roistering cronies in the saloons began to treat him coolly, then coldly. It was evident that his prestige was on the wane. He resigned as editor on February 14, 1863 and soon thereafter the paper closed down. This was Joaquin's last sponsorship of the Confederate cause, but in the meantime there was danger that he and other Rebel sympathizers might be lynched. There was talk of running the REVIEW editor out of town on a rail, but the action was postponed because Minnie Myrtle was about to have a child.

The baby, a girl named Maud, was born in mid-summer, and a few weeks later Joaquin and his family quietly stole out of Eugene at dawn. Once again he was striking out for new country, intent on starting a new life, this time in the mining camp of Canyon City in Grant county toward the eastern end of the state.

5

Finding one's way to Canyon City is difficult enough even today, as there is no rail or bus connection, but the trip undertaken by Joaquin and his family was painfully laborious, for it meant following on horseback a winding trail of some two hundred miles. The route displayed the scenic grandeur that is Oregon's—through deep dark forests of Douglas firs, across sparkling trout streams, over rolling prairie land and lush wheat fields, and cutting through the spurs of the picturesque Blue Mountains—but it is doubtful if the travelers had time to appreciate the beauty of the country. Minnie Myrtle was nursing a month-old baby, whose cradle was a willow basket swinging from her saddle-bow, and Joaquin was driving a herd of cattle to sell in Canyon City.

The Canyon City of today as compared to the Canyon City of 1863 is enough to shake the confidence of the most optimistic Chamber of Commerce. Gold had been discovered at Whiskey Flat outside the town and ten thousand people were living in the new Eldorado. Today Canyon City has settled back and numbers only a few hundred inhabitants, about as many as it had before the gold rush began.

Joaquin set up a law office in the town and, if he did not make much money, for the first time he won the esteem of his fellow citizens. That they thought a great deal of him is shown by the fact that in the spring of 1864, when the Utah and Nevada Indians went on an ugly scalping bee, Joaquin was elected Captain of a company of fifty-four volunteers sent to aid the U.S. Army in fighting the marauders. This was quite a tribute to Joaquin, who at the time was twenty-six years old.

In this expedition Joaquin became a true Indian Fighter,

whose bravery was witnessed and acknowledged, and yet, perversely enough, he seldom in later years could be persuaded to mention the war, but preferred to dwell on his participation in non-existent battles.

The U.S. Cavalry commanded by Lieutenant J. A. Waymire pursued the Indians, who were well armed and far superior in strength, south of the Harney Lake region. There, because they were so outnumbered, the soldiers hesitated to engage in the fight. At this juncture Captain Miller and his volunteers came riding down the trail. The battle started immediately. There was a comic touch when one volunteer received a scratch wound only to find seven members of the Miller company dismount, throw down their weapons and carry him, and themselves, safely from the field; but Joaquin's conduct as an officer was irreproachable. In 1929, a survivor of the fight still remembered the heroism of "Capt. C. H. Miller," who tied his hat to the saddle and, his long hair streaming about his head, led the charge on a mule against the Indians fortified on a ridge. Joaquin's mule was shot out from under him and he continued up the slope on foot.

The Indians retired from the battlefield, with the cavalry chasing them down, and that was the end of the war. Later on, at the site where the troops of Lieutenant Waymire and Captain Miller had met, Fort Harney was built, and the route followed by the cavalry in pursuit of the defeated Indians is known today as Joaquin Miller Trail.

6

Shortly after Captain Miller returned to his Canyon City home he found himself the father of his first son. The boy was named George Brick Miller. Joaquin's third and last child by his marriage with Minnie Myrtle was born two years later and named Harold.

Despite the presence of children, which is supposed to cement a marriage, Joaquin's life was now disturbed by a crisis commonly known at the time as "wife trouble." In later years he was to blame his marital incompatibility not on a clash between two poetic temperaments as many people thought, but on the fact that he was ambitious to make his name in the world, while Minnie Myrtle deserted the sacred muse and settled down to the humdrum business of raising a family.

With the discovery of a series of ledgers that Joaquin kept at Canyon City it appears more likely that the marriage eventually broke up because the handsome Captain Miller strayed. The ledgers contain mostly law case reports, bits of verse and ideas for poems, but there are scattered diary entries showing that Joaquin was in a tormented state of mind, and he made enigmatic references to a "Mrs. E."

"Man is apt to do things in life which he afterwards regrets," Joaquin wrote somberly on August 2, 1865. "I surely have. Life, brief as it is, has been inconsistent enough . . . So much for *friends*."

"I am about to undo that act," he wrote a few days later. "God help me! I have thought over it long and earnestly!"

On August 18 he was in anguish because "All is lost—the last hope is gone." And the final entry reads: "Things have gone worse financially and domestically."

It is difficult to guess exactly what was torturing Joaquin. The most logical assumption is that his troubles stemmed from his dallying with the mysterious "Mrs. E." Perhaps he had concluded that his marriage had been a mistake; perhaps Minnie Myrtle had threatened to leave him; perhaps he was belatedly harassed by guilt feelings for deserting his *pocono* and Indian daughter Cali-Shasta. We do not know. In any event, the crisis lingered and passed, and he and Minnie Myrtle stayed together—for a while.

It may be that the marriage was mended because Joaquin was able to solve the financial difficulties he mentioned, and with that stroke his domestic problems were temporarily shelved. For the first time in his life he secured a job that guaranteed him a steady income. The post of Judge of Grant county fell vacant and, as Joaquin frantically pulled strings to be appointed, he found after a few months that he had been awarded the political plum. He was aided in his quest by an old friend, the powerful politician George D. Williams. Williams, who had been Chief Justice of Oregon Territory, and who soon would be a Senator, had smoothed the way for Joaquin's admission to the bar in 1860, and he now saw to it that Joaquin got the Judge's job. The appointment was approved by the citizens, who regarded it as a reward for his leadership in the Indian War. It meant that Judge Miller would have a regular salary from June, 1866, when he was appointed, to the fall of 1869 when the term expired. Then he would have to win an election to keep the post.

Grant county at the time comprised almost one-third of all Oregon, so the territory under Joaquin's jurisdiction was vast—almost as large as his native Indiana. Not a great deal is known about Joaquin's activities as County Judge, and the only stories that have been handed down concern his atrocious handwriting on various court documents. "The best you could say for it was no man in the world could read it," an oldtimer recalled. "It was just as if a turkey had stepped in ink and walked over the paper."

Joaquin himself seldom reminisced about his three years

as magistrate, except to mention that he usually favored the underdog in a case, and in later life he frowned on being called "Judge Miller." He did love to tell one story of those Canyon City days, a story familiar enough on the frontier. It was about a miner who had been sentenced to death by hanging, a fate Judge C. H. Miller himself may well have escaped. The doomed man was riding in a wagon on his way to the gallows when a boy ran breathlessly by, headed for the place of execution. "Don't hurry, son," the prisoner cried. "The fun won't start till I get there."

Joaquin was, perforce, a solid citizen. The gay and exuberant young man now had to behave sedately, as befitted a magistrate. In a few short years his life had changed drastically. The horse thief, the squaw-man, now handed down important decisions and was respectfully called Your Honor. The evidence shows that he did not care much for the role, but what pleased him greatly was that his duties were none too demanding, so that he had leisure time on his hands. He wasted much of this time in "doggeries," as saloons were quaintly known in Oregon. But he used some of it more profitably by reading and writing and planting trees, a new hobby. His orchard was the first in Canyon City, and it still bears fruit today. All the rest of his life, whenever he had an opportunity, Joaquin was to plant trees.

7

Now that he could devote more time to poetry, Joaquin founded and headed the Literary Society, using it as a proving ground for his verse. The spectacle of a grownup man, and a Judge at that, immersing himself in such an esoteric art was not calculated to appeal to voters at election time, and yet, when Joaquin had accumulated a comfortable backlog of verse, he defiantly had them published. He issued two skinny volumes of poems while serving as Judge, and, as no publisher was willing to go along with him on a royalty basis, he had to pay all printing and distribution costs himself. When news got around Grant county that Judge Miller had written not one but two books of "pomes" there were a great number of citizens who announced they would be candidates for his post when the term expired.

These two books of Joaquin's are today rare and collectors' items. Both were signed "Cincinnatus Heine Miller." Perhaps Joaquin hoped he might be confused with the German poet, but alas, the thought was to occur to no one else.

His first book was titled *Specimens*. It was dedicated to his "bunchgrass constituents," for, said the author, the poems were written where "painted savages are oftener met than savants and where riming is considered a mild type of insanity." It was a thin volume, scarcely more than a pamphlet, with many fattening fly leaves, and it was pretentiously bound in leather. *Specimens* was published in 1868 in Portland, and Joaquin paid to have five hundred copies printed. He vastly overestimated the consumers' market. He priced the book at one dollar, later reduced it to fifty cents, and eventually gave away copies free, and thus he could truthfully announce that the first edition had been exhausted. Only two copies of *Specimens* are known to exist today, although others may come to light.

Specimens was just what the title implied—samples of his fugitive newspaper verse—and it made no splash in the literary world, not even in Oregon, for few critics bothered to review the book. Undismayed, Joaquin the following year published his second offering, called *Joaquin, et al*, which he dedicated to his daughter Maud. This was a volume of 124 pages, nearly twice the size of *Specimens*. *Joaquin, et al*—the title is taken from the poem he wrote on the Mexican bandit, Joaquin Murietta, whose name Judge C. H. Miller was soon to adopt—also went unnoticed, and again the copies were distributed free. In this collection, as in *Specimens*, Joaquin dwelled lovingly and insistently on the glories of the Sierra Nevada mountains, and gradually he became known as "Poet of the Sierras," and this sobriquet clung to him the rest of his life, although Joaquin himself preferred to be called "Byron of the Rockies."

Both *Specimens* and *Joaquin, et al* were diffuse and verbose, filled with the redundancies that characterized most of the poetry he was to write in the future. Joaquin sent a review copy to Bret Harte, editor of the OVERLAND MONTHLY in San Francisco. "Try and *condense*," Harte wisely suggested.

In later years Joaquin said that when he was learning to write poetry in Canyon City he was greatly impressed by an Indian Chief who said: "White man talks too much. It does not take many words to tell the truth." While this may have impressed Joaquin, he never followed such excellent advice. Ambrose Bierce admired Joaquin personally, but he shuddered at his gabbiness in print. "He requires no fewer than one hundred and fifteen lines to relate the landing of a ship in fair weather with nothing to prevent it," Bierce wrote.

We know today the setting in which Joaquin nearly a century ago composed his poems, for the "cabbin" where he lived is now a museum open to the public ("Apply at Courthouse for admittance"). Situated on a hillside overlooking Canyon City, it has four rooms. There is a small front room, furnished with a reed organ, a table and home-made chairs presumably put together by Joaquin. Sentimental colored

prints and daguerreotypes of the Millers and a tattered flag
with thirty-eight stars adorn the walls. At one time Joaquin's
Bible was prominently displayed, but it was stolen by a visitor. If the souvenir-hunter who took this relic was religiously
inclined, the chances are he was deeply shocked, for Joaquin
pasted newspaper clippings, cooking recipes and above all
whiskey advertisements into the Good Book. All his life Joaquin was a man who liked to try out new brands of whiskey.

The front part of the cabin was the family parlor, where
company was entertained, and Joaquin used it as his workshop. The stone jug of "the fluid" that always was by the side
of Joaquin's writing desk is not on display today. In the
middle of the cabin there is the kitchen, equipped with an
iron range and dining table. The back is divided into two
tiny bedrooms. A caretaker proudly escorts visitors through
Judge Miller's home and talks nostalgically about the old
days he never knew, when Canyon City was booming and
Joaquin was just one of ten thousand citizens. Recently a
visitor innocently inquired about Joaquin's Indian "wife."
"That's one thing we don't talk about," snapped the cus-
todian.

Today, Joaquin's shabby little cabin in Canyon City has
been turned into a shrine, and the three backless ledgers in
which he scribbled diary entries and made notes for speeches
are displayed by the Oregon Historical Society. If Joaquin
could have known this in 1869, how delighted he would have
been!

8

When his juridical term came to an end Joaquin announced he had set his political sights higher and aspired to
serve the people as a Supreme Court Judge. "I ask the nom-

ination first because I am competent and second because I desire it," he declared, and he went earnestly to work to secure the nomination. Joaquin at this time was described as "large and imposing" with "keen, penetrating eyes peering out from shaggy eyebrows," a man equally at home in a lady's parlor, or with one foot on the bar-rail of a doggery. It was noted, too, that he exhibited a quality that never was to desert him and which was invaluable for a politician running for office—he impressed people. "No one who saw Miller easily forgot him," declared Herbert C. Thompson, an Oregonian who knew Joaquin. "An impression remained of a big, powerful man, handsome in a virile way . . . and there was about him a proud gleam of the eye and a fierce dignity that marked him apart from a snake doctor. People called him a poseur. He was."

A poseur is seldom handicapped in seeking public office, and it was believed Joaquin would be a vote-getter, even though he did write poetry. He was waging an energetic campaign when the blow fell. And, once it had struck him, he withdrew his candidacy.

He was away from home, making stump speeches, when his wife Minnie Myrtle suddenly left him, taking the three children to her parents' home in Port Orford where she announced she would file suit for divorce, charging Joaquin with desertion. As if this was not enough to kill him politically, the "Sweet Singer of the Coquille" warbled to everyone who would listen about her intolerable afflictions: Joaquin had been selfishly ambitious, so devoted to poetry that he not only neglected her but also his children, in whom he took no interest. Joaquin had been a niggard when it came to paying household expenses and supporting his family in general. Joaquin seldom spent any time at home, but always could be found in the nearest doggery carousing with his cronies.

Joaquin never denied any of these unofficial charges (they were unofficial because Minnie Myrtle did not sue for divorce, but obtained a separation), and it is quite likely that they were true. It was noted in Canyon City that Joaquin was becoming more eccentric, that he was obsessed with poetry and particularly with the beauties of his own verse, and that he had even begun to limp—not because of his Indian wounds, but because Byron had limped. As for being stingy, Joaquin later had the reputation of being a scatter-good in a saloon, but a miser in the home. It undoubtedly was true, too, that Joaquin spent much of his time in doggeries. In many a reminiscence of the old Oregon pioneers we find remarks about the Judge's great and overwhelming love for whiskey, and yet there always occurs the same refrain: "Yes, Joaquin Miller drank lots, but no one ever saw him with more than he could carry."

All things considered, he probably was not a good husband. There is the testimony of Herbert C. Thompson, who, it should be remembered, was a friend of Joaquin and not of Minnie Myrtle: "She was regarded as a patient, long-suffering woman, commanding respect as well as sympathy." Minnie Myrtle at a later date was to air the charge on a public platform that Joaquin had married her not because he loved her but because he was captivated by her reputation as a poet, and that once he felt he had overtaken her and had no further use for her tutelage, he let the marriage go to pot. Joaquin did not deny this accusation, either.

Granting that all her charges were true, it is evident that Minnie Myrtle deliberately and vindictively timed the break-up so as to blast forever her husband's chances of mounting the Supreme Court bench. But, what Minnie Myrtle did not know was that she unwittingly did Joaquin a tremendous favor. If he had won the election he undoubtedly would have settled down in Oregon, to become a respected public official, never to be heard of outside the courtroom. What Minnie Myrtle did was to push him out into the world, to the fame he so much desired.

"She was not so ambitious as I was," Joaquin afterwards said candidly when he explained how his marriage had broken up. "She had not such a strange, wild life behind her to haunt her." This presumably refers either to his half-Indian daughter, or to the indictment issued against him. At another time he described Minnie Myrtle as "a strange, unhappy woman." Then again he revealed that his love for his spouse began to wither away when he discovered that she had lied to him about her age! Lying about one's age was then, as now, the natural prerogative of a woman, and such a show of indignation coming from Joaquin, the man who cut down his real age by five years, can only be described as hilariously absurd.

9

Joaquin was at a loss as to what to do next. There was no future in Canyon City, for the gold veins were running low and the boom days coming to an end, and so he decided to establish himself elsewhere. (Joaquin was not to return to Canyon City until thirty-eight years later, when in 1907 he was feted as the "home boy who made good." Joaquin grandly invited the whole town to Sell's Brewery for free drinks, but Sell was the man who paid the bill. There, late into the night, he reminisced about the old days in Canyon City, and many an oldtimer who decades before had guf-

fawed at the idea of Joaquin writing "pomes" sat in awe as
the poet recited his verse.)

For more times than he cared to remember, Joaquin once
more was on the march—again leaving one town in hopes
of "finding himself" in another. He went to Eugene and
found no job, then on to Portland, a big town of eight thousand, and found no job. He darkly considered shipping
around the world as a deckhand, but first he wanted to see if
he could profit from what he believed was Bret Harte's appreciation of his poetic talents. Joaquin thought Harte had
written a halfway encouraging review of his second book in
the OVERLAND MONTHLY. Actually Harte had penned a
merciless attack on the poems, but Ina Coolbrith, a co-editor,
had persuaded him not to print it, and then she herself had
written a more favorable notice. Joaquin did not know these
circumstances and he submitted by letter two of his newest
lyrical compositions to Harte.

"Although I shall not be able to use either of your poems,
I think that I fairly appreciate the merit of their performance," Harte temperately wrote back. "I should be glad to
receive something else from you."

Joaquin was delighted. He was further heartened when he
received a long-overdue letter from Charles Warren Stoddard, the well-known writer. In March, 1869, Joaquin had
written to Stoddard in San Francisco. "Knowing you to be a
true poet," his message began, "I venture to lay before you
a little plan of mine to show you how you can do me a signal
service." He had then revealed that the little plan was for
Stoddard to review and praise his *Joaquin, et al* in OVERLAND.
Stoddard was in the South Seas when the letter arrived but
now, early in 1870, nearly a year after the message had been
sent him, he courteously replied, explaining his delay in an-

swering and mentioning with routine politeness that it would be a pleasure for him to meet Joaquin should he ever happen to be in San Francisco.

It was at this time, too, that Joaquin was fortunate enough to be introduced to a visiting celebrity, George Francis Train, a well known minor figure of American history, noted for his eccentricities (he omitted all articles from his grammar, considering them as weakening his style, and he advised Joaquin to do the same) and abilities as a promoter. Train read his poetry and pronounced it superb. He advised Joaquin to quit provincial Oregon and live in an atmosphere more congenial to his esthetic art—London, preferably, "where genius is recognized." Whenever Train became enthusiastic over a man or a project he did so to the point of fanaticism. Train was delivering a lecture on the first tramway system in London, which he had built, when he cut short his speech and began to read Joaquin's poems. He then told the citizens of Oregon that despite his esteem for them he considered them at the same time somewhat obtuse, for they had in their midst another Shakespeare and didn't know it, and he railed at his audience for not appreciating true genius. Train described Joaquin as a man of unlimited powers, lofty principles and extraordinary mental endowment.

The chances are that the only person who listened to Train and was honestly impressed by this grandiose tribute was Cincinnatus Hiner Miller. Train's judgment happened to coincide exactly with Joaquin's. He decided to leave Portland immediately.

He wrote to Stoddard, informing the astonished man with disarming naiveté that the "Byron of the Rockies" was accepting his "invitation" to visit him in San Francisco, and he advised his host exactly at what time to meet the Oregon steamer at the wharf. Joaquin added he was extremely sorry that he was unable to be Stoddard's guest for any length of time as he was on his way to London, where, incidentally, his poetry was greatly appreciated. One can but imagine Stoddard's feelings on receiving this extraordinary message; it must have made him curious, however, for he did meet the Oregon boat.

Joaquin had had trouble in finding his true vocation. He had been a cook, a miner, a squaw-man, a lawyer, a pony express rider, a newspaper editor, a judge. Now he intended to be a Poet, a Poet with a capital P, and a Poet he was to remain to the end of his long life.

On June 6, 1870 Joaquin left Oregon, seldom to return. He sailed from Portland (on borrowed money; it is not known who supplied it), bound for San Francisco, and the world.

10

Joaquin carried with him a poem especially written for and dedicated to "The Bards of San Francisco Bay." It started off:

> I am as one unlearned, uncouth
> From country come to join the youth
> Of some sweet town in quest of truth;
> A skilless northern Nazarene.

The bewildered Joaquin was to find that the bards of the "sweet town" would burst into roars of laughter on conning what was intended as a serious if somewhat ingratiating eulogy. But if they laughed at the arrival of the "unsophisti-

cate," as they called him, that was more than they had done
eight years before when Joaquin had been unable to attract
any attention whatsoever in San Francisco.

Stoddard, the gentleman who had "invited" Joaquin to
visit him, was at the dock, and he saw at a glance that the
"northern Nazarene" was destined to be regarded as a peculiar character, even in unconventional San Francisco. Joaquin
strode down the steerage gangplank wearing a broad sombrero, blue denim pants that were too small for him, beaded
moccasins and a white linen duster that fell to his heels. Stoddard noted that the man was handsome with an impressive,
commanding air, and that his first words were: "Well, let us
go and talk with the poets."

Stoddard, a worldly man who had met his share of the
eccentrics who swarmed about San Francisco, strangely
enough found himself driven to apologize for the rude conduct of their fellow poets. He mentioned with some embar-
rassment that he was the only literary master who had come
to meet Joaquin. This did not please Joaquin, but he graciously ignored the lack of courtesy and handed Stoddard the
manuscript of "The Bards of San Francisco Bay." Then, as
Joaquin took a nip of whiskey from a bottle he extracted
from his voluminous duster and rocking back and forth on
his heels, he waited for Stoddard to read the poem there
and then on the wharf.

"Never had a breezier bit of human nature dawned upon
me this side of the South Seas than that Poet of the Sierras
when he came to San Francisco in 1870," Stoddard was to
remember.

While Joaquin stood by watching him intently, Stoddard
read the entire ode carefully, and then, as he recalled three
decades later:

In vain I assured this untamed poet that the "Bards of San Francisco Bay," whom he had so naively saluted, had taken the vows of neither brotherhood nor sisterhood; that they feasted at no common board; flocked not; discoursed with no beaded rills; neither did their skilled hands sweep any strings whatever, and he must, therefore, listen in vain for the seraphic song.

The affable Mr. Stoddard soon introduced Joaquin to Ina Coolbrith and Bret Harte. Joaquin and Miss Coolbrith were to enjoy a long friendship, but his relations with Harte were cool from the outset. Harte was hostile because he correctly sensed him to be a rival, while Joaquin did not care for the dapper editor solely because he thought that the man dressed like a dude. Sooner or later Joaquin met all the select literary set in San Francisco: Ambrose Bierce, Prentice Mulford, H. H. Bancroft, John Muir, Henry George and others, and each eventually was to recall in memoirs how stimulating and even lovable he had found Joaquin, though it must be admitted he acted somewhat queer at times. Mark Twain, a quasi-member of the colony, was not in town, but Joaquin became his friend later. Almost all of these writers in San Francisco made a point of acting and dressing flamboyantly and theatrically, and there is little doubt but that the impressionable Joaquin was influenced by them to live a consciously picturesque life from then on.

During his short stay Joaquin lived (undoubtedly to the relief of his "host" Stoddard) on Russian Hill, among the Bohemians, the writers and artists. He was usually seen in the company of Ina Coolbrith, the beautiful poet with dark red hair and clear, gray eyes, and she became enamored with the raw Oregonian. She appreciated his poetic potentialities as well as his masculinity, and she was as far as we know the first in what Harr Wagner guardedly described as a long, long series of "lady friends." According to West Coast legend, Ina also was the sweetheart of Mark Twain, Harte and Stoddard.

Miss Coolbrith praised Joaquin to the literary circle, pointing out that he was poetically precocious at twenty-eight (for she did not know or suspect he was thirty-three), but in the privacy of her apartment she was sternly critical and was a taskmaster. In her review of *Joaquin, et al* she had likened Joaquin's oft-repeated love for the snow-peaked Sierras to "Diana's hanging all her clothes out to dry." Now she tutored him, made him rewrite and again rewrite his sprawling verse, while she introduced him to poetry that he had not known existed—that of Swinburne, the Rossettis and other "moderns."

Ina Coolbrith was also responsible for two invaluable suggestions which were to be accepted by Joaquin. She pointed out that the easiest way to make himself known in England, where Joaquin insisted he was going, was to be "different" from the run-of-the-mill American, and that this could be accomplished by showing no inhibitions in conversation and by wearing some colorful (even if outlandish) costume that Britishers might identify with that of a true Wild Westerner. Joaquin instantly agreed, for he already had acquired a taste for the fanciful and bizarre.

He did not at first, however, appreciate the advantages of Miss Coolbrith's second scheme. She told him that he should discard the faintly comic name of Cincinnatus Hiner and adopt one reeking of the West—Joaquin, perhaps, after the bandit he had celebrated in verse. No person likes to lose his name, but after long debates the visiting "Nazarene" agreed, and from 1870 on and for the remainder of his days he was known only as Joaquin Miller.

In later years, when Ina Coolbrith did not loom as great an authority as she had seemed during his San Francisco debut, Joaquin was prone to remember that he himself had selected the nom de plume. This choice was made, he said, after critics had reviewed his *Joaquin, et al* and sneered particularly at the title poem. "I kept both the name and the poem and made them respect both," Joaquin declared. There are too many witnesses to the contrary. There were to be half a dozen people who remembered Ina Coolbrith arguing heatedly with Cincinnatus Hiner Miller, pointing out: "How can you expect to conquer England with a name like yours?" Stoddard thought Miss Coolbrith's choice of the name Joaquin was "inspired." Bret Harte declared that she "did Miller a good turn when christening him Joaquin."

Joaquin had every reason to be pleased as he prepared to leave for England (on borrowed money, and again it is not known who his patron was), for in a month's time he had been accepted as a refreshing character, and even as a fair poet. And the self-styled "Byron of the Rockies" was jubilant when a magazine thought "He is as impulsive and reckless as Byron," even though his lyrical talents were not compared to those of his great god. Now, in following Train's advice to "try out" London, he was to be the first of the Western writers who invaded the British capital, and, because he was to be successful, he was to be followed by many an ambitious Westerner—Bierce, Harte, Mulford, Stoddard and Twain. But it was Joaquin Miller, the "unsophisticate," who paved the way.

Joaquin Miller, Poet, left San Francisco early in the summer, bound for the Isthmus, which had to be crossed on foot. He then intended to sail to New York by steamer and, after acquiring a following there, sail on to England. When he had arrived in San Francisco only the courteous Mr. Stoddard had greeted him at the dock, but when he left the town a large crowd toasted him with good wishes. "In his farewell he predicted that he would have 'a name among the princely few,' " the CALIFORNIA MAIL BAG reported. And the weekly magazine added a prophecy of its own: "which may yet be verified."

CHAPTER FOUR

The London Adventure
1870-1871

I

*J*OAQUIN boarded the steamer *Europa* in New York har-
bor in August 21, 1870. He was in no mood to participate in the usual farewell festivities, going instead directly to
his $65 second-class cabin to ponder on the brutality of fel-
low man when it came to recognizing true genius. We know
from a diary he kept that during the voyage to the port of
Glasgow he was overcome by a black fit of melancholia and
that the self-confidence he had acquired after being so favor-
ably received in San Francisco all but disappeared. Joaquin
had ample time on his hands to be despondent, for the trip
took nearly two weeks, and he had much to be despondent
about.

His visit to New York had not been quite the triumph he
had visualized back in San Francisco. Immediately on arriving in the city he had walked to the TRIBUNE office and confidently sent one of his newly printed cards to Horace
Greeley:

JOAQUIN MILLER: BYRON OF THE
ROCKIES

for Greeley long had been partial to Westerners. As Joaquin
had planned it, he first would read aloud a few of his choicer

poems to the editor, then consent to have them printed, and then graciously agree to serve as TRIBUNE correspondent during his "tour" of Great Britain and the continent. But, peculiarly enough, Greeley had never heard of him and had no desire to meet him. Joaquin always believed that the insanity that was to strike Greeley down two years later began to make itself evident back in those August days of 1870, since it was manifest the editor was mad when he refused an audience with the Far West's Byron.

Nor had it helped to bolster Joaquin's ego when he failed in a second attempt to get friendly with a public figure. This was on the occasion of his visit to Henry Ward Beecher, when the famous preacher refused to come out of his study for a man-to-man chat. Joaquin later liked to recall that this snub was administered solely because Beecher at the time was worrying about the noisome scandal that Victoria Woodhull would bring down on his head. Joaquin did the next best thing to seeing the Brooklyn divine: he reverently plucked a leaf from a tree in front of Plymouth Church and carefully stowed it away in an envelope. History has not recorded what ever happened to this precious memento.

In short, Joaquin had not been received by anyone of consequence in New York, and not even the hangers-on he met in saloons had appreciated the poetry that he had insisted on reciting to them. It was clear that New York had not the warm friendliness of San Francisco, and for the rest of his days Joaquin was to dislike the giant city, terming it "a great place for cheap books, and a big den for small thieves." And, as the *Europa* continued its plodding course, his gloom surely must have deepened when he considered that he was arriving among the aloof Britons without money, without letters of introduction, and without a single friend in the London town he intended to conquer.

There could have been but one consoling thought—the knowledge that, in the scheme to change his luck by starting a new life in a new land, Joaquin Miller had nothing to lose.

2

The dreary voyage ended—"I don't think I spoke a dozen words in the whole desolate twelve days"—Joaquin found no Stoddard to greet him as he stepped down the gangplank in Glasgow, and he did not stop long in the Scottish town. "It looked too much like New York," he bitterly noted in his journal. Joaquin set out on foot to visit the nearby Robert Burns country. He permitted himself some "silent devotions" before Burns' grave and then declaimed a poem he had conceived in honor of his fellow poet. Inasmuch as it was delivered in stentorian voice, the oratory attracted the attention of other visitors at the shrine, and so Joaquin felt called upon to repeat the threnody for their benefit. The notice he gained was quite pleasing and prompted him to improvise a number of poetic obituaries at other graves he visited.

He trudged on to the Tweed, spending the night amid the ancient ruins of Dryburgh Abbey where Scott was buried. He slept there not so much because of reverence for the ruins, nor for Scott, but because he could not afford to patronize an inn. Standing before Scott's tomb, he loudly recited another poem in homage to the writer beneath him. Joaquin offered to sell the manuscript copy of the ode to the bystanders who gathered curiously around him, but without success. The canny Scots would listen, but they would not buy.

The next stop on the grave-visiting agenda was the most important of all: obeisance before Byron's tomb in Notting-ham. During the spring of 1870 Joaquin had rowed out to the isle of Sausalito in San Francisco Bay and picked some leaves of laurel. These he had made into a wreath which he carried with him to England. In a gesture of worship he placed the garland on the tomb of the man whom he con-sidered the world's greatest poet (or at least the second great-est), and then the self-imposed schedule called for the in-evitable poem penned specially for the occasion. But first, in order to draw the other Byron pilgrims closer, Joaquin threw back his head, cleared his throat and intoned:

> O my poet! Worshipped where the world is glorious
> with the fire and the blood of youth! Yet here is your home
> —ah well!

We know that these are Joaquin's exact words, for he tells us so in his journal. Then, when he was surrounded by the somewhat puzzled onlookers, Joaquin planted his foot on Byron's grave and, for the benefit of his fellow spectators, as well as for the dead poet, proclaimed:

> O master, here I bow before a shrine,
> Before the lordliest dust that ever yet . . .

Despite the solemnity of the occasion, he could not resist the impulse to pun poetically. Joaquin recorded that he gave the caretaker a sovereign to nail his wreath above the tomb, and that the man promised to keep it there on receipt of a sovereign each succeeding year. It is not known how long the wreath remained.

London now was one hundred and twenty-five miles dis-tant and, having little money, the touring American walked the distance. When he reached the outskirts of the city he heard that the famous Thomas Carlyle had lived nearby. Joaquin briskly composed an ode to be delivered at the author's grave. This, unfortunately, was a wasted poetic effort, for he was informed that Carlyle was very much alive. Joaquin sought an interview, but the terrible-tempered Scot refused to see him. "I like Carlyle—that is, the parts of him which I don't understand," he candidly wrote. "And that is saying I like nearly all of Carlyle, I reckon."

He arrived in London on November 2. It had taken him almost two months to walk from Glasgow to England's capital. On entering the city he immediately headed for Westminster Abbey. As Joaquin remembered it, he who had never been to London before, who had no guidebook and asked no directions, unerringly made his way through the crooked streets to the historic shrine. Joaquin explained, as if he could scarcely believe it himself, that this was accomplished by the unusual expedient of following not his nose, but his heart. "My heart was in the Abbey," he said, "going out to the great spirits, and the immortal dust gathered there."

It can safely be presumed that Joaquin reveled in Westminster Abbey, with its several hundred tons of immortal dust before which he could indulge in silent devotions and recite his dedicatory dirges. In England Joaquin Miller was irresistibly drawn to visiting graves, and yet, strangely enough, when he himself died his ashes were scattered over the Sierras at his request, thus depriving disciples of his own from paying homage to his remains.

Joaquin would have liked to have spent the night in Westminster Abbey to save lodging expenses, as he had done in the Dryburgh ruins, but the attendants informed him this could not be arranged. Reluctantly he left and rented a small and grimy but inexpensive room for five pence a day at 52, New Street. An over-fastidious visitor described the neighborhood as "dingy, depressing and unprosperous," but Joaquin was happy with his surroundings. There was a pub right next door and soon he found that the customers of this "reeking gin-mill" liked to listen to him—"Poetry, *pure* poetry is my life" he would declaim before he started to read his verse— and his performance usually was rewarded with free drinks. He also was very fond of his landlady, a Mrs. Brady, who regarded him as an artist and as such not a person to be plagued with the prosaic problem of meeting the rent. Mrs. Brady was six feet tall and bony, built on the lines of a telegraph pole, and her main satisfaction in life was beating up her husband. Brady was the employee of a brewery—"short and stout as one of his beer-barrels, and a good-hearted soul," as Joaquin described him—and he enjoyed being knocked around by his wife. They were as happy a couple as Joaquin had ever met.

In later years Joaquin liked to reminisce how he sallied over to France in his capacity as correspondent for "one of the leading New York newspapers" to, as he casually put it, "see the French and Germans fight." It is doubtful, however, that he visited the Franco-Prussian battlegrounds or was as he remembered "caught between the armies and in danger of being shot by the Germans or sabred by the French." There is no record of his articles from abroad in any New York newspaper at the time. Besides, by Joaquin's own admission, he was without funds, and the struggle to buy a single skimpy meal was a daily problem that often went unsolved. At this stage Joaquin was, as he wrote with his congenital weakness in spelling, "hartbroke." Yet he intended to stick with poetry—pure poetry, that is.

During this dark period, Joaquin devoted himself to two pursuits—visiting literary shrines and seeking to interest publishers in his poems. A pilgrimage on foot to Camberwell where Robert Browning had lived and the retracing of the travels of Washington Irving were sheer pleasures; but the search for a publisher was unmitigated drudgery. Joaquin had brought with him copies of his two books of poetry. He hoped to select the cream of these volumes and add to them a few verses of more recent inspiration to interest a publisher. Everywhere he was rebuffed, and his encounter with Murray, son of the founder of the house that had published Byron, was typical. Murray refused even to glance at the poems, declaring in a flurry of negatives, "No, no, no! No use, no use. Don't you know poetry won't *do?*" Joaquin was so enraged that he shook his fist at Murray, but only, as he tells us, after he had left the building and was out in the street.

3

Joaquin's luck changed the day he knocked on the door of the editor of FUN, a magazine modeled after PUNCH, in search of a job. There he met "my first, firmest friend in London." This was Tom Hood who, though not having much of a literary reputation himself—he had stood so long in the shadow of his father, the famous poet—did have a wide acquaintance, and Joaquin knew here was the man who could introduce him to the mighty. Tom Hood, an Americanophile and a convivial, gregarious man, took an instant liking to Joaquin. He first was attracted to the American because of the formidable gusto with which Joaquin attacked a bottle of whiskey at lunch, and as their friendship grew, he found the visitor a wonderful drinking companion at any hour, for Joaquin, like Hood (who actually was christened in a punch bowl, and of whom it was said he never got far from one the rest of his life), liked to start drinking early and finish late, and in the interim, talk, talk, talk. As Hood got to know his new friend better he was greatly taken with his candor and breeziness, and, being a writer of sorts himself, he was sympathetic as he listened to Joaquin's stories of being snubbed by publishers.

Tom Hood read the poetry and liked it fairly well—though he decided that he preferred Joaquin the man, Joaquin the gay pub-crawler. Nevertheless, Tom Hood set out to launch his friend into the London literary river. This he was able to accomplish brilliantly, first, by exploiting Joaquin's natural talent for showmanship, and secondly, by introducing him to his own literary set, which was composed in the main of the Pre-Raphaelite Brotherhood members, who were easily persuaded to spread the news of the glories of the visiting genius.

When Joaquin had landed in Glasgow he had been wearing moccasins and a sombrero, tight pants and flannel shirt, partly because of Ina Coolbrith's advice to be "Western," but mostly because that was his entire wardrobe. He soon discarded this outfit, reasoning that it was too American, too backwoodsy for staid Britain, and besides not too comfortable during the long walk ahead of him. Once arrived in London he managed to attire himself more suitably, if more conservatively: the white stock, the dull black coat and trousers. Tom Hood quickly changed all that. Tom Hood knew, just as Ina Coolbrith had known, that people who wore drab costumes were a shilling a dozen in London.

But before he changed Joaquin's manner of dress, Tom Hood considered his friend's personal appearance. Joaquin was six feet tall and weighed a solid 190 pounds; he was handsome with a broad forehead, hard jaw and firm chin and clear blue-gray eyes set under bushy eyebrows, although his nose was a little too strong. He wore a wisp of a tawny goatee, but otherwise was clean-shaven.

Under Hood's supervision Joaquin let the goatee edge out into a distinguished Imperial, and above it grew a flowing mustachio. His hair was permitted to grow long so that the yellow locks flopped about on his shoulders. Gradually he came to resemble more and more Tom Hood's idea of a frontiersman. (The imaginative Hood,who never set foot in America, nonetheless anticipated this "Western" style, for some years later, when Buffalo Bill came to London and made such a sensation, he affected the identical get-up.)

Next came the matter of clothes. The black garments were cast aside. The basic costume Joaquin Miller was now adopting was the one he would wear forever. But alas, it was not the one he preferred. Joaquin pleaded with Hood to let him wear a Byronic open-collared shirt, to become the mysterious and glamorous figure out of "Don Juan," untamed and yet aloof. This, Tom Hood decided, would not do. There were thousands of open-collared Byrons walking in Fleet Street; but there were no frontiersmen or Indian scouts in all London.

Joaquin now wore a sombrero, with the brim updashed in front, and he carried a riding quirt. The shirt was a flaming red, and a blue polka dot bandanna was loosely knotted around the neck. An enormous red kerchief was in the hip pocket, ready to be whipped out and flourished. Sometimes he wore cowboy pants with chaps, and then again pantaloons stuffed into his boots. The boots were always high-heeled, with jingling spurs attached. Jingling spurs in an English drawing room were quite a spectacle in this year of 1871, particularly when there was nowhere a horse in sight. On occasions, Joaquin would wear a red sash over this costume, but, it must be admitted, this extravaganza puzzled even the Britishers, who wondered if this actually was standard wear in the United States.

Joaquin, carried away by the spirit of the masquerade, wanted to tote a pistol in holster, but Tom Hood thought this was going too far. However, he did impress upon Joaquin the necessity of adapting his personality to his costume. He advised him never to walk normally, like any other mortal, but to swagger; never to hesitate to talk authoritatively on any and every subject, but to be cocksure; never to be daunted by fact in telling a story when his imagination and fancy could do just as well, or better. Tom Hood's idea was Joaquin Miller should become different, should always be colorful and flamboyant. Joaquin had been practicing at this for some years, and so the instructions were easily followed. What may have been a mere pose at the start was to become for the rest of Joaquin's life an integral part of his temperament and character. From then on, no matter where he was, in the mansions of duchesses, in clubs and surrounded by celebrities, in the streets, or even when alone with himself, Joaquin always was to act the role of the superbly heroic Man of the Plains, the authentic gen-u-ine frontiersman— and it paid off.

Once his transformation had been completed, Tom Hood introduced him, as Joaquin said, "to almost everybody." Many of these everybodies were the Pre-Raphaelites, with whom Joaquin became a great favorite, and he, in turn, was impressed by them. The Pre-Raphaelites were scornful of the academic style of writing and painting then in vogue, and were generally regarded as a dangerous, radical crew, interested only in the subversive. They had "discovered" Hugo, Baudelaire, Verlaine and Blake, and now they "discovered" Joaquin Miller. The squaw-man, the horse thief was in select company.

All of the Pre-Raphaelites were considerably older than Joaquin, and each was a pronounced individual in his own right, so it was quite a feat to stand out among them. Those who became his friends and boosters included Dante G. Rossetti and his brother William, Burne-Jones, Ford Madox Brown, William Morris, William Holman Hunt and George Frederick Watts.

Dante G. Rossetti became an ardent Joaquin Miller fan and could not get enough of his eccentricities. Rossetti would stand wide-eyed when Joaquin stuck two cigars in his mouth, lit them and then cried, "That's the way we do it in the States!" All these artists listened to Joaquin with jaws agape when he told of his experiences in Boston, of the time he had chased down and lassoed a herd of buffalo trampling through Beacon Street. This certainly would have amazed any Bostonian, let alone a sedate Beacon Streeter, but then it must be remembered that Joaquin was talking to Englishmen.

4

In the spring of 1871 the obscure firm of Whittingham and Wilkins, which specialized in putting out "vanity" editions for writers who could find no publisher, agreed to issue Joaquin's verse. Joaquin pawned his gold watch, which he had held on to tenaciously through his destitute days, and borrowed money from his Pre-Raphaelite friends to meet the costs.

This work, titled *Pacific Poems*, was a slim book of 107 pages plus twelve pages of preface matter, and was put out anonymously, and did not even bear the publisher's imprint. The edition was limited to one hundred copies; one was given to a bookseller as a token that the book was on sale to the public, and the remaining ninety-nine were sent to reviewers and to people of prominence in the social as well as the literary world. Only two copies of *Pacific Poems* are known to exist today.

Joaquin had written all the poems himself, but after he had received page proofs his friends advised him against publishing the volume, at least in that form. They thought that the verses had originality, but that their meter was execrable, so much so that the critics were bound to attack the book savagely in their reviews. Joaquin yielded to the advice. Two friends he met through Tom Hood were persuaded to "polish" his poems. They were George Francis Savage-Armstrong, who later was to become a well-known professor at Cambridge, and "an Irish poet." The Irishman's identity is unknown, and it is presumed that he had some standing in literary circles and did not want his name associated with the outpourings of an unknown American. Walter M. Hill, a bibliophile, stated in 1915 that the Irish poet (who was "still living") told the following story of aiding Joaquin:

> One day he came to me and said, "Look here, do you mind taking a passage—this passage"—pointing to it in his proofs—"from the poem Oregonia, and putting it into what you call correct meter, but altering my words as little as possible."

Joaquin had Armstrong perform the same service for him with other poems.

Hundreds of books of verse were being published in London at the authors' expense, and none of them ever attracted any attention. There was no reason to believe that Joaquin's offering—the third book he had paid to be published—would fare any better. But, to the amazement of everyone except possibly Joaquin Miller, *Pacific Poems* was hailed delightedly by a unanimous press. Joaquin at once announced he was the anonymous author. Like his idol Byron—and how often Joaquin must have dreamed that the hope come true—overnight he found himself famous in London. "His time was come, he ran his race."

There was a certain amount of puffery written by reviewers who were Joaquin's friends—Walter Thurnberry, his tavern companion, went so far in the London GRAPHIC as to acclaim the American as one of the great poetic geniuses not only of the age but of all time—but there were many critics known for their implacable impartiality who also touted *Pacific Poems*. As Joaquin jubilantly jotted down in his diary: "Eureka! The ST. JAMES GAZETTE says 'Arazonian' is by Browning!" The most popular poem in the book was "The Arazonian," and it was destined to be translated into several foreign languages. All his life Joaquin spelled by ear, and, since he pronounced "Arizona" as *Arazona*, "The Arazonian" it was. Certainly no Englishman knew the difference. The poor public, which read all the laudatory reviews and yet could not buy a copy of the book, soon was reciting two favorite lilting lines from "The Arazonian":

> For what is all, in the worlds of fire
> But a vexing of soul, and a vain desire?

This prompted Joaquin to announce that, instead of issuing a second edition of *Pacific Poems*, within a few weeks' time he would publish an entirely new volume, containing all of the *Pacific Poems* together with many, many more splendid

verses. And there was a good deal of excitement when the
original manuscript of "The Arazonian," written on the
backs of old bills and letters, was presented in a formal ceremony to Tom Hood. Hood evidently misplaced the manuscript for it has not survived.

Today *Pacific Poems* is judged as considerably less than
second-rate. Why then did these effusions captivate London?
How was it possible that, as one, the English critics abandoned so completely the high standards of their profession?
Perhaps Van Wyck Brooks has the best explanation, for, as
he wrote of Joaquin in *The Times of Melville and Whitman:*

> His verse had a certain melody and swing and he seemed
> to express with his new scenes all that was wildest and
> woolliest in the little-known West . . . Verbose and
> banal as he often was, rough-hewn and melodramatic, he
> evoked the romantic, heroic life of the plains and espe-
> cially the mountains that appeared in the popular pictures
> of Albert Bierstadt. Here were the great open spaces, the
> dust and taste of alkali, the giant California trees, the
> miners and their cabins, the wigwam and the outlaw's
> camp, the gambler, the vaquero, the white buttes flashing
> in the light of the moon. One saw the coyote in the chapar-
> ral, the rattlesnake in the manzanita, the fleet-footed mus-
> tang, the hawk, the deer and the bear, the prairie fire, the
> Indian lodge, the Spaniard's hacienda, the pack-train
> stringing round the mountain its long gray line. This was
> the world, with its picturesque settings and vigorous prim-
> itive life . . .

5

The new literary lion soon was a familiar figure in drawing
rooms and clubs. With a change of his fortunes, Joaquin
moved to more respectable lodgings in Camberwell. Mrs.

Brady was so sorry to see him leave that she stopped halfway through beating her husband to wish him a fervent farewell. Now Joaquin would stroll over to the Endsleigh Gardens to see William Rossetti (but without formal invitation), or to the finely named Queen's House in Cheyne Walk to see brother Dante G., but most of his time was spent in the homes of the rich and titled. The dowagers and the duchesses thought his Oregon accent was wonderful—it sounded so Scottish to them—and they were astonished at his capacity for food and liquor. Joaquin had a stomach that could digest anything, even English cooking, although he claimed that pemmican was his favorite dish. It was difficult, however, for the hostesses to get pemmican in London.

As for liquor, Joaquin regarded the English brand of whiskey as a doubtful intoxicant, gulping it down by the tumblerful as if it were beer while he discoursed on various "fluids" and "hard stuff" to which he was accustomed in the Wild West, where whiskey was not whiskey unless 180 proof. Even his name intrigued London. It had such a romantic ring. Joaquin explained that it had been conferred on him by Joaquin Murietta, whom he once had sheltered. Murietta, he said, was not an ordinary bandit, but an American Robin Hood, a man who had called him "his son." It was not mentioned that Murietta died when Joaquin was a boy.

The dowagers were enchanted by Joaquin's attire. They had not realized that Americans dressed so colorfully. Joaquin varied his costumes. One day he was an Indian scout, the next a rugged old frontiersman, and then a '49er of Gold Rush days. Often it was difficult to determine just what Joaquin was, or meant to be. Occasionally he would appear in a velvet jacket, embroidered pantaloons, with silver bells jangling at the seams, and with two, maybe three, giant

Bowie knives stuck into a broad leather belt. "Miller proved something of a revelation to the people of England," as an American magazine recorded.

His appeal seems to have been exotic. The wild Sierras were far removed from London, halfway around the globe, but there in their drawing rooms the British could see an authentic Westerner. Joaquin became London's "character," but it is doubtful if such an act would have intrigued anyone in the United States. Wild Westerners were thick in America, but in England they were a novelty, and the British thrilled as Joaquin stomped about in front of them, his sombrero tilted back on his head, his riding crop slashing out at a marble fireplace to emphasize a particularly flawless rhythm in one of his poems. They were in ecstasy when, his voice booming and rising, then dropping to a whisper, he recited a verse from "Kit Carson's Ride," which he promised would be in his new edition of poems:

> Room! room to turn round in, to breathe and be free,
>   To grow to be a giant, to sail as at sea
> With the speed of the wind on a steed with his mane
>   To the wind, without pathway or route or a rein.
> Room! room to be free where the white border'd sea
>   Blows a kiss to a brother as boundless as he;
> Where the buffalo come like a cloud on the plain,
>   Pouring on like the tide of a storm-driven main.

The story of "Kit Carson's Ride," in which the Indian scout and his "brown bride" escape from prairie fires with the "red Comanches hot on their track," never failed to arouse the twittering hostesses, and we have the word of an eyewitness that they were on the verge of swooning dead away by the time Joaquin reached what was considered then as a most daring, erotic passage:

We lounged in the grass—her eyes were in mine
　　And her hands on my knees, and her hair was as wine
In its wealth and its flood, pouring on and all over
　　Her bosom wine red, and press'd never by one.

As an older generation of school children in the United
States can testify, "Kit Carson's Ride" became a "must"
when it came to reciting at commencement time or when
performing before teachers in elocution classes. Today some
serious poets take the harsh attitude that such a "classic"
antagonized countless children toward verse and set back
poetry fifty years.

Joaquin, like his hostesses, was at times overstimulated if
not uncontrollable, and the "bosom wine red" stanza particularly went to his head. One evening, overcome by the
splendor of his verse, he became so ecstatic that he rolled on
the drawing room floor in a frenzy, biting the ankles of various aristocratic women. It is even said that he bit first the
ankle of a Duchess, then of a Marchioness, then of a Countess,
then of a Lady, in strict observance of their rank, but perhaps this is a canard. "It enlivened the dinner—dull before,"
Joaquin remarked when asked about the incident. The noble-
women looked on in amazement, but they found they were
delighted too, and when news of the ankle nipping got
around the social set was in a furore. Joaquin was in demand
everywhere, to bite ankles. To the British, it was "a demmed
good show." Even Queen Victoria heard of these shenani-
gans, but, unlike her subjects, was unamused.

Joaquin and his antics so tickled the English that he was
admitted to the exclusive Savage Club, its only other American member being Julian Hawthorne, although Mark Twain
was later accepted. Hawthorne, son of the famous novelist,
in his memoirs described Joaquin as "a licensed libertine,"

adding rather loftily that he also was "charming, amiable, and harmless, amusing the club and himself by costuming his part as Poet of the Sierras." The patronizing Julian Hawthorne did not know it then, but he was destined to have a certain affinity with Joaquin: Joaquin had been indicted as a horse thief. Hawthorne would be indicted for fraud. But there the affinity ends, for, unluckily for Hawthorne, *he* had to serve a jail sentence.

Joaquin frankly explained to Hawthorne the necessity for wearing his sombrero, red shirt, scarf and sash, long hair. "It helps sell the poems, boys!" he cried, "and it tickles the Duchesses!" Plainly, Joaquin relished the idea of putting something over on the British.

Hawthorne remembered how Joaquin would tell the open-mouthed members of the Savage Club his "tall tales of 'My California,' of his wild adventures with Walker of Nicaragua, his big hat tipped on the back of his head and a nip of whiskey at hand." "When his tall figure appeared in the doorway," Hawthorne reminisced, "up would go an arm with the Indian sign, 'How!' The club understood him and approved of his dramatizations and Munchausenisms, though to the uncredited outsiders it was apt to be a little frigid." Ten years later Hawthorne was to meet the gaudy Buffalo Bill and listen to the same "weird tales of his triumphs," just as he had listened to Joaquin Miller.

With the upsurge of Joaquin's fame (some called it notoriety), he made other new and important friends. He met Ruskin, who thought he "would pass," and Sir Charles Dilkes, powerful editor of the ATHENAEUM, who introduced him around. The visit with Tennyson that Joaquin remembered in some detail probably did not happen. Joaquin said he went to Tennyson's residence at Farringford, on the Isle of Wight, and that the great man generously praised his poems. (Mark Twain said Joaquin referred to the poet as a "dear old peanut.") Strangely enough, Professor Savage-Armstrong, a more reliable authority, also remembered making the trip with Joaquin to Farringford, but in his version of the visit the two were too awed to approach Tennyson's door. This is puzzling: Tennyson had left the Isle of Wight a year before Joaquin reached London.

Joaquin did meet Browning, and he recorded for posterity the tremendous wit of this wonderful man. "Browning was just back from Italy, sunburnt and ruddy," Joaquin said. " 'Robert, you are browning,' smiled Lady A. 'And you are August-a,' bowed the great poet grandly." Such were the high jinks of the literary set in 1871.

Browning invited Joaquin to dinner. The poet, whose fame was at its peak with the success of his "The Ring and the Book," was interrupted in his conversation by a servant who said the cart had arrived to take the books to the hospital. "I am sent so many books by young authors that there is no room for them in the house," Browning explained to his guest. "I send a cartload every few weeks for the hospital." When Joaquin returned to his lodgings he hurriedly took off the wrapping of his new book that he had intended to send to Browning.

The meeting with Swinburne was a more important event to Joaquin, for he admired the poet more, and tried to imitate his verse. The encounter took place at Number 9, the Pines, Putney Hill—that much we do know. But there are two conflicting versions of what happened. Joaquin said that he was accompanied on his visit by a well known, but unnamed, poet whom Swinburne regarded as a rival, and that Swinburne shouted, "Bring the American poet up, and tell Blank to go to hell."

This is at variance with the situation as Theodore Watts-Dunton remembered it. Watts-Dunton, a literary leech who lived with the unmarried Swinburne and who has been most unkindly described as the man who debauched the poet (this means nothing—the names of such debauchers are legion), said that Joaquin sent up his card and promptly had it returned, as the great man had no desire to see stray Americans. Suddenly inspired, on remembering Swinburne's admiration for Walker the Freebooter, Joaquin cried, "Tell Mr. Swinburne that I'm the man who took part in the Walker expeditionary force a while ago." Whereupon, according to Watts-Dunton, "By way of reply Swinburne himself appeared on the stairs, and welcomed the hero with outstretched hand," for Joaquin "had found the sesame to Swinburne's heart."

Joaquin was now popular everywhere—popular where the British congregated, that is, for certain members of the American colony in London were suspiciously watchful. Back in the United States, the San Francisco NEWS-LETTER stated on August 6, 1871 that "California's new poet is making a sensation in every London paper except EVERY SATURDAY, which is edited by Harte, who is jealous." And the CALIFORNIA MAIL BAG in considering the great fame of "California's New Poet" said Joaquin was "commended by every other publication with the exception of EVERY SATURDAY, which is edited by Bret Harte, who is exceedingly jealous of the new candidate for literary honors." The first stirrings of discontent and animosity in London's American colony would soon begin to rumble.

6

All his life Joaquin was to remember the outstanding experience of his London adventure, when he was the guest of honor at a dinner given by Dante G. Rossetti. The celebrated poet-painter had adopted the visiting American unreservedly and was generous in extolling his poetry and person, just as he had done a few years before when he introduced Walt Whitman to London literary circles. To Rossetti, there was no difference between Miller and Whitman when it came to poetic genius. This must have been extremely gratifying to Joaquin, but, vain as he outwardly seemed, he was under no such illusion himself. He had his own opinion as to the width of the gap between a Whitman and, not only himself, but any other contemporary American poet. "I often think of you as the one lone tree that tops us all, battered by storm and blown but still holding your place, serene and satisfied," Joaquin was to write the good gray poet a few years later.

Joaquin attended the Rossetti feast merely as *a*, and not *the* guest, and we know a great deal about the affair because Joaquin often wrote and talked about it. But we do not know who the other guests were, for Joaquin, though singularly impressed by the evening, was at the same time strangely close-mouthed about it. "The home is entirely a castle," he wrote. "One may not give names and dates and details. The secrets of the board and fireplace are sacred . . . I should be in disgrace forever if I dared set down any living man's name."

This reticence from a diarist—a far cry from a Boswell or a Pepys—is perhaps explained by Joaquin's great awe when confronted by anyone who claimed to know much about poetry. According to the letters of Watts-Dunton, published more than half a century after the Rossetti party took place, Joaquin was astonished at anyone's "profound knowledge of the art of poetry." "It's amazin'," Watts-Dunton quoted Joaquin as saying. "He seems to know everything about poetry that was ever written, and much more. And here am I, a poet with a big name, and I'm damned if I could tell the difference between a hexameter and a pentameter to save my scalp."

Watts-Dunton undoubtedly gave a correct rendering of the conversation, for Joaquin doted on the expression "to save my scalp." It had such an authentic, earthy, Western and Indian ring, and it delighted the Britishers. But, if we can believe Watts-Dunton, the man who possessed this profound knowledge of poetry was not Rossetti or Swinburne or any other poet, but was Watts-Dunton in person. And if Joaquin actually was impressed by the superficial Watts-Dunton, it is easy to understand why he was so overwhelmed when face to face with Rossetti and his entourage.

We may safely reconstruct from Joaquin's diary and his other recollections just what happened during this "scintillating" evening.

"I cannot forget that dinner . . . nor can I hope to recall its shining and enduring glory," Joaquin fondly thought back. "I am a better, larger man because of it."

Joaquin tried to recapture for his readers the "golden grain" of the conversation that passed over the table. It turned out that among "a few of the pearls picked up as they were tossed about the table at intervals" was a deep observation made by none other than Joaquin Miller, né Cincinnatus Hiner Miller. This splendid opportunity presented itself when Rossetti—the "Master," as Joaquin called him—commanded him to give his definition of poetry.

Joaquin was not at a loss for words. "To me a poem must be a picture," he quickly replied.

The way Joaquin remembered it, the guests leaped to their feet, applauded wildly, showering huzzas on him. This may or may not have happened, for Joaquin's memory at times was short, but if there was such a response it must have met with the approval of Rossetti—of whom it has been said that he wrote his canvases and painted his poems. In any event, for the rest of his life Joaquin was to use the same glib formula whenever he was asked what poetry meant to him.

Inasmuch as this dinner reputedly was so remarkable for its wit, Joaquin is peculiarly reticent when it comes to quoting anything that actually was witty. (When he tried, the sample is one of exaggeration, not of wit. For instance, Joaquin revealed that when the Master stated no great poem could ever be written in a city he, Joaquin Miller, instantly seconded the dictum, saying, "You might as well try to grow a California pine in the shell of a peanut," and he added that the sheer brilliance of his metaphor stunned the assembled guests.) The chances are it was merely another stag all-night drinking party, for as Joaquin said, "We dined so late that we missed all relish for breakfast."

"If I could remember and write down truly and exactly what these men said," Joaquin stated, "I would have the best and greatest book that ever was written." He did, however, write down and thus permit us to glimpse a flash of what he called the philosophy of the Master, who, apropos of nothing, declaimed: "Let us see the beauty in the world, and we will see nothing that is ugly." This remark too, it seems, was so profound that for a few minutes the guests were breathless with admiration. Rossetti let the shiny epigram echo in their ears and then relapsed into moody contemplation.

Eventually, as the bottles began to pile up on the table, the conversation resumed. From then on, having delivered himself of his sparkling bon mot, "the Master sat quiet for the most part," Joaquin noted. The others of the party were equally glittery, however, as witness the description of the following conversational flurry:

"What is poetry?" cries a neighbor.
"All true pure life is poetry," answers another.
"But the inspiration of poetry?"
"The art of poetry is in books. The inspiration of poetry is in nature."
To this all agreed.

There was a lull, but soon the talking picked up—"Heard melodies are sweet, but unheard melodies are sweeter," came a voice from the end of the table—and it finally reached almost its zenith. As Joaquin recorded:

A painter, ruddy-faced and a rollicking gentleman, remarked merrily to me as he poured out a glass of red wine: "When travelling in the mountains of Italy I observed that the pretty peasant women made the wine by putting grapes in a great tub and then getting into this tub, barefooted, on top of the grapes, treading them with their brown, bare feet. At first I did not like to drink this wine. I did not think it was clean. But . . . I noticed they always washed their feet after they got done treading out the wine."

This commonplace observation, which the English had been making for centuries, seemed to cause a sensation. But there still was one further gem to come, namely when the Master emerged from his reverie and spoke words. Joaquin had just begun to quote from Longfellow, then much in vogue in certain circles, when, to his surprise, someone at the table commented rather superciliously: "I never read 'Evangeline' but once."

Here was a man who had failed to read "Evangeline" two, three, four times! Joaquin was aghast. He rose to his feet in defense of a fellow American, of a great fellow poet. But, before he could point out the error of the Philistine's ways, Rossetti the Master coughed, paused significantly, and then uttered a pronouncement that silenced any further comment on the subject:

"It is a waste of time to look twice at a sunset."

This brilliant *aperçu*, Joaquin thought, topped the evening, and he sat down. From then on, there was nothing to be looked forward to. And so Joaquin desisted from describing whatever else happened. "I have gone too far in this already," he wrote. "I have profaned this great man and occasion quite enough, and shall attempt to quote no more of his wonderful utterances."

All in all, as is clearly seen, it was quite a party!

7

The critical success accorded *Pacific Poems* meant that Joaquin could have his pick of publishers to issue his second book, for the public at large was clamoring to read his verse. The distinguished house of Longmans, Green, Reader and Dyer was selected and the book, consisting of 301 pages or nearly three times as long as *Pacific Poems*, was published in May, 1871, a month or so after his first production. And Joaquin gave Savage-Armstrong generous credit for assisting him "to tune up" the poems.

"Now, the new book must come out!" Joaquin wrote in his journal. "Yesterday I submitted a list of names for it— nine names—and one of my Irish friends settled on 'Songs of the Sierras.' And that, it is agreed, shall be the name of the new baby." Joaquin added, with his usual fondness for exclamation points: "Good! Good!"

Songs of the Sierras embodied all of the *Pacific Poems* and much new material, and was dedicated "To The Rossettis." It contained five long poetic tales, all dealing with the Far West, a semi-dramatic poem, and a eulogy on Burns and Byron. The choice of the title was really excellent. Joaquin had sometimes been referred to as the "Poet of the Sierras," but from now on this was to be the sobriquet that instantly identified him. Joaquin himself never was too pleased with the nom de plume. He thought it too confining, geographically speaking, and preferred the more resounding appellation "Lion of the North," but people felt that the phrase had been preempted and it never caught on.

Many modern critics consider *Songs of the Sierras* as Joaquin's best book of poetry. However, this is not to say that it deserved one-tenth of the praise lavished on it by the British critics. If these gentlemen were to be believed, Joaquin had no equal as the greatest American poet, dead or alive, and this included Poe, Whitman, Emerson and Whittier. Only Shakespeare the Englishman was admitted to be superior.

"This is truly a remarkable book," Joaquin's friend, William Rossetti, declared in the ACADEMY. "It contains picturesque things, picturesquely put." This pronouncement, so sweet to a poet's ear, was followed by the astounding assertion that the "excellent and fascinating" versifier ranked "among the distinguished poets of all time, and could greet them as peers." Savage-Armstrong also did some mighty log-rolling for his American friend, devoting nine fat pages, no less, to eulogize the poems in a periodical called DARK BLUE. FRASER'S MAGAZINE prophesied that Joaquin Miller the poet would live through the ages, but warned Joaquin Miller the man to "keep clear of modern mysticism," meaning that he should not associate with the Pre-Raphaelites. Joaquin cannot have been displeased when one critic coupled his name with Victor Hugo, and his dream of dreams came true when the influential SATURDAY REVIEW not only compared him to his idol Byron but pronounced him superior, saying that the few faults he had were those inherent in Byron's work, but that Joaquin possessed "a ring of genuineness which is absent from Byron's poetry." The WESTMINSTER REVIEW and the PALL MALL GAZETTE were little less glowing. All in all, Joaquin could not have gotten more flattering reviews if he had written them himself, and his *Joaquin, et al,* ignored in Oregon, was republished in London by the Hotten house in Piccadilly.

Here and there, it is true, a reviewer who perhaps felt ashamed when he considered the extravagance of his praise, would condemn certain stray faults (even Rossetti noted some "odd and inadmissible words" and "platitudes of phrase," while FRASER'S MAGAZINE, although commending Joaquin as a most remarkable poet, pointed out that "his philosophy is still crude . . . his rhythm irregular"), but nearly all comments were highly favorable, thus assuring a good sale for the book.

At the time, and for years to come, *Songs of the Sierras* sold tremendously in England, and a favorite poem with British readers was Joaquin's tribute to his old "comrade-in-arms," the valiant William Walker, a poem that is regarded today as perhaps the finest he ever wrote. Horace Gregory, the modern critic and poet, declares that "Behind a rhetorical gesture that has now become quaint and was never as brilliant as it once seemed, one may detect the genuine note of pathos, with a suggestion of a dignity that had never been fully expressed." He is referring to the following passages on General Walker:

> He lies low in the level'd sand,
> Unshelter'd from the tropic sun,
> And now, of all he knew, not one
> Will speak him fair in that far land.
>
> . . . . .
>
> I said some things with folded hands,
> Soft-whisper'd in the dim sea-sound,
> And eyes held humbly on the ground,
> And frail knees sunken in the sands.
> He had done more than this for me,
> And yet I could not well do more;
> I turned me down the olive shore,
> And set a sad face to the sea.

And yet, such examples as these were offset by innumerable doggerel verses. One, titled "Comanche," an excerpt of which is printed below, is a jingle that reminds one of the dialogue in a Lone Star Ranger program as staged today for children—little children—on television:

> A blazing home, a blood-soaked hearth,
> Fair women's hair with blood upon!
> The Ishmaelite of all the earth
> Has like a cyclone, come and gone—

and also:

> "To horse! To horse!" the rangers shout
> And red revenge is on his track. . . .

Following its tremendous success in England—where, despite its price of $1.50 it immediately sold 11,000 copies in two editions, and a third was ordered—*Songs of the Sierras* was published in the United States, and the critics as one were as savage in censure as the English were oppressive with acclaim. Joaquin's heavy-footed romanticism was not accepted as any true picture of the West by the people who knew the West. Some reviewers automatically assumed that Joaquin was totally illiterate, gleefully pointing out that he rhymed *Goethe* with *teeth*, and this was a poetic howler that was to haunt Joaquin for decades.

The American critics found Joaquin's philosophy cheap, his rhythm clumsy, his meter uncertain. They sneered at his "false vigor" and his lack of subtlety, his "blemishes arising from early want of culture," and were generally inclined to treat *Songs of the Sierras* as second-rate imitations of Byron. They declared his characters were Byron's in a different guise, that Kit Carson was another Don Juan dressed as a scout, that Walker was Lara with a revolver on hip. They pointed out that all the poems were more or less alike, that the cast of the characters inevitably numbered four: the superb hero, the beautiful heroine, the good Indian, the dirty villain. "There are people of all nationalities whom a pinch more brains and a trifle more of diffidence would not hurt," the NATION declared, and the magazine sneered at "William Rossetti's latest discovery."

As for the topheavy compliments bestowed on Joaquin by the English, well, some people were naive to the point of stupidity. The critics attributed the success of the book in London to the fact that the poems were different—as compared to the stodgy seriousness of the run-of-the-mill poetry of the Victorian age. They believed, with reason, that the

British were prone to like poetry of the Wild West because it was a far-away place that most of them could never hope to visit; but right there in London, before their eyes, they had a real romantic frontiersman—at least he dressed like one —the living image sprung from the fantasies they read. "It has carried our English cousins by storm, because the life itself is all so novel and strange to them," HARPER'S NEW MONTHLY pointed out. "Its fatal fault is that in its portraiture of American character it sacrifices truth to the poet's conceit."

The feeling among critics of our own age is that Joaquin Miller's talent was merely thin and that most of his poetry is close to trash, and they can point to the inescapable fact that none of his work has survived. This opinion, of course, may change; many a poet and writer has been resuscitated after years of oblivion and disrepute. One thing, however, cannot be denied: In spite of the unanimously unfavorable reaction of the American critics, the American public of the 1870's, the 1880's and the 1890's responded differently. It adopted Joaquin Miller the poet and took him to its generous and uncritical heart, and, as generations of schoolchildren have known, the pedagogues considered his works as "classics."

8

Joaquin was a healthy exhibitionist, and posturing was second nature to him. Of course he seldom wasted a performance on one or two people. He needed an audience, the larger the better, which would spread the news of his latest antics. In public he would go to any length to play practical jokes on friend or foe, and once he even went to the extreme of shaving off his Imperial, merely to attract attention.

As Julian Hawthorne recalled, this came about one day in the Savage Club, when:

A person obviously of exotic interest, a typical Pall Mall exquisite, twirling a slender, ebony cane, seated himself on a chair, dusted it off with a monogrammed handkerchief, crossed his aristocratic legs, revealing patent leathers with spats, unbuttoned the black Prince Albert, and took out a silver cigar case from the pocket of his white waistcoat. After patting the white camellia in his buttonhole, and without removing his silk hat, he held up a gloved finger to the waiter, "A whiskey and soda."

The waiter was embarrassed by this self-possessed hot-house flower, for the rules of the Club forbade the serving of drinks to anyone not previously introduced. Willie Dixon, the manager, glided forward to explain the iron-clad regulation. The stranger stared insolently at Willie, putting a monocle to his eye to peer at him more intently. He stroked his smooth chin and gave a tweak of his waxed mustache in disgust. And then, dropping his role, Joaquin cried with a shout of laughter:

"What's eatin' you, Willie? Don't you like my new rig?"

Joaquin then turned to the clubmen clustered around him and commanded—

"Move up, boys. I guess the drinks are on you!"

There was a curious mixture of childlike naiveté and Davy Crockett brag in Joaquin's makeup, and while the former was engaging and easy to take, the latter wasn't. Hawthorne mentioned that Joaquin occasionally was humble—but only occasionally—when he thought about the fact that he, only a few years removed from a squaw-man, was being welcomed as a guest in Britain's most splendid castles.

"Once, as we were sitting before an English fireplace one

evening," Hawthorne recalled, "he said 'Wonderful, that while I sit here gold is being given me thousands of miles over yonder!' " He also recorded Joaquin's rather obscure afterthought: "Genius works night and day and the antipodes do not affect it."

Constant braggadocio can be an unnerving experience, even when tempered with humbleness. And for some reason Joaquin was driven to more and more bragging, outlandish bragging, until it became a compulsion. In after years there would be printed the repetitious reminiscences of those who had watched Joaquin in action at a party, teetering on his high-heeled jackboots, hitching away at his red sash, gulping down his whiskey, and boasting, boasting, boasting.

Much of Joaquin's wild talk, which centered mostly on his exploits in the Wild West, was true. Some of it was tinctured with fancy. And a large portion of it was simply the product of a loose imagination. Perhaps he had learned Tom Hood's lesson too well, for now he overplayed his hand. So much had happened to Joaquin during this thirty-four years that he could have safely amused his audiences merely by telling the truth, but he had to embellish, to embroider, to exaggerate, and what Mark Twain later was to describe as the "muddy torrent" poured out relentlessly:

He had driven a covered wagon across the plains and saved his entire family by his indomitable courage in repelling Indian attacks. Joaquin Murietta had found him such an invaluable lieutenant that he had bequeathed him his name, and called him "my son." He was "born to the saddle," had mastered the art of taming wild horses as no living man before him. ("One morning Trollope hinted that my immunity was due to my big Spanish saddle," Joaquin recorded. "I threw my saddle on the grass and rode without so much as a blanket; and I rode neck to neck, and then left them all behind and nearly everyone unhorsed.") He had founded an Indian Republic, had established the first pony express service in the West, had dealt out impartial justice as a Judge in Oregon "with one law-book and two six-shooters." He had been so successful in mining for gold that he always threw away all the undersized nuggets. He had . . . and so on, and so on.

The stories had been heard before. Many of his listeners were greatly entertained, for Joaquin could tell the same tale twice, but so differently as to make it a new experience; but others shrugged and walked away. Some became downright bored and were apt to voice their bitterness about the tedium to which they were exposed. Once this began to happen, certain members of the American colony led by Bret Harte began to chime in with direct attacks on their fellow countryman. They ridiculed Joaquin's extravagant behavior, his showy dress, his semi-illiteracy. They snickered at this "tame frontiersman" with his high heeled boots and red shirt, and they circulated reports that Joaquin chewed tobacco, he spit on the floor, he kicked puppies, and he didn't believe in God.

9

Joaquin wisely sensed that the slight decline of his popularity might degenerate into a complete downfall. He decided to return to the United States and profit by the wave of publicity he had received there, and to reconquer England at a later, a more propitious time. He announced that he was off to America to visit his dying sister Ella, and in September, 1871 he left abruptly. However, his silent exit—the most inconspicuous thing he ever did while in Britain—should not blind us to his very real accomplishments:

This splendid poseur, Joaquin Miller, had arrived in Great Britain in September, 1870—penniless, an uncouth American, a backwoods wanderer, a wife-deserter and horse thief, a man virtually escaping from his native land. Twelve months later, on his way home, he had emerged from obscurity to fame with one giant stride. If he had a few enemies, he also had many powerful friends. He had a popular reputation as a great poet, with adulatory comments in print to prove the high opinion the English critics had for him.

It had been a rewarding year.

CHAPTER FIVE

The Wanderer
1871-1875

I

 OAQUIN took an expensive suite at the Astor House on his arrival in New York and invited the press for an interview. The reaction of the reporters concerning the return of this native was mixed. Some thought that if he seemed perhaps too expansive and glittery it was probably due to his unpredictable poetic temperament; to others he was merely a bundle of affectations and even a freak. But all agreed that Joaquin Miller was good newspaper copy.

When Joaquin told the story of his London success he casually mentioned that Browning, Swinburne, Tennyson and the Rossetti brothers especially admired him and his poetry; and then he started name-dropping on a higher level. There were "a Duke or two" so close to him as to be almost his brothers, while he had met socially such mighty personages as Queen Victoria, Princess Louise, the Prince of Wales and Lord Gladstone. The reporters were not curious about "Lord" Gladstone, but they were interested to hear about the encounter with the Queen. Joaquin thought back. He had met Her Majesty at some castle, at some sort of a reception. No, he did not remember the name of the castle or when the meeting had taken place—he had attended so many receptions in England. Joaquin (who, incidentally, *was* to be introduced to Victoria two years later) said the Queen took such an instant fancy to him that she impetuously stripped a ring from her finger and gave it to him. "I felt like hugging her," Joaquin added.

This bit of news intrigued the newspapermen, for they had heard of no such incident, and they asked Joaquin to go into the matter more fully. Joaquin pondered and pondered, then explained what had happened:

> She took a little ring of three small diamonds from her finger, and handing it to me said seriously, "This will remind you of one who is prouder of a book she has written than the crown she wears." I wear the ring on my watch chain—it's too small for my finger.

The reporters wanted to know the name of the book the Queen had written and which had established such marvelous affinity between the two authors, but Joaquin could not remember the title. He suggested perhaps she had written it, but had not published it. Joaquin was asked if he could show them the royal ring. He said he had forgotten to wear his watch chain. When a newspaperman pointed out he was wearing the chain, Joaquin smoothly explained that he meant he had forgotten to put the ring on the watch chain.

The next day, the interviews with America's new poet were all faintly hostile, for some of the reporters seemed to feel that Joaquin was prone to exaggeration. The episode of Queen Victoria's largesse was all but ignored. That was the last that was ever heard about the "little ring of three small diamonds." The ring Joaquin was to display from here on would be the one he wore on his left hand, inlaid with a stone the size of a pigeon's egg, which, as the poet said, "was given me by Napoleon the Prince Imperial."

Joaquin moved out of the suite and took a cheap hotel

room. He realized it would be to his advantage to keep in the public eye and so, in an open letter sent the New York TRIBUNE and other newspapers, he addressed the poetic admirers he had left behind him in Britain.

"As I left England suddenly, barely saying good-bye to a few friends at hand," Joaquin wrote, "I have ever since felt like making some public expression of my gratitude to that country for its noble treatment of me and my crude 'Songs of the Sierras.' . . . I had neither money, name, nor influence . . . England! the terms of expression of my thanks are threadbare."

Joaquin admitted in the letter that "the American press has been more cautious and qualified in its reviews." This was decidedly an understatement, for when Joaquin arrived in his native country he found that the critics were trying to outdo each other in their caustic comments. HARPER'S NEW MONTHLY sourly advised Joaquin to "put off his uncouth dress, and attire his thoughts in respectable habiliments." The three kingpins of the American critical world were savage in their condemnation of *Songs of the Sierras*. William Dean Howells wondered in the ATLANTIC MONTHLY how the English could overlook the "dreary unreality," the "dreadful prolixity," the "chasmal vacancies" of Joaquin's verse. Edmund Clarence Stedman the poet and critic bluntly stated that Joaquin was "a mountebank." "I've no use for a poet who turns up at a reception looking like a scout or gambler from a Rocky Mountain mining camp," he frigidly declared. Richard Watson Gilder felt the same. "While in London Miller wore jackboots, Mexican serape, broad-brim hat, and long hair like a scout," he sneered. "Similarly attired, he called on me at the CENTURY magazine, all for the advertising which resulted."

Yet, as often happens, the persistence and violence of these attacks redounded to Joaquin's advantage, for the general public became sympathetic to the man under fire and sided with him. They read his verse and it appealed to them. They liked Joaquin's *poetry* and felt no need to go into a pet just because the poet himself dressed extravagantly or behaved in unorthodox fashion. People who ordinarily disliked verse became fond of reading Joaquin Miller, for his ideas were simply, though at times crudely, expressed, and he glorified the golden West they liked to hear about. Throughout the years that followed—and this again has often happened—the more the public rallied to Joaquin, the more choleric the reviewers became.

Joaquin decided that New York was a dull place to live in —he had never cared for the city anyway—and, with winter coming on, he contemplated a trip to the warm South. First he went to Boston and presented a letter of introduction from Jean Ingelow to the publishing firm of Roberts Brothers. Miss Ingelow, whose morocco-bound volumes of verse decorated American parlors for so many decades, urged the company to add Joaquin to its stable of writers. Joaquin was given a liberal advance, and both poet and publisher were to profit by the alliance, for his books were to sell well.

While in Boston Joaquin made an effort to counteract what he termed "unwarranted charges against my reputation, which nearly question my veracity." He was referring to a story in the New York Herald a few weeks before, in which the writer not only doubted Joaquin's participation in the Nicaraguan filibuster, but wondered if he actually had even met or seen General Walker. It was pointed out that in one of his poems Joaquin had described Walker as "a tall man," whereas as everyone knew the General was a dumpy little fellow.

Joaquin was appalled by this distrust—this distrust displayed so publicly. He considered suing, but decided against it. Instead, in a letter to the HERALD, he said that of course he knew his old comrade-in-arms was no giant, but as he explained it: " 'A tall man,' I believe, in the old term, as used by the poets, did not always imply a man of uncommon stature." Sadly enough, this had been generally regarded as less than a lame reply, as the public apparently had little use for poetic license. Years later, Joaquin was to use what he considered the perfect answer to the question of being with Walker in Nicaragua. "Was Milton ever in hell?" he would ask.

Now, in an effort to mend the damage, Joaquin summoned for an interview one Clint Parkhurst, an itinerant journalist, to whom he gave the true inside story—never before told—of his fighting background. Joaquin revealed in detail his bravery in Nicaragua, where he had been wounded and commended by General Walker on the field of battle for his heroism, and, though he said he was loath to do so, he related some of his "experiences" in California, such as his founding of the Indian Republic.

The article that resulted, "The Border Days of Joaquin Miller," appeared in LAKESIDE magazine in 1872, and is mentioned here only because it has a certain unique value of its own: it was the first of a long series of planted stories concerning the mythical episodes of Joaquin's career, and these yarns would appear periodically for sixty years, up to the 1930's.

An ironical and grim incident delayed Joaquin's trip to

the South. In England, he had given the illness of his sister Ella as the excuse for his hasty departure. Whether he knew it or not, Ella had died in Oregon six months before he sailed. But now, after he had arrived in the United States, Joaquin was informed that there was indeed a serious illness in the family—his elder brother, John De Witt Miller, was on his deathbed.

Joaquin went to Easton, Pennsylvania, to be with him. John had volunteered for service in the Union army during the Civil War, and he reproached himself for not having seen his mother and father since. He urged Joaquin to visit their parents, while they were still alive. On September 15, 1871 Joaquin wrote his brothers James and George Melvin in Oregon that John had died "very peacefully and in his full mind." "I think I will be in Oregon soon, but am not certain," he added. "I may do well on my books."

A few days later Joaquin wrote to "My dear Mr. Whitman" from Easton. "I have many messages for you from your friends in Europe which I promised and so much desired to deliver face to face," he said, but, he added, "I am weary and want rest, and I cannot rest in cities." Joaquin said he was going straight from Easton to San Francisco and that he was taking with him only one book, "a Walt Whitman" that Rossetti had given him. "Grand Old Man!" he saluted Whitman. "The grandest and truest American I know, accept the love of your son, Joaquin Miller."

2

In contrast to the aloof reception he had in New York, Joaquin was warmly greeted in San Francisco and hailed as "California's Own," the man who had put one over on the British.

On the Christmas holiday of 1871 he visited Ambrose Bierce, who on that day had taken a new bride. He advised Bierce to leave San Francisco and try out London where, he said—just as George Francis Train had assured him a year before—"true genius is appreciated." He assured the writer that through such friends as Tom Hood he could guarantee that Bierce could make a living in journalism. Bierce took the advice and was in London the following summer.

On New Year's Day of 1872, Joaquin and his old friends celebrated the occasion in the Grand Hotel, and it was noted that although the whiskey flowed freely down his throat he successfully "assumed the grand manner which was expected of him." His friends believed he would stay in the city at least until the applause ran out, but he received word his father was ill, and hurried to Eugene.

Joaquin found, as might be expected, that the old school-teacher was inordinately proud of his literary son, but he also found that he was expected to take care of his Pap—who was in poor financial as well as physical shape—for the family took it for granted that his wealth matched his fame. Joaquin had to confess that he had little money—it must be presumed he had spent the generous advance Roberts Brothers had given him, or else he preferred to keep it for current expenses. He went to his brothers and explained that royalties on *Songs of the Sierras* would not be paid him until later in the year, and James loaned him a sum of money which Joaquin turned over to his father. Thus Pap Miller no longer had to worry over finances during the last months of his life. He died in his sleep the following year.

Joaquin did not linger long in Oregon, thanks to the activities of Minnie Myrtle Miller, who had obtained a legal separation in 1869 but, as far as can be ascertained, never got a divorce. Joaquin had been heartily welcomed by the Oregon newspapers and many a story was printed about his stupendous successes in London. This prompted the "Sweet Singer of the Coquille," who once upon a time had been recognized as the Poet in the family, to deliver on February 29, 1872 a lecture in Portland on the all-inclusive subject of "MAN, his PAST, PRESENT and FUTURE."

The MAN under consideration was Joaquin Miller, and Minnie Myrtle took a rather gloomy view of him. Joaquin's PAST, she declared, was terrible. He had lived with that Indian girl, had made love to other women, and he had treated his true wife with "coldness and neglect." Joaquin's PRESENT, according to Minnie Myrtle, was if anything worse. He refused to support her and his three children, leaving them to starve in the streets of Portland. As for Joaquin's FUTURE, Minnie Myrtle darkly predicted it would include a trip to the gallows. Those attending the lecture were led to feel that the marriage was on the rocks.

There was nothing Joaquin could do about these public accusations. The spectacle of a man fighting back at an outraged woman and making countercharges had to be avoided. As for making a plausible defense of his conduct, this was impossible for Joaquin had to concede that, with one exception, the charges were true. Joaquin did not and would not provide for the upkeep of his wife and two sons—we know that the sons later were to be alienated from him for that reason—but he did send his daughter Maud to a finishing school in Canada, though it is not known how long he paid her expenses.

So, while Joaquin kept silent, Minnie Myrtle toured the state and gave her lectures. It was noted that the women in her audience appreciated the talks more than did the men.

There were a few high-minded editors in the country who refused to publicize the quarrel, believing as Edward Everett Hale did that a poet should be criticized for his poetry, and not for his "character and antecedents." Practically all journalists, however, devoted considerable space to the wrangling and then added cutting editorial comments of their own, deploring the plight of a deserted wife, declaring that Joaquin Miller was a wealthy, wealthy man. The attacks on Joaquin became, as Harr Wagner said, so "coarse and unscrupulous" that Joaquin decided to drop completely out of sight.

We know that Joaquin first went to northern California, where he searched for and found his daughter Cali-Shasta. He took the beautiful young girl, then fourteen years old, to San Francisco and installed her in the home of his friend Ina Coolbrith. Inasmuch as Joaquin did not return to California for years, Miss Coolbrith shouldered all the costs of her upbringing, and did so cheerfully.

And then Joaquin dropped out of sight so successfully that we do not definitely know where he was or what he did for the ensuing six or seven months. It is possible, though there is no proof of it, that, as he claimed, he went to Brazil.

According to the way Joaquin told the story, he made a trip to South America, where he said his poems were well known and even beloved, and being a celebrity he was given an audience by Dom Pedro II, Emperor of Brazil, who took an instant fancy to him—perhaps it was the same kind of instant fancy that so gripped Queen Victoria. Joaquin wrote *Isles of the Amazons*, a long narrative poem which he graciously dedicated to Dom Pedro, and the Emperor was so impressed by the quality of the verse that he himself translated it into Portuguese. Dom Pedro pleaded with him to live forever in Brazil, right in the royal palace, but Joaquin felt that "visiting anyone for long, especially a Court with its routine, would kill my Muse." Desperate to enjoy his company, Dom Pedro then offered him the poet-laureateship, but Joaquin reluctantly declined the honor. A poet-laureate had to compose in the language of the country, and there were many unkind souls who, when they heard Joaquin's tale, thought that it was difficult enough for him to write a poem in English, let alone in Portuguese.

Now, Joaquin did write an Amazonian poem, and in reading it one might suppose that the author had a knowledge of the country. But there is no record of its having been translated into Portuguese, nor is there any mention of Joaquin Miller in the memoirs by or about Emperor Dom Pedro II. Nonetheless, it is possible that Joaquin did make such an excursion into Brazil, for his whereabouts during the six-or-seven-month interval cannot be traced.

3

The Poet of the Sierras returned (from somewhere) to London early in 1873. At first he lived in the garret of what was known as "The Poet Cowley's House," because Cowley had stayed there briefly two centuries before. Later he moved to No. 11, Museum Street, Bloomsbury Square, which was to be his permanent address in London. The fussy Watts-Dunton came to Museum Street and found the rooms "very diminutive and dingy in character," but Joaquin liked the location because, being close to the British Museum, many of his fellow writers lived in the neighborhood.

Following Joaquin's spectacular success during his first stay in London, the American literary colony in the city had increased, and practically all of its members were Westerners. Mark Twain, Bret Harte and Ambrose Bierce were in London. Joaquin secured Bierce a job as assistant editor to his close friend, Tom Hood. The American who later became so famous for his savage and sardonic writings was to spend the next few years working part-time on the comic magazine called FUN, a fact that most of the biographers of "Bitter Bierce" are apt to skip over hastily.

There were two new arrivals from San Francisco, and Joaquin took them to live with him, "diminutive" as his rooms might be. They were Charles Warren Stoddard and Prentice Mulford. The arrival of Mulford was a stroke of luck for Joaquin, as he was now trying to write a book of reminiscences and a volume of verse at the same time, but found that he was making small headway. Joaquin hired Mulford as his amanuensis and ghost writer and dictated to him the story of his amazing experiences with the Indians—as he remembered them, and when he failed to remember, Mulford remembered. Stoddard replaced Savage-Armstrong and the unknown Irishman as a "polisher" of Joaquin's verse—a development he could not possibly have foreseen when he first met the "unsophisticate" at the dock in San Francisco.

The reason why Joaquin could not devote himself to his own literary efforts is incredible, considering that writing was his livelihood: he simply did not have the time. For now Joaquin once again became the social lion, being in demand in all the better drawing rooms, and his reinstatement in the old familiar role was accomplished quite easily. One year's absence had served him well. Joaquin found the Britishers had a renewed appetite for the company of a genuine frontiersman of the West, and it was fortunate for him that his compatriots in London had not aspired to step into his shoes—indeed, they had shunned the idea. "I was introduced and went everywhere," Joaquin said, and for once he did not in the least exaggerate.

It was during this second invasion of England that Joaquin met and became the fast friend of Lord Houghton, a man powerful in literary and social circles. Before being elevated to the peerage Lord Houghton had been known as the poet Richard Monckton Milnes, a rich patron of letters who had championed Swinburne and Whitman at a time when they were ignored and even in disrepute. The rich Lord Houghton had many interests. He was a leader of the society set, a biographer of Keats, an art connoisseur and bibliophile (after his death it was revealed that the heart of his "collection" was the largest pornographic library in all Europe), and he liked eccentrics so much that he posed as one himself. Lord Houghton knew everybody, high and low, and was another of the many persons who supposedly "corrupted the more-than-willing Swinburne." According to Henry Adams, Houghton was Falstaffian, with the laugh of a Silenus, "a maker of men—of a great many men."

Lord Houghton could not make Joaquin's reputation—it already had been established, though the foundations were a bit shaky—but he could and did introduce him to a wider society. "Dickie," as Houghton was known to his intimates, was instantly attracted to the big and virile American, whom he described in a letter to Prime Minister Gladstone as "most interesting as poet and man."

Joaquin in turn seemed almost infatuated with the rakish Lord, who incidentally was twenty-eight years his senior. "He is besotted with Richard, has neither eyes nor ears for anyone else when he is present," said a leering guest who saw the two together at a cozy breakfast, "and Richard is very devoted to him in return." In reciprocating the compliment of introducing him to the upper stratum of society, Joaquin presented him to his American friends, and Houghton felt amply repaid. Joaquin arranged for "Dickie" to meet Mark Twain, a move he was to be none too happy about, for in time Houghton was to conceive the queer notion that perhaps Twain was an even greater genius than Joaquin Miller.

We know from the letters Joaquin sent Houghton (the Lord had such faith in the talents of his new friend that he carefully preserved them for posterity) and from the recollections of various Victorians that, at the same time while Prentice Mulford slaved away at writing Joaquin's book in Museum Street, the poet was caught up in the social whirl. For instance:

He had midnight supper with the Shah of Persia, dinner with Tennyson, tea with Dean Stanley, lunch with Browning, and breakfast in Albemarle Street with the Archbishop of Dublin, and he was pretty nonchalant about it all. (Joaquin stated that he received three letters signed "Dublin," which he threw aside, but that a friend excitedly pointed out: "His Grace, the Archbishop of Dublin! He wants you to breakfast with him! Why, your fortune is made!" Joaquin remarked that he found this sort of thing quite boring.)

He drank whiskey while Swinburne drank his port, and he had evening chats with all the Rossettis. He was often seen having drinks with Willkie Collins and Charles Reade and Mark Twain at the Langham Hotel bar's sacred "Poets' Corner." Anthony Trollope thought the American obstreperous, but he liked him. "Two of your wildest countrymen —Joachim Miller and Mark Twain—dine with me at my club next week," Trollope wrote Kate Field. Joaquin, in turn, informed Houghton in his best blasé manner that "Trollope's dinner at the Garrick was very pleasant indeed. Twain there. Member Cabinet. Parliament."

The great Mark Twain was then known as a funny lecturer. To the flamboyant Joaquin Miller, his compatriot was the shrinking violet type. "He was shy as a girl, although time was already coyly flirting white flowers at his temples," as Joaquin later described it so fancily, "and could hardly be coaxed to meet the learned and great who wanted to take him by the hand."

He met, liked, and was liked by the hero of the day, aged Edward John Trelawney, the buccaneer who was the friend of Byron and Shelley. "I visited him at a very humble hut up the Thames, where he lived alone, ate vegetables, drank water from the river only," Joaquin wrote, "and, notwithstanding his wild sailor life and lively days in the Levant, never touched either rum or wine or tobacco." Joaquin could not understand that Trelawney would never take a drink when he "used to drop in on us at the Savage Club," but nonetheless he thought that he was "the most picturesquely remarkable man I ever knew."

He visited Whistler and, though the painter was hard to please, the bluff and breezy American charmed him. He invited Joaquin to his Chelsea studio to sit for a sketch, and the poet liked it because it made him look so romantic, mysterious and Byronic. Joaquin traveled to Stoke Poges to muse in the graveyard where Gray wrote his "Elegy," and from there he wrote wearily to Lord Houghton that Gladstone (he did not refer to him as "Lord" Gladstone) again had begged him to be his guest at his country estate, but that he was unable to accept the invitation. A few weeks later Joaquin informed "Dickie" that at last he had arranged his schedule so as to visit "Gladstone the Great," as he called him, and that he had held the people there spellbound, being the last guest to leave the castle. Mrs. Gladstone took a particular liking to Joaquin, as often happened with the wives of men he met. She asked him back to breakfast and sat enthralled as he told of his experiences as Chief of the Modoc Indians—the story would be told in his forthcoming book, he assured her—and of his long stay with his dear, dear friend, Emperor Dom Pedro II of Brazil.

And, with a few hundred other guests, he was introduced to Queen Victoria ("Has a queenly bearing," Joaquin acutely noted) at a reception. The Queen graciously allowed that she had heard of his poetry, but she did not give him a ring of three small diamonds. Shortly after this historic encounter a magazine printed a cartoon showing Joaquin Miller sitting at a table, the dominant member of his company—and the company consisted of Victoria, the Prince of Wales and the Shah of Persia. Joaquin was represented as wearing his usual Wild Western garb, but for once the costume did not seem so striking, for the swarthy Shah was attired in billowing Oriental robes. Joaquin never cared much for the Shah of Persia. He thought the fellah was a show-off.

As he made the hurly-burly rounds to fulfill his social obligations, Joaquin's comportment was about the same as it had been during his first visit to England. There was no reason to change a successful formula. The "Byron of the Rockies" always remembered to limp—just as the other Byron, the English one, had limped—when he paced about a drawing room and honored his poetic ancestor with such lines as:

> In men whom men condemn as ill
> I find so much of goodness still

and the doting Duchesses were deeply stirred, for they found the doggerel highly philosophical.

Joaquin, while adhering to the basic formula, did however add a refinement to his "entrance" into London's illustrious townhouses. Previously, he had been content to pause ever so slightly when the butler announced his name, so as to give the guests the chance to take in his costume. Now he found that the audience reaction was more gratifying when he strode forthwith into the room, as if disdainful of all formalities, and at the same time giving the impression that there was no need for Joaquin Miller to be identified by a flunky. Joaquin now began, too, to wear a shaggy bearskin around his shoulders, the identical hide, he assured his listeners, that the giant grizzly had worn before he had stabbed him to death in mortal combat high amid the peaks of the Rockies. He would carelessly throw the bearskin to one side and then, without preamble, squat on the floor and start chanting an old Indian song that he had learned when Chief—the adopted Chief, that is—of the Modoc Indians:

> Tah-tey-ahyay-te-ho-tu-lelo!
> Lelo! tu-ho-te-ahyay-tey-tah!

Joaquin then would stop, as if choked with emotion at the memory of his beloved Indian comrades and of their lovely language, which he knew so well. Sometimes there were a few carping guests who argued that Joaquin's Indian vocabulary—if it were Indian—seemed to be confined to these two short lines; but the hostesses were delighted.

So, while Joaquin's behavior had changed little, the same was true for his costume, for he retained his old frontier dress. He did experiment to the extent of wearing a red fez, to the consternation of English students of the West, but, finding that it clashed with the crimson of his sash, he returned to his floppy sombrero. At this time, however, Joaquin made a change in his personal appearance: he let his Imperial and mustachio blossom out into a closely-cropped beard. This beard, which much later he was to let grow, he was to wear the rest of his life.

In 1871, when Joaquin was the social success of London, he had admitted that he found life in the drawing room a stimulating and exhilarating experience. Now, in 1873, he professed that he was tiring of the gilded salons that held him captive. He yearned for the Wild West, for the open spaces, for his frisky horse, for the campfire in the purple hills under the soft moonlight. But no matter how often he voiced his complaints, the denizens of the salons did not find *him* boring. Not yet.

4

Two books were published under Joaquin's name in the summer of 1873. The one for which he had the most hopes was *Songs of the Sun-Lands*, a volume of new and old verse. The poems had been "gone over" by Charles Warren Stoddard, but unfortunately Stoddard, who had become Mark Twain's secretary, had not had much time to devote to Joaquin's work. Simultaneously with its publication in London, Roberts Brothers in Boston issued the book, and Joaquin sat back tensely waiting for the verdict of the critics.

The second product was a prose work, *Life Amongst the Modocs*, which purported to be an autobiography. This book at first was not regarded with much pride by Joaquin, for Prentice Mulford had been hired to manufacture the volume after listening to Joaquin's tales of adventure—"Mulford did all the work," Joaquin freely admitted. The book was called *Life Amongst the Modocs*, and not, as would have been more correct, "Life Amongst the Diggers," because the Modocs were known in England as a proud and warlike tribe, whereas the Digger Indians that Joaquin had "married into" were a tribe of low culture, too lazy to till the soil, who fed on the roots they dug out of the earth.

This highly romanticized version of life among the savages, as Joaquin and Mulford remembered it, was an immediate success. The English public was deeply impressed by what it regarded as Western naturalism, and by the idyll of a white youth living with the picturesque redskins, a life which the hide-bound, fog-bound Londoners thought was utterly fascinating. The book, put together so carelessly and with such total disregard for veracity by the Mulford-Miller duo, soon became tremendously popular and, as one of Joaquin's biographers, Martin S. Peterson, noted, "was accepted as gospel truth, and in time Joaquin Miller began to believe it himself." It was issued in France (as *Scènes de la vie des mineurs et des Indiens de Californie*) and in the United States, and in the latter country it ran through countless editions over the decades, being known under various titles: *Unwritten History; Paquita, the Indian Maiden; My Own Story;* and *My Life Among the Indians*. In each of these successive volumes Joaquin would eliminate a few incidents and add some new ones, but each edition remained substantially the same. Toward the end of his life, when this book was under steady attack by scholars of the West, Joaquin at last admitted that much of the material had been embroidered. Today this "autobiography" is indexed in many libraries (the New York Public Library, for instance) under the heading of fiction.

Prentice Mulford, once his writing stint had ended, decided to return to America, and Joaquin advanced him the passage money. (Joaquin at this period was financially well off. He dined out so often that his food cost him nothing, and, being the most lionized personality of the day, he was besieged by editors willing to pay high prices for his poems.) The aftermath of Mulford's departure provided Joaquin with a romantically tragic tale that he was to tell often, a tale that was an appealing mixture of truth and fantasy and one that eventually was to thrill the American theatre-going public.

Prentice Mulford was a man who liked to be unhappy—Bierce labeled him "Dismal Jimmy"—and so the events that followed after Joaquin invited him to live at 11, Museum Street must have been sincerely gratifying to him, for he was plunged into some real sufferings. The story is this:

At the fairly advanced age of thirty-nine, Mulford fell in love with the landlady's daughter. Despite all obstacles—the girl was an adolescent of fifteen and semi-illiterate while Mulford was a man of culture; she was a Catholic while Mulford was a Protestant—the elderly suitor insisted upon marriage. His American friends tried to point out that he probably could enjoy the pleasures of her body (the girl had what was described then as a "magnificent carriage") without going through the formality of Holy Matrimony, but Mulford would not listen to them. Indeed, such talk seemed to anger him. And so the ill-matched couple were married.

Mulford and his wife sailed for New York, where he secured a job as reporter for the EVENING GRAPHIC, but the pay was small, and Mulford liked to drink, and he always was in need of money. His child bride became an artist's model, but she did not tell her husband that she posed in the nude, an unforgivable sin for a "lady" in the 1870's.

Bierce, in discussing Mulford's life in London, remarked that "He married there a fool named Josie—forget her other name—with whom I think he lived awhile in hell, then freed himself." To Joaquin, however, the marriage and its consequences were a matter far more complex. In 1885, according to Joaquin, who never tired of repeating the story, he attended a reception at the White House in the company of Mrs. Mulford. Rose Elizabeth Cleveland, the President's daughter and hostess, was informed by an indiscreet and perhaps vindictive guest that Joaquin's companion was a bad, bad woman, probably a whore, because she actually had posed in her bare skin. Miss Cleveland allegedly recoiled in horror, summoned Joaquin to her and peremptorily demanded that the harlot leave the sanctity of the White House. "If my guest is not acceptable," Joaquin said firmly, "then I am also an undesirable and will withdraw."

But this was not the end. "Mulford learned what happened," according to a magazine version of the incident, "and, being very sensitive, rowed out on the ocean in a small boat and never returned."

Joaquin told the tale to Herbert Bashford, a California playwright, and it became the basis of a play that was a sensational success—*The Woman He Married*.

There is a modicum of truth to the plot, for Mulford did commit suicide. But his "sensitivity" was generally overestimated, for he did not kill himself until 1891, five full years after the alleged incident in the White House, when he was fifty-seven years old and long after his wife had deserted him.

5

As Joaquin's popularity in London continued, it was noticed that the American would capitalize on almost anything that happened to him, and that he could even turn a fault that people laughed at into a publicized triumph. There was the matter of his handwriting. Joaquin could write as neat a script as anyone if he wanted to, but usually his handwriting was practically undecipherable. One time a printer was puzzled when he came across a poem titled "The Bodin." This, he learned, was meant to read "The Bedouin." Another printer could not make out a title intended to be "The Skirmish." Knowing that Joaquin was an authority on Indians, he set it to read as "The Comanches," and that is the title by which it is known to this day. And when these stories made the rounds in London, people noted that Joaquin's handwriting got worse, so that even he himself could not read it.

Joaquin's handwriting—the handwriting he presented to the public—never improved. Van Wyck Brooks in his essay "Byron of the Sierras" tells of his encounter with the bard's chicken-track script:

> When I was a boy a friend wrote the poet for his signature. He replied not with one signature but with twenty: scraps of verse he had written, portraits of himself clipped from newspapers, "sentiments" scrawled on bits of paper and signed with Indian hieroglyphics. A bountiful harvest indeed for one stilted boyish note! What did it matter that, turn it about as we might, we could scarcely decipher a word of all this extravagant script the poet had showered on us?

Brooks remarked that Joaquin's "appropriately barbaric" handwriting was—for instance, when he wrote a letter dealing with a real estate venture—"very legible." "But what literary man is without his vanity?" asked Brooks.

There can be no question about it: when Joaquin tried hard enough, it took a Rosetta stone to decipher what he meant. Some of Joaquin's acquaintances thought his hand-writing was worse than his spelling, and that his spelling was even worse than his poetry. Others concluded that his oc-casional flashes of good writing were due not to the law of averages, but to the fact that the printer could not read the manuscript and so was forced to improvise the poems him-self. Joaquin had an alibi for his wretched scribbling. It was caused by the terrible wound he had received on the right wrist, after he had been pinked by an arrow in one of his numerous battles against the Indians.

Actually, apart from his deliberate efforts to write as poorly as he could, the illegibility of his script can easily be traced to Joaquin's persistent use of the then outmoded quill pen, and his quill was usually split.

A dinner was given in his honor to celebrate the success of his Modoc book. After being saluted with many toasts, Joaquin came to his feet and flourished aloft a copy of the volume. "Gentlemen," he cried, "when I die and go to heaven, this book will be my vindication for having lived."

There was present at the dinner the foreman of the print shop, who had set all the type of the book by hand, and he was not carried away in like fashion. "I hope that when you die and go to heaven, Mr. Miller," the printer declared, "you will take along a printed copy of the manuscript, for God Almighty himself could not read your writing."

6

It was at one of Lord Houghton's lawn parties that Joaquin was presented to the one person he desired above all to meet, and here his feeling was shared by millions of Americans and Englishmen. She was Miss Emilie Charlotte, better known as Lillie Langtry, the fabulous Jersey Lily. Miss Langtry,

A sample of Joaquin Miller's handwriting. (*Courtesy of the Manuscript Division of the New York Public Library*) whose beauty has been captured for us in the paintings by Millais and Burne-Jones, was then a lovely young woman of twenty-one and was popularly considered to be the most ravishing person that ever wore a bustle.

The thought could never have occurred to Joaquin, and in spite of his egocentricity he would have been startled beyond belief if he had known it, but the Jersey Lily was yearning to meet Joaquin Miller. In common with others of the social crowd she was curious about the Wild West poet she had heard so much about, and, when she met him, he lived up to her expectations, for Miss Langtry found Joaquin a "child of nature and perhaps the most picturesque personality of the literary world."

"He had lived a life adventuresome," the Jersey Lily was to write later. She then related the "facts" of Joaquin's life that so intrigued her and all London: "He ran away from school to mine for gold, he had been adopted by the Indians, imprisoned for some imaginary offence, had escaped from jail by the aid of an Indian girl, swam a river with her to freedom, and married her—all before twenty! At least, that was the story which circulated in London, which added piquancy to the interest created by his virile personality."

Miss Langtry left an interesting account of her meeting with Joaquin. During the lawn party she idly picked up a volume of sonnets written years before by Lord Houghton and: "I laughingly asked my host if I couldn't inspire him sufficiently to write *me* one. He looked at me whimsically, a wee bit pathetically, and said, 'My dear, I am too old.'"

Lord Houghton (he was then sixty-four) did the next best thing in an effort to please the celebrated beauty. He pointed out Joaquin Miller and said that there was the man to write a poem to her. As Miss Langtry described it:

He led me up to a very tall, lean man, with a pale intellectual face, yellow hair so long that it lay in curls around his shoulders, a closely cropped beard, and a dreamy expression in his light eyes. I don't remember what he wore, except that it was unconventional . . . He left, soon returned, and read me from a torn sheet of paper the following verse:

TO THE JERSEY LILY

If all God's earth a garden were,
   And all the women flowers,
And I a bee that buzzed there
   Through all the summer hours,
Oh, I would buzz the garden through
   For honey—till I came to you!

When he had finished, he added, with a dramatic gesture, "Let this verse stand; it's the only one I ever wrote to a living woman."

Now, Joaquin had written many poems to living women, and Miss Langtry did not get the sonnet she wanted, but, considering that this pleasant jingle was written on the spur of the moment, she was deftly rewarded with a tribute to her beauty. She kept the scrap of paper all her life, and years later Joaquin included the verse in his printed works.

Julian Hawthorne, who witnessed the incident, congratulated Joaquin on his ability to manufacture the rhyme so promptly.

"Well, I was always pretty quick on the trigger—when I had to be!" he declared proudly.

The intrepid Joaquin, undaunted by the fact that the Lily was the "boon companion" of none other than the Prince of Wales, the future Edward VII (Miss Langtry was to horrify all England by committing one of the most atrocious acts of lèse majesté on record: she poured cracked ice down the Prince's neck), attempted to court the Jersey Lily, and, as he was to hint to his American friends, with considerable success. This is so unlikely that it can be dismissed as wishful thinking, although Joaquin enjoyed the reputation of being a great lover, who was successful because he excelled in amorous gestures that fanned and flattered the imagination of women. His various liaisons will be discussed later; but we do not know of more than one affair of the heart he had during his stays in London.

Joaquin did have at least one more encounter with Miss Langtry in London, and on that occasion he paid her a compliment which was a charming mixture of old-world courtesy and new-world spontaneity. As the lady herself told it:

> A few evenings later I went to Lady Brassey's, and at the foot of the broad staircase stood Joaquin Miller awaiting me. I walked upstairs to greet my hostess and he backed before me, scattering rose leaves, which he had concealed in his broad sombrero, upon the white marble steps, and saying with fervor, "Thus be your path in life!"

Joaquin and Lillie Langtry were not destined to meet again until each was a little older—forty years later—and under circumstances which were touched with sadness. The Jersey Lily, by that time an actress, and also a properly married woman known as Lady de Bathe, called on him and asked if he remembered the strewing of rose petals in her path. Joaquin said he remembered the incident. In fact, after the success of the maneuver in London, and when the time came when he had the luxury of a rose garden of his own, he had repeated the performance many times, to the delight of at least a dozen ladies.

7

The reviews of Joaquin's two books began to appear, but, the pity of it, they were uniformly censorious. In the United States the critics were about as cynically irreverent as might have been expected, but surprisingly enough the English pundits, who two years before had saluted Joaquin as a genius, now became almost as acrimonious as their American brethren.

Of the two volumes, *Life Amongst the Modocs,* dedicated "To the Red Men of America," fared best, though it was brutally assailed. But *Songs of the Sun-Lands* just was not treated as anything resembling serious poetry. The consensus was that while it was natural for a poet to study his rivals and perhaps faintly echo a line here and there, Joaquin Miller had come dangerously close to stealing entire stanzas. It was noted that Joaquin Miller had abandoned Byron and was now slavishly imitating his new idol, Swinburne, and to a lesser degree Browning and Tennyson—to his great disadvantage.

Soon the quips began to circulate: The poetic J. Miller seemed to be some sort of a comic Joe Miller; the American made his living in dealing with second-hand verse; the poet was acutely "sensitive"—he could tell hot soup from cold soup. "It is not difficult to write nonsense verse in this meter," John Addington Symonds, the distinguished critic, declared. As an example of Joaquin's primitive rhyme and shallow depth of thought, Symonds reprinted the following verse in the ACADEMY:

> In the place where the grizzly reposes
> Under peaks where a right is a wrong
> I have memories richer than roses
> Sweet echoes more sweet than a song.

As for *Life Amongst the Modocs*, the critics conceded that it had a certain amount of originality, but the general feeling was expressed by the authoritative ATHENAEUM. "Mr. Miller's so-called book about the 'Modocs' turns out to be a monstrously dull volume," the magazine declared. "We do not hesitate to call this a 'got up' book." Joaquin's life with the Indians now was regarded as anything but idyllic. "He is a scoundrel by his own admission," the ATHENAEUM flatly charged.

Joaquin thought that this passage was libelous, but he did not sue. Instead he wrote a raging letter to the editor, demanding to know the name of the anonymous critic who wrote the review. Joaquin hinted that a duel would follow, but that in any event he wanted the satisfaction of "telling him to his teeth that he was a liar a cowrd and a cur."

The magazine's only reply was to point out the mistakes of punctuation and spelling in Joaquin's letter. "Mr. Miller is sadly wanting in the courtesies of life and the advantages of education," its editor coldly remarked.

In the United States the reviews were so unanimously unfavorable that Joaquin refused to read them. Even the CALIFORNIA MAIL BAG, which alone of all American periodicals had wished him success when he left for England in 1870, now contemptuously concluded that "We fear Mr. Miller lacks the power of growth, unless it is the power to grow worse."

At first Joaquin was inclined to be supercilious over the yappings of the critics, and yet the about-face of his old standbys, the English reviewers, disturbed him. He could have taken refuge in the fact that Prentice Mulford had interpolated inventions and excesses in the Modoc book, which was true; but he did not. It was the criticism of his poetry, which meant so much to him, that hurt most. Here, too, Joaquin could have blamed his collaborator, Stoddard; but he did not. He admitted that he knew little of rhyme and meter and that Stoddard had helped him over some rough spots, but he assumed full responsibility for all the faults noticed by the man-eating critics.

8

A few weeks after the devastating reviews had appeared, Joaquin fell from grace. He had reigned as a favorite for more than a year.

Now, just as in 1871, the members of the American colony began to back-bite. It appears that their rancor was in a measure justified, for Joaquin had begun to behave toward them in a rather overbearing way. His compatriots had other grievances, too. They were tired of continually hearing the name of Joaquin Miller, as if he were the only American man of letters living in London. They knew the West, and they knew it did not in the least resemble the land he so often described. They resented the ease with which Joaquin had acquired popularity and prestige. Bret Harte (whom Joaquin described as "my mascotte, my good genius," at a time when Harte was regarded as a literary nobody in London) was the ringleader in undermining Joaquin's reputation, and he openly pronounced him as "impossible." "Joaquin Miller is the greatest liar ever known," "Bitter Bierce" bluntly asserted in one of his bitter moments, writing in San Francisco. "He rewrites his life from reading dime novels."

The Americans now began to ridicule Joaquin openly. They referred to him as Cincinnatus, or as Hiner; and when they did use the name Joaquin they were careful to pronounce it "Joe-aah'-kin" instead of "Wah'-keen." They said he bought his Wild West costumes from a London theatrical supply house, and the rumor was spread that Joaquin believed he "owned" California and had warned off all other poets not to write about the state. "He calls it 'My California,' " the Americans pointed out. Once more the familiar stories that dogged Joaquin all of his life began to circulate—his Digger squaw, desertion of his wife, his refusal to support his children. It was brutally stressed that he had been imprisoned not for "some imaginary offence," as Lillie Langtry had so naively put it, but for being a horse thief.

Such was the whispering campaign as conducted by his countrymen, but the coup de grâce itself was administered by the leaders of English society. For, either because Joaquin could no longer curb his eccentricities or because his conduct became more flagrant in the course of his ceaseless campaign to impress the British for all time, he overplayed his hand, just as he had in 1871. The hostesses who once had sat so entranced now were merely amused, and, finally, plain bored with him. There is ample evidence that their attitude was justified.

For instance, there was the grand reception given by Lady Constance Rothschild, which was attended by the elite of society in formal dress. Joaquin appeared wearing a red flannel shirt and blue overalls, and carrying a miner's pick. That, in itself, would have been acceptable and certainly was expected; but what followed was calculated to chill the heart of the most forgiving hostess. Joaquin, his sombrero set firmly on his head, elbowed his way impatiently through the crowd, refusing to acknowledge any of the salutations addressed to him. He made his way to a recessed window, took a book from his pocket and became immersed in reading. He made it clear that the Master preferred to be alone. And Lady

Rothschild decided she would leave him alone—forever.

Jean Ingelow, too, was taken aback by the poet's conduct when she invited him for lunch at her home. Joaquin sat at the table with his host, Edmund Gosse and Mrs. Nathaniel Hawthorne, without bothering to take off his cumbersome sealskin coat. He professed to be astonished when word got back to him of Miss Ingelow's distaste for his get-up. He explained that he could not have done otherwise because he was wearing nothing underneath his coat but an undershirt.

"Dickie" Houghton was not particularly amused by the antics of his good friend, either. During a lawn party Joaquin threw his bearskin on the grass, squatted on it and peremptorily summoned the guests to sit down with him. But when he insisted that they huddle alongside him, as if they were confined in a wigwam, and join him in chanting his Indian verse, well, the Britishers began to rebel. It wasn't "the demmed good show" that they had remembered.

Joaquin acquired another idiosyncrasy that was not likely to make friends. He got into the habit of appearing at soirees and, after coldly surveying the guests from the doorway, turning on his heels and vanishing, as if he had detected something extremely distasteful about the company. A guest who witnessed this entrance-exit act said Joaquin stretched out his hand to the hostess and, "as if talking to a sea-lion," roared: "Give us your flipper—goodby." Also, when the English read the reviews of his two latest books they could not help but wonder if Joaquin Miller was the genius they had imagined. And, when they heard the ugly rumors of his youthful years, they began to wonder (forgetting, no doubt, that these rumors had been circulated before) whether he was a Gentleman.

"Joaquin Miller would have been thought unsufferably

vulgar if he had not been a notoriety," Augustus Hare the Victorian declared, "as it was, everyone paid court to him." But now the wheel was turning. Even as close a friend as Lord Houghton shied away from questioning Joaquin about his early career. "I have known and asked nothing of his private life," Houghton wrote Gladstone, and here apparently he was protecting himself in case his intimate friend became involved in a scandal.

Ambrose Bierce had never met Mark Twain and asked Joaquin to arrange for an introduction. The poet reserved a table at the Whitefriars Club early in the autumn of 1873 and invited Stoddard to attend the party. Joaquin the host did not arrive at the appointed hour, and so Stoddard introduced the two, and the trio waited for Joaquin to make an appearance. They suspected the poet would make a "stage entrance," and all agreed not to notice any of his eccentricities.

Forty-five minutes later, Joaquin strode into the dining room. He was arrayed in his knee-high boots, his buckskin shirt, his sombrero; around his middle he wore a huge leather belt into which he had stuck a brace of Bowie knives. The three guests greeted Joaquin casually, pretending not to notice his late arrival or the costume. The poet was put out. As soon as they were seated at the table Joaquin began to gesticulate and flourish his Bowie knives to make a point. Each of the trio regarded him blandly, almost with indifference, and then continued their talk.

Finally, in desperation, Joaquin leaned over the table, plunged his hand deep into the fishbowl, and pulled out a wriggling goldfish. He rose to his feet, held the goldfish aloft and, to the amazement of the Britishers who were staring at him from the neighboring tables, swallowed the delicacy whole. Joaquin sat down and roared, "A wonderful appetizer!" Twain and Bierce and Stoddard nodded politely in agreement, then turned to each other and resumed their conversation. This was too much! Joaquin stalked from the room in a rage.

About this time Anthony Trollope staged a dinner in Joaquin's honor, with Twain, George Leveson-Gower (also known as Lord Granville the diplomat), Thomas Hughes, author of *Tom Brown's School Days*, and many others in attendance. Though it was Joaquin who was being feted, Twain noted that "He was a discordant note, a disturber and degrader of the solemnities." Twain was ordinarily a gracious man and certainly not envious of a fellow American's success, and he was friendly toward Joaquin all his life, and yet at times he was irritated to the point of disgust at the poet's behavior. As Twain wrote:

He was affecting the picturesque and untamed costume of the wild Sierras at the time, to the charmed astonishment of conventional London. He and Trollope talked all the time, and both at the same time, Trollope pouring forth a smooth and limpid and sparkling stream of faultless English, and Joaquin discharging into it his muddy and tumultuous mountain torrent—well, there was never anything just like it except the Whirlpool Rapids under Niagara Falls.

(It was at this time, according to Twain, that the poet lost not only the respect of his English friends, but also the love of his English fiancée. Neither Joaquin nor any of his acquaintances, with the exception of Mark Twain, ever made any mention of this fiancée. All we know is that, according to Twain's letters, the lady was Iza Hardy, the daughter of Sir Thomas Hardy, who was "about twenty-six, goodlooking, goodhearted, affectionate . . . thoroughly English, and very much in love with Joaquin." While Mark Twain must be considered a reliable witness, it is nevertheless extremely curious that Joaquin—indiscreet, talkative and forever bragging about his feminine conquests—never alluded to what must have been a rather significant episode.)

The cumulative effect of this anti-Miller movement was that Joaquin soon was invited nowhere by the Britishers. He had to fall back on the company of his American friends, and they were none too eager to be seen with him.

Joaquin, never a man to brood over personal setbacks, decided to make another strategic withdrawal. In October, 1873, two months after the reviews had appeared and a few weeks after his fall from grace, he announced he was off for Italy, where there was wide interest in his poetic works, and where at the graves of Keats and Shelley he intended to commune with their spirits.

9

Joaquin spent a few weeks roaming through northern Italy. He was the guest of Lorimer Graham, the American Consul in Florence, he visited Browning in Venice, and retraced the footsteps of Shelley and Byron. He was entranced at the sight of Lake Como, where he wrote the well-known lines—the once well-known lines:

> From out the Alps the moon came wheeling through
> The rocky pass the great Napoleon knew.

He considered settling permanently on the beautiful shores of the lake, but his audience—and Joaquin Miller could not breathe without an audience—was composed of Italians, and as he did not know the language, he went south to Rome where there was a large American and English colony.

Joaquin did not care much for Rome, although he was to stay there for a year. He complained in a letter to Lord Houghton that the Holy City was crowded with "Priests and painted Virgins," but he did not mention his compatriots scoffed at him as "Childe Miller." "I send you a rose from the grave of Shelley and a sprig of hedge from that of Keats," he wrote Houghton. "Next week I go on to Greece, then Egypt or elsewhere, I suppose."

In his letters from Rome, Joaquin was always on the verge of leaving for other lands. In later years he recalled his impressions of the antiquities of Greece—where he was "in and about the tombs of buried empires and forgotten kings" —of Egypt, and once he even remembered having immersed himself in the study of Buddhistic mysteries while in India, but there is no evidence that he visited these countries. It was Charles Warren Stoddard who made a trip to the Near East, in 1876–77, and wrote a book about it, which may have caused a confusion in Joaquin's mind. Joaquin did, however, visit Palestine and stayed for a few weeks. He went to Jerusalem to write "A Life of Christ," but after a few chapters he gave it up and never completed the project. It was there that he wrote much of "Building of the City Beautiful," a tribute to the spirit of the Jewish people through the centuries, but the poem was not published until two decades later.

Joaquin could have well afforded a journey to Egypt or even to India. Although *Songs of the Sun-Lands* was a critical and financial failure, his Modoc book was selling tremendously in England and in America too, and his royalties were correspondingly high, but he was content to spend most of his time idling in Rome.

Joaquin attracted a good deal of attention from touring Americans as he lounged in a *bèttola*, where he was as much at home as in a doggery of Oregon, glass in hand and declaiming poetry in front of his admirers, or walking on the Corso and the Pincio, or driving afternoons with the ladies. Joaquin startled his compatriots (and the Italians, too) by his facility for gulping down bottle after bottle of the stoutest *vino* (he always claimed any dishwater of the Shasta county mining camps had more bite to it than the strongest wine), and he amused them by his grotesque attempts to cope with the language. One morning at breakfast he was being served by an Italian who knew not a single word of English. "What is the word for 'hard' in Italian?" Joaquin asked of an American. He was told that it was *duro*. "Take away these biscuits," Joaquin roared at the waiter who stood blankly before him. "They're too god-damned *duro*."

Stoddard came to Rome and again Joaquin offered him the hospitality of his board, but Stoddard was puzzled because his friend acted so mysteriously about revealing exactly where he lived. This was all the more strange as anyone who wished to see or talk to Joaquin could find him at almost any hour of the day in a *bèttola*. In a book of reminiscences published thirty years later Stoddard described Joaquin's peculiar agitation before he conducted him to their lodgings: " 'Swear!' cried the poet, as we paused on the Spanish steps,— it was very like a travesty on the ghost of Hamlet's father,— 'Swear that under no circumstances will you at any time or place reveal to any one the name of the street and the number of the house in which we lodge. It is a dead secret!' "

Stoddard swore and he easily kept his oath, for no one ever asked him for the address.

Joaquin was asked one day why it was that he always could be found drinking in the Café Greco, the famous haunt of the Bohemians, instead of making the rounds of all the art galleries, as did his fellow Americans. "My eyes were weakened by snow blindness when I was a pony express rider in the West in my youth," Joaquin patiently explained. "And I later overstrained them by poring over old manuscripts in the British Museum." And yet there were some people who claimed Joaquin's eyesight at times was piercing, that from seventy-five yards, maybe a hundred, he could read the label on a whiskey bottle.

Joaquin did do a certain amount of literary work in Italy, as he was writing his first novel, but he did not overstrain himself as the book was not completed and published until two years later. The locale of this novel, *The One Fair Woman*, was in Rome and its heroine, known as "The Lady in Pink," was modeled after the brilliant and beautiful Creole, Mrs. Frank Leslie, the brand-new wife of the founder of LESLIE'S WEEKLY, and one of the most talked about women in America. Her husband published many other highly popular magazines in the United States besides the WEEKLY. Joaquin Miller was a writer, and the Leslie magazines needed writers. When the Leslies visited Rome he resolved he would get into their good graces, and he achieved this goal so successfully that Mrs. Leslie became his mistress. This was somewhat astonishing in that Victorian age, all the more so as the lovely lady was on her honeymoon when she met Joaquin. Mrs. Leslie, a gay and uninhibited soul, who casually took on and survived four husbands, never placed much importance on a honeymoon.

Joaquin later was to tell American journalists that while in Rome he had made a speech before the Italian parliament —a command performance ordered by the King. He had explained to the rapt legislators exactly just how they should go about draining the swamps of the Campagna, a problem to the Romans since before the days of Caesar. As Joaquin had little experience in this field (unless we consider him qualified as an expert because he once worked in a sluice-ditch in California), it can safely be assumed that his memory betrayed him.

There seems to be a greater core of truth to another story Joaquin told about his Roman holidays, for others also have mentioned it. Joaquin and one of his drinking companions, an Englishman (whose name we do not know), heard that a small island in the Mediterranean was for sale, and that with the island went the title of Duke. The two decided they would share the title. They pooled their money, intending to build a race-track on the isle for tourists, but the deal fell through when the Englishman inconveniently died of malaria. For many years Joaquin liked to refer to himself jocosely as "Half-Duke Miller."

10

After a year's absence, Joaquin returned to London in October, 1874. He stated that he had come back to England solely to serve as escort for the body of his departed English friend, and that he had no ambition to play any role in society. He invited Lord Houghton to be his guest at the Savage Club, and the Lord accepted, but he was not particularly eager to renew their friendship. Joaquin made tentative efforts at becoming, for the third time, a reigning celebrity, but no one was interested in him. He half-heartedly tried to conform, to use new tactics: he wore a less garish costume and he shaved off his beard, but society and the literary set remained apathetic. Joaquin immediately lowered his colors. "Yes am letting my beard and hair grow long again because my doctor counsels it," he resignedly wrote Houghton in November.

There was little he could do in London. His countrymen from America were cool toward him, and he lost a loyal friend when his original sponsor, Tom Hood, died. Joaquin took cheap quarters in the Langham Hotel, as his money was running low. "Am just back from Saulsbury [*sic*]," he wrote Lord Houghton on New Year's Eve of 1874, but the noble Lord he once had so familiarly addressed as "Dickie" did not reply.

Soon after the new year of 1875 got under way the lonely Joaquin Miller decided to leave forever the unresponsive, callous capital of England. Fame, and with it fortune, he now decided, lay in New York, the city that in retrospect seemed to him such a lovable place, and where there was a wide interest in his poetic works. And so, after scraping together enough money to buy steerage accommodations, he sailed for America. A few years later Joaquin was to return briefly to London, the city that twice had almost hysterically hailed him as the supreme genius, and again he would be totally ignored. ("Mr. Joaquin Miller, the American poet, arrived in London two or three weeks ago," the ACADEMY, the same magazine that once had saluted him so effusively, would remark at that time. "He is not likely to remain long.")

"Never go back to a city where you were successful, nor to a sweetheart who gave you ecstasy," Joaquin later said, and he knew what he was talking about. "You will never find things the same as they were."

CHAPTER SIX

The Rootless Years
1875-1886

I

THE second homecoming of Joaquin Miller caused little journalistic stir in New York. The poet told the reporters that he had been received by Queen Victoria, but the newspapermen—traditionally people with notoriously long memories—seemed to have heard the story before and were skeptical.

Asked if he planned to go back to England, Joaquin said, no; he would settle permanently in New York, where there was a great demand for his poetry. If he traveled anywhere, he added, it would be to Arabia. Why Arabia? Joaquin said that Arabia fascinated him. How so? Joaquin explained that he had just returned from the deep dark interior of that country, where he had headed a scientific expedition to study inscriptions on the ancient tombs, and that he had explored districts never before seen by any white man. In honor of this expedition he would title his next book of poems *The Ship in the Desert*. A ship of the desert, he confided, was a camel.

The journalists agreed that the publication of a new volume would at least make the reviewers happy. "Mr. Miller always has been fair game for the critics," one of them noted.

If Joaquin did not enjoy the favor of the reviewers, he

was avidly sought after by the decaying dowagers of the town, and, though he caused no such social furore as in London, he was so busily engaged in dining out that he scarcely found time to finish his book of poetry. Joaquin continued to dress extravagantly as he made the rounds, but now that he was in America he did not act quite so violently Western. He seldom, for instance, carried a miner's pick to a soirée, or walked down Fifth Avenue with Bowie knives stuck in his belt. Most of the time he was more conservatively attired: the rippling military cloak, the silver-headed cane, the bell-crowned hat, the huge solitaire diamond stud glittering on his shirt—presented to him, as he admitted without false modesty, by his beloved comrade, Emperor Dom Pedro II of Brazil.

Indeed, when Joaquin sat for an oil portrait by Benoni Irwin, as did so many of the fashionable of the day, he emerged almost the fop. Gone was the miner, the Indian fighter, the frontiersman. The poet was shown holding daintily aloft one of the new-fangled cigarettes—certainly a far cry from his Shasta corncob pipe days—while gazing dreamily into the distance. The portrait, a three-quarters view, eventually found its way into the collection of Mrs. Frank Leslie.

During one of the many receptions attended by Joaquin there occurred an odd coincidence. He met and became friendly with General Ambrose Burnsides, the man who is quaintly responsible for the word "sideburns." Burnsides told of his triumphs as a military leader in the Civil War and as a Senator from Rhode Island, and Joaquin in turn related his European experiences. And then, to their mutual astonishment, they discovered that each had been born in the same tiny hamlet—Liberty, Indiana. Apparently, Joaquin by now had forgotten about his legendary birthplace—that famous covered wagon, in Millersville, named in honor of his Pap.

The socialites found that the gregarious poet never played hard-to-get, even though he had been lionized by the aristocrats of London town, and that he was not only easy to meet but eagerly accepted invitations to dine. John Henry Johnston thought him if anything a bit too approachable. Johnston was introduced to Joaquin at a Saturday evening reception given by Mary Mapes Dodge, editor of ST. NICHOLAS magazine, and he casually mentioned he hoped to receive the poet at his home some day. Johnston forgot all about the routine invitation until the following Monday afternoon when a messenger arrived at his business house with a note from his perplexed wife. "Do hurry home," she begged him. "Joaquin Miller is here, and is staying for dinner." Johnston hurried, and he found that his guest was a most entertaining man, and also an extremely thirsty and hungry man.

2

Joaquin went to Boston to confer with his publisher about his new book of verse, and there he was welcomed as a great fellow poet by Longfellow. Now, although Longfellow's squashy poems were the rage of the day and their author was regarded as America's Homer (this estimate has since been sharply revised), Joaquin did not seek to extend their friendship. Instead, he spent as much time as he could with Walt Whitman, who was visiting in Boston, and for whom Joaquin felt a poetic affinity.

This caused much supercilious sniffing in the Cambridge literary set, for some people (Longfellow included) suspected that the Westerner had entered a drawing room with a cud of tobacco in his cheek. It must be remembered that this was at a time when it was the fashion to sneer at Walt Whitman as a guttersnipe. To Joaquin's great credit it must be said that all his life he staunchly defended and praised the good gray poet, and that he recognized Whitman's genius in the days when he was summarily dismissed as a lyrical impostor. He publicly scorned "all the little wits of America [who] were trying to stick pins in stout-hearted, empty-handed, and harmless old Walt Whitman."

Whitman acknowledged Joaquin's valuable allegiance. "I ought to be very grateful to him," Whitman said. "He has always gone out of his way to show that he stood with me— that the literary class would not find him aligned with them in their assaults on me." But when it came to appraising Joaquin's poetry he did not permit their friendship to color his judgment. "Miller never did quite the work I expected him to do," Whitman reluctantly told a friend in 1881. "He may do it yet."

During Joaquin's last dismal days in London, when his popularity fell away so completely, he had not found Lord Houghton much of a friend in need. However, when "Dickie" came to the United States in August, 1875 and wanted to meet Whitman, Joaquin made instant arrangements, and Whitman was to find that Houghton "showed an unmistakable warmth of friendship for me." (Joaquin never held a grudge, and it was often remarked that he spoke well of everyone; as for Houghton, Joaquin later dedicated a book to him.)

It was at this time that Whitman received a letter from Joaquin which he could not in the least decipher, even though in desperation he tried to read it upside down. Whitman prided himself on reading the most outlandish of scrawls, but, as he said: "I always had the devil's own time reading Miller—in fact, I always left the half of him unread. I could catch the drift but no more."

Joaquin's letter, dated September 5, 1875, read in part:

> I have been wandering up and down the house and waiting to hear from Lord Houghton so as to get you two together here on the banks of the Hudson, but he has gone West the other way. I am off today for Boston on biz and pleasure.

In 1888 Whitman came across the note and once more tried to decipher it. "If you can read this letter you beat me," he said, handing it to a friend. "I did my best at it again this morning, but it left me out in the cold."

After many laborious hours, the friend succeeded in decoding the missive. "That's the first time the letter has been read in full—the first time," Whitman marveled. "Why, it is thirteen years old."

3

Joaquin's new book, *The Ship in the Desert* (which was a single long poem, and dealt not with Arabia or camels as he had promised, but with the Great American Desert), was published late in 1875, and the critics gleefully rolled up their sleeves.

"This last volume," the New Englander declared with tongue in cheek, "has not given us as much pleasure as *Songs of the Sun-Lands,*" and the magazine seemed to think that this criticism was devastating enough. Other reviewers pointed out that Joaquin's latest verse were full of the usual mandatory clichés, and that the poems were disfigured by many flagrant faults of style. His lack of education was emphasized with the customary uncivil sneer, and the fact that he used antelope as a plural was pettily regarded as a mistake of the worst sort (here the learned scribes were in error).

APPLETON'S JOURNAL thought Joaquin Miller wrote more incoherently than even Bret Harte, a comment which evidently was considered the apex in slander. APPLETON'S declared it was one thing to try and find something good, as Harte did, in harlots, roués and border-ruffians, "but it is quite another to laud these people as, by reason, apparently, of their very 'primitiveness' and 'savagery' an exceptional praiseworthy species of the genus man. Mr. Miller makes a parade of condemning everything that civilized and decent men hold in respect; and his social code seems to be that men are 'noble,' and 'grand,' and 'earnest,' and 'sincere,' and 'admirable' in exact proportion to their barbarisms."

Before publication of *The Ship in the Desert* Joaquin confidently predicted that the poem would outlive everything he had written. But now, after the reviews were in, he announced that, while he was not forsaking the sacred muse, his next two books would be works of prose—novels. There was a great public demand for him to write novels, he said.

4

Soon after the year 1876 got under way Joaquin once again become a target of abuse. This time it was not the critics who were on the firing line, but, instead, various members of the wealthy business set. On April 10, Alexander T. Stewart the merchant prince died, and apart from his relatives, who were understandably curious about his will, he was mourned by no one. Stewart, the owner of the largest department store in the country, had been a slavedriver. The fourteen-hour day was his idea of bliss for the workingman, and he had a heavy hand when it came to fining employees for "lapses," which might include anything from being a few minutes late to tieing their shoelaces during working hours.

On hearing of the death, Joaquin like most people was pleased, so much so that he sat down and penned a poem. The last stanza, which is printed below, was widely circulated and quoted for many years:

> He got some gold, dug from the mud,
>   Some silver, crushed with stones;
> But the gold was red with dead men's blood,
>   The silver black with groans.
> And when he died he moaned aloud,
>   "They'll make no pocket in my shroud."

Joaquin took this bitter tribute to the grasping merchant to the New York HERALD, which promptly accepted it. He was given $3 for his composition, which he presented to a scrublady in the lobby.

The response from the mercantile families in the town was instant, and outraged. After all, the man was dead . . . *de mortuis nil nisi bonum* . . . It was even suggested that proceedings should be instituted to deport Joaquin Miller back to his native land. Whether he was to be sent into exile to his native Indiana, or to Oregon, or to California, we do not know. Joaquin was also accused of being a Communist, an epithet then coming into vogue.

As any student of Joaquin's career knows, he was not against businessmen *per se,* but he despised the robber barons as personified by Stewart, as did practically all writers and poets of the day, let alone other decent though less articulate people. A few years later, another immensely wealthy merchant died, and again Joaquin was quick to write some lines about him. Here, too, he was attacked, but this time because he eulogized the millionaire. The man was Peter Cooper, beloved today, but regarded then by his fellows as a traitor to his class. Cooper, in contrast to Stewart, believed in the equality of man, he paid his employees well and cut their working hours, and he was a philanthropist.

Joaquin's poem about Cooper was also widely quoted— and it may be that here was the reason for his popularity with the ordinary reading public:

> And wisest he in this whole wide land
> Of hoarding till bent and gray;
> For all you can hold in your cold dead hand
> Is what you have given away.

5

As he had promised, Joaquin made his debut as a novelist with his *First Fam'lies of the Sierras*, published in 1876. Its plot was interesting and well constructed, being concerned with the machinations of the Mormons, a people much in the public eye and in disfavor, at the time. The book received little critical acclaim, for it was felt that the characters were "Bret Harte types," but it sold well and in a matter of months Joaquin was to make a fortune because of the plot he had used.

In that same year the prolific Joaquin published a second novel, *The One Fair Woman*, on which he first had started to work in Italy. It was a long romance of five hundred and forty-eight pages, advertised as "Three Volumes in One" when it was put out in London and New York, and therefore sold for the high price of $2.

The background was Italy, with life in Genoa, Naples, Venice and Rome being sketched for the reader. The hero was Joaquin himself, as he fancied himself to be, and to make sure there could be no mistake about it, he named him Alphonse Murietta. The heroine, known as "The Pink Lady," was modeled after Mrs. Frank Leslie, and the book was dedicated to that powerful figure in the publishing world.

One of the few favorable reviews of *The One Fair Woman* appeared in the Providence Press. "One of the most brilliant, original, and impressive novels read for many a year," the newspaper declared, but the value of this judgment is marred by the fact that it was written by Joaquin himself. Other critics took a colder view. "No plot, no action, no characters—in short, no novel," was one verdict.

The climax of the book, the last throbbing paragraph as written by Joaquin, was often quoted derisively as an example of his fictional powers. *The One Fair Woman* ended as follows:

"No, do not think women blind," she said at last. "Men do not deceive women as often as they suppose, either for good or evil. I understand you better than you understand yourself. Had you flinched from your duty to that lady when she needed your help, I should have hated you, my hero."

Joaquin's second incursion into the field of fiction did little to increase his reputation. He announced that his next book would be a volume of verse.

6

The One Fair Woman may have aroused little public interest, but Mrs. Frank Leslie, to whom the book was dedicated, thought it was wonderful, and her opinion counted. Mrs. Leslie was a valuable friend for any writer to have, as she had much to say about buying manuscripts for the many magazines her husband published.

Their affair cannot be related in detail, as of course neither party was so indiscreet as to describe their passionate relationship for posterity, but the romance flourished off and on for thirty years, and the liaison was an open secret. Joaquin undoubtedly had a versatile lover in Mrs. Leslie, for many gentlemen found her technically perfect in bed, but perhaps more important, she also proved a financial asset for a writer. Mrs. Leslie bought many of his poems and stories for the various Leslie publications, paying top-market prices, and even before Joaquin had started to write his next book of verse she bought the pre-publication rights, sight unseen.

Not too much is known today about Mrs. Frank Leslie. She deserves a biography of her own, for she was one of the most amazing and most talked-about women of her era. Throughout her life she attained whatever goal she set for herself, whether in the pursuit of husbands and lovers (she had four of the former, a gross of the latter), or in her business ventures. Born obscurely and in poverty, she was to leave a $2,000,000 estate, and she herself earned every last dollar of it as America's first woman magazine editor—at a time when ladies were relegated to the nursery, the kitchen or, at best, the front parlor.

She was born Miriam Florence Follin, but it is not known exactly where or when. *Who's Who in America* accepted her story that her antecedents were Huguenots of aristocratic origin, but it is more likely that she was born about 1836 in New Orleans of Creole parents, probably as the illegitimate daughter of one Charles Follin and Susan Danforth.

After the father had decamped, young Miriam and her mother went to New York, where they ran a boarding house for men. At the age of eighteen the girl met and married a jeweler in Maiden Lane named Peacock. It is quite probable that this marriage was brought about by *force majeure* as the wedding was announced in the HERALD, vehemently denied the next day by Peacock, and a few days later confirmed by him. But, if the marriage came suddenly, so did the divorce.

In 1857 Miriam's life changed after she met the glamorous Lola Montez, renowned for her verve and beauty and fire and her lovers, but not for her acting or ballet dancing. Miriam's brother Noel had fallen in love with Lola in California and had accompanied the actress on a tour to Australia, acting as her manager and standby bed partner. On the return voyage, Follin was so distressed by the attentions Lola gave other male passengers that he dived overboard, and was drowned.

Lola Montez went to New York, sought out Mrs. Follin and dramatically cried, "I have killed your son!" She offered to give all the money she had to her lover's surviving children (for Follin had left a wife and family in Cincinnati), but mother Follin had a better idea. She suggested that, if Lola took her daughter on the stage, the slate would be wiped clean. This was done, and Miriam was billed as Lola's "sister." A woodcut illustration of Lola Montez and Miriam was printed in the March 7, 1857 issue of the ILLUSTRATED NEWSPAPER owned by Frank Leslie. Little did the publisher know that fourteen years later he would marry Miriam Follin.

Lola and Miriam parted (it was said that the Countess—for she was one—found the teen-age girl cuddled in bed, entirely naked, with an actor, entirely naked; but unless the man was a favorite of Lola's this is an unlikely reason for their quarrel, because La Montez was never bothered by such trifling lapses in morality).

Miriam promptly married a man known as a "catch,"

Ephraim G. Squier. Squier, fifteen years her senior, had served as Minister to Peru and was the author of several respected books on archaeology, and, though he had the reputation of being a heavy drinker, he was hired as an editor by Frank Leslie. Miriam began to contribute articles to the Leslie publications, and before she was twenty she was a recognized writer. She then went to work for Leslie—in more ways than one, it would seem—as editor of the first illustrated ladies journal in the country.

Unfortunately for the elderly Squier, who loved his wife almost as much as he loved his whiskey, his boss Leslie also became fond of the irresistible and gifted Miriam. Leslie divorced his wife, handing her a $28,000 settlement, and moved in to live with the Squiers. Squier's feelings about the arrangement are not known, but Miriam thought the situation was utterly delightful, so much so that at one time she startled her intimates by admitting that she was "exhausted." The members of this *ménage à trois* lived happily together— but not forever after. The day came when the young Miriam and the fifty-two-year-old Leslie decided they would be even happier if husband Squier could be forced to desert the field.

This was easily accomplished. Squier was persuaded to attend a "thrill party" staged by Miriam and Leslie in what was described as "a high-class whorehouse" in 27th Street. The duped and drunken husband participated in the orgy that followed, being attended by no less than five houris. But, a few days later, his wife announced she was outraged, and filed suit for divorce. She submitted affidavits—from the "ladies" who had been present at the carousal—which revealed that her husband had been unfaithful to her. The judge was as horrified as Miriam. A divorce was granted, and soon Miriam married Leslie. Squier died a few years later, forgotten, penniless, a hopeless drunkard.

Despite this lurid background, Mrs. Leslie was accepted by society, for after all her new husband was powerful and a millionaire, but she was best known in New York as the "Lioness of Bohemia," a sobriquet as famous as her literary salon. "I have met at the same time under her roof more eminent men and women than at any other one place I can now recall," Joaquin stated. He said one dinner was attended by Joaquin Miller, President Grant (his old fishing partner), Dom Pedro II of Brazil (his beloved friend), Don Carlos the Spanish Pretender, and four United States Senators—with Mrs. Leslie "entertaining us all with an ease of indifference that now seems to me incredible."

Strangely enough, Joaquin, who dressed so flashily, was rather taken aback at Mrs. Leslie's penchant for appearing in a blaze of diamonds. (When she was presented to New York's Governor Tilden she wore $70,000 worth of diamonds, and it was considered the height of refinement that she had refrained from putting on *all* her jewels.)

The more Joaquin saw of Mrs. Leslie, the more his poems appeared in the Leslie magazines, which numbered twelve, and the publisher-husband did not seem to mind his attentions. Mrs. Leslie (whose motto was, significantly enough, *tout ou rien*) often invited him to her Fifth Avenue palace, and for weekends to her vast Interlaken estate in Saratoga Springs, where according to Joaquin she lived in "royal splendor." "Perhaps the most interesting of her private conquests was that over Joaquin Miller, to whom she was more than a publisher," wrote Madeleine Stern. According to this literary historian, Mrs. Leslie was "the bright particular star that governed his life for many years." Joaquin, asked years later why he had not taken her as a wife, answered: "I was single when she was married, and vice versa," and this was true.

All her life Mrs. Leslie had exacting standards. She liked men who were first of all big and sturdy when it came to bedding down, and they had to be handsome creatures. Joaquin fulfilled these requirements perfectly. He was at the height of his physical powers at the time. He was thirty-nine (though he posed to be thirty-four), and a comment made about him by the Washington correspondent of the New York TRIBUNE conveys an idea as to his good looks and attractiveness:

He was an intent listener during the reading of the returns, and I had a fine opportunity for studying his appearance. His soft, fine hair is of a richly golden hue, his beard tawny, and his eyes finely blue. In sunset light Joaquin Miller is a perfect picture that an artist would despair of reproducing.

The long poem that Mrs. Leslie obligingly printed before book publication was "The Baroness of New York," a work of uncertain rhyme and meter. Joaquin had recited the opening stanzas at the Dartmouth Commencement of 1876 and they had been received well, so he had great hopes that the entire verse would retrieve and even enhance a reputation that was slowly slipping away. However, the finished product was regarded by readers as too rambling, too tedious and too long—two hundred and thirty-three pages, plus eleven pages of preface matter.

"A monstrosity, an outrage," the EVENING MAIL of New

York termed the book, probably referring to several cutting couplets attacking the respectable professions of the day, such as:

> A lawyer? liar? much the same
> In practice, quite as well as name.

but most critics were puzzled as to what it was all about, and they condemned the shallow insight of the poet. To give an example:

> Men are not shrewd as women are;
> 　A woman feels an atmosphere,
> Sees all, where man sees naught at all
> 　Her instincts lead where reasons fall.
> Now it may be the reason is,
> 　Her little feet are set more near
> The light of golden gates ajar.

Joaquin himself was to realize that this effort was a complete failure. There is today a presentation copy in the University of Chicago library signed by Joaquin with the gratuitous comment that it "isn't worth a damn." Twenty years later, he revised this composition, easily cutting 1,800 lines to 800; but it remained a book not worth a damn.

7

Toward the end of 1876 Joaquin and other celebrities were invited to Greenwood cemetery for the unveiling of the Horace Greeley monument. On the journey to Brooklyn, Joaquin found himself in a coupe with the city editor of the Tribune, and the next day the newspaper printed an amusing account of their conversation.

Joaquin enthusiastically told the editor about the new poem he was working on. He described vividly the burning of a Fifth Avenue mansion (Mrs. Leslie's, probably), and of the dramatic arrival of an intrepid California ranchero (Joaquin, probably), who dashed to the scene on horseback. The ranchero leaped from his horse, scaled the front of the house and rescued the heroine from the flames.

When he had finished, Joaquin excitedly asked the newspaperman what he thought of the idea.

The editor automatically reacted as an editor. "How do you get your hero inside the police lines at the fire?" he asked.

Joaquin was at first puzzled, then annoyed. He had never permitted trivial details to interfere with his visions of poetry —pure poetry, that is.

The journalist patiently explained that a cordon was drawn whenever a fire broke out; that everyone except police, firemen and reporters was barred, and that a man on horseback certainly would not be allowed to cross the lines.

Joaquin seemed to think these were petty points—it was evident the editor never had written poetry. "Besides," the newspaperman continued realistically, "by the time you bring your ranchero to the scene the insurance patrol would have obstructed the street with rescued goods from the burning mansion. Your hero would have no chance to get inside the lines."

Joaquin was, as the editor phrased it, "equal to the occasion" in solving the impasse. "Bravo!" he exclaimed, clapping his hands. "He shall ride 'em down!"

8

The new year of 1877 was to prove a busy one for Joaquin. First in an effort to supplement his steady income from the Leslie publications, he tried out lecturing, an occupation so profitable to writers at the time. Joaquin's subject was

"Literary London," but his trial performance, held in Philadelphia, was a failure. For reasons known only to himself, the poet discarded his Western garb and appeared in full evening dress, and monocle. To Philadelphians, this costume, as worn by Joaquin Miller the frontiersman, was ludicrously unsuitable.

"He is not an orator, and as a lecturer he cannot be conscientiously called a success," the Philadelphia Press stated. "Mr. Miller appeared about eight, attired in full evening dress. His personal ornaments were confined to an eyeglass and a button-hole bouquet." His listeners did like Joaquin's definition of poetry: true poetry, Joaquin said, was "a succession of beautiful pictures." But this esthetic credo was too insubstantial to sustain their interest throughout a whole evening.

Joaquin soon forgot his platform failure for, a few months later, as he jubilantly noted, he "hit a gold mine," and this for once was no exaggeration.

Plays with a Western setting were enjoying a boom. Mark Twain and Bret Harte attempted to capitalize on the vogue, but their efforts had come to nothing. Then Joaquin tried his hand—and he was successful beyond all his dreams. With the help of P. A. Fitzgerald, a Philadelphia playwright, he turned out a dramatization in five acts of his *First Fam'lies of the Sierras*. This play was called *The Danites, or, the Heart of the Sierras*, and when it opened on August 22 at the Broadway Theatre it was an immediate and tremendous hit. The Times critic complained about "the superabundance of Mr. Miller's prose," but he had to concede the play was "original and racy." The paying public thought it was wonderful.

The play could not have been staged at a more timely moment, for Brigham Young had just died and the newspapers were full of lurid stories about the Mormons. The Danites themselves were euphemistically referred to by the Mormons as "avenging angels," but actually they were members of a secret police branch of the church—one might say, a latter-day Gestapo of the Latter-Day Saints. The play was full of action and suspense. The plot was well constructed, dealing with the massacre of a party of Mormons by a band of "gentile" emigrants, and the subsequent remorseless search for the murderers by the revengeful Danites.

McKee Rankin played the title role of Sandy McGee the honest miner ("a king, this man," as Joaquin described the character), and so achieved stardom for the first time. Rankin and his wife were to appear in this vehicle for the next quarter-century. Others in the cast of eleven were Billy Piper, known as "that cussed boy," a Parson, a Judge, a Danite Chief and his underling, a Widow, Captain Tommy ("a woman with a bad name but a good heart"), her companion Bunkerhill, and Washee-Washee, a "heathen Chinee" who provided the comic touches.

Sometimes the action was held up when Joaquin's poetic penchants got the better of him (he had Billy Piper, an adolescent, declaim on nature: "Oh, what a miracle! The moon and golden stars, and all the majesty of this calm still world to love. Oh, life is not so hard now."), or when he extolled the charms of California (one of the characters exuberantly praised "the glorious climate of Californy," thus making Joaquin one of the first among the millions who would exalt the Golden State), but in the long run the drama held its audiences tense and enthralled.

The Danites had been scheduled to run for only a few days, but its opening-night success was so great that it was held over for seven straight weeks at the Broadway, when the production was transferred to the Grand Opera House for two more weeks. Season after season the play was given by road companies in hundreds of thousands of performances, rivaling the popularity of *Uncle Tom's Cabin* in some sections of the country. As late as 1898, twenty-one years after its original production, *The Danites* was revived in New York, and still was a hit.

The play appealed to the public even in printed form, and it ran through many editions which Joaquin revised from time to time—there were four different copyrights. In the preface of one of these editions Joaquin wrote that "millions of people crowded, first and last, to see the dreadful Danites glide stealthily across the mimic stage." That the drama had genuine merit is shown by the fact that it was deemed good enough to be included recently in Halline's *American Plays*.

Part of the play's popularity was no doubt due to the bitter feeling against the Mormons. Years later, after this animus had died down, Joaquin regretted the anti-Mormon tone of the play. "I have always been sorry I printed it," he said, "as it is unfair to the Mormons and the Chinese."

9

Joaquin had money in his pocket and he decided to spend it on a quick visit to London. While there he published *Songs of Far-Away Lands*, a collection of poems dealing with Italy and the Far West. "Civilized life has done little for him," the ATHENAEUM remarked in reviewing the book. "He is still the half-reclaimed savage he has chosen to represent himself." Other critics thought Browning should sue Joaquin for plagiarism.

Joaquin did not stay long in England, and all we know of

his activities at that time is what he mentioned in his letters to Lord Houghton, to whom he dedicated the *Songs*. A dream came true when he was invited to spend a week at Byron's historic home, Newstead Abbey in Nottingham, as guest of the owner, Colonel William Frederick Webb.

He inspected some manuscripts and thought Byron wrote "a sorry scrawl." "By special favor I have had Lord Byron's rooms," Joaquin wrote Houghton on August 30, 1878. "They are said to be haunted, you know. I believe in ghosts; but I have waited in vain for any visitant . . ." In a postscript Joaquin informed "Dickie" that he had not returned to London as planned: "Am at present here in what was Sherwood Forest, with the Duke of St. Albans."

It will be remembered that Bret Harte was the ringleader of the group that had virtually driven Joaquin from London a few years before. Joaquin, who was not prone to petty grudges ("I have never known him to speak an unkind word of *anyone*," Stoddard declared, a statement which has been echoed by many others who knew the poet), not only was friendly toward Harte but went out of his way to make a valuable social contact for him. "I got an invitation from Mrs. Webb, the hostess of Newstead Abbey, to visit her there," Harte wrote at the time. "I think I am indebted somewhat to Mr. Miller for this first introduction to some of the best people in England—for he was visiting the Abbey at the time." A few years later Harte was publicly sneering at Joaquin as a "literary nothing."

Joaquin stayed in London only a month or so, and then returned to New York, where he found a letter from Lord Houghton awaiting him. Joaquin replied in a message dated October 16. "I have just returned from the Rocky Mountains where I spent months with the Indians," he wrote. This must have mystified Houghton, who but a few weeks before had seen Joaquin in London. "My destiny," Joaquin confided, "is a cattle ranch."

The poet was mistaken. His destiny was to stay in New York and enjoy the prestige accorded a successful playwright. He established a bachelor household with Charles Warren Stoddard, who, since the day when he met the unknown Joaquin Miller on a San Francisco pier, seems to have spent much of his life following Joaquin around and living with him. On this third stay with him, Stoddard found his friend a comparatively rich man because *The Danites* had returned in 1878 to New York for another run, and would come back in the following year, too. Despite Joaquin's affluence, the two men lived simply. "He had a knack of slapping a steak into a bed of live coals in the parlor grate and then tossing it over with the tongs that was my delight and my despair," Stoddard recalled. "Big mealy potatoes roasting in the ashes, plenty of good bread with butter and cheese." Stoddard claimed he and Joaquin drank cup after cup of tea, but this is hard to believe, for Joaquin's fondness for whiskey grew as the years passed.

In 1878 *The Danites and other Choice Selections from the writings of Joaquin Miller, "The Poet of the Sierras"* was published. It was "Dedicated to all who admire, even to the humblest extent, the writings of Joaquin Miller." This unusual inscription was probably inspired by the book's editor, A. V. D. Honeyman. "I am aware of the merciless denunciations of this author's verse at the hands of a few American writers of 'book notices,'" Honeyman wrote. Sure enough, the critics assailed the volume for its pretentiousness, but it sold extremely well. On the other hand, Joaquin's *Songs of*

Italy, published the same year, went unnoticed by reviewers and public alike.

Joaquin began to be seen less and less in the company of Mrs. Frank Leslie, for he was busy wooing a wealthy young lady of such great respectability that she shunned Mrs. Leslie's Bohemian circles. However, when the TERRITORIAL ENTERPRISER, a newspaper in Virginia City, Nevada, issued an extra entirely devoted to the many loves and the many sins of Mrs. Frank Leslie, he came to her defense. The sheet, which was irritated because Mrs. Leslie had written slightingly about the women of Virginia City, viciously suggested in this exposé that the publisher's wife was a bastard and a few grades below a whore, whose mother had let out rooms to "single gentlemen by the day or week, with no questions asked."

Joaquin answered these and other below-the-belt charges by publicly pronouncing Mrs. Leslie "pure," and to his eternal credit it must be said that he did not add, "as the driven snow."

The rich and respectable lady Joaquin was courting was Miss Abigail Leland, the daughter of a hotel chain owner, whose jewel was the vast Union Hotel in Saratoga. Joaquin was introduced to Miss Leland, who was an amateur elocutionist, after attending one of her performances. Abbie, as Miss Leland was generally known, and Joaquin fell in love at once.

Abbie liked Joaquin's poetry for a thoroughly personal reason. During one of the panics of the 1870's, Alexander T. Stewart had foreclosed mortgages on two of the Leland hotels in New York, the Grand Union and the Metropolitan. The action had brought Leland close to the wall, and though he recovered and even increased his fortune, all of the Lelands bitterly remembered Stewart's action. Abbie thought that Joaquin's sentiments about Stewart were commendable and perfectly expressed.

The couple evidently had other things in common, too, for on March 12, 1879, the two were quietly married in New York. Strangely enough, the newspapers did not comment on the wedding, although Joaquin was a celebrity, and Miss Leland well known as an heiress. According to the *Dictionary of American Biography*, Joaquin at the time apparently was not formally divorced from his wife, Minnie Myrtle Miller. This usually authoritative publication cannot be accepted here, however, as its sketch of Joaquin's life is shot full of errors.

Mr. and Mrs. Cincinnatus Hiner Miller moved into quarters at 109 West 33rd Street, but a few weeks later Joaquin took rooms nearby which he used as a workshop and as an occasional sleeping-out place.

Superficially at least the marriage might be called a success inasmuch as there never was a divorce; nonetheless, the two seldom lived together, and during most of their married life the distance of a continent was to separate them. Little is known of Mrs. Miller, reputedly a beautiful woman, but a deliberately shadowy character who shied away from the spotlight as determinedly as her husband sought it. One child was born of the union, Juanita, who in 1953 is the only direct living descendant of Joaquin Miller.

10

When Joaquin made his fourth visit to England in 1880, there was an important reason for the trip. McKee Rankin has the distinction of being the first actor-manager in the United States to take a complete American cast across the

Atlantic to stage a play in London—and the vehicle chosen was the popular *Danites*. But before he left, Rankin coolly informed Joaquin that no royalties would be paid him while the troupe was in England. When Joaquin threatened to go to court, Rankin pointed out that the poet had received royalties in the past merely because of the goodness of Rankin's heart: Joaquin in fact did not own the copyright to the drama and so was entitled to none of the profits.

Joaquin learned that, incredibly enough, this was true. A few years before, when he had finished the play, the slippery Rankin had told him he would take care of the wearisome details of obtaining a copyright. He then had taken the adapted stage version and secured the copyright under the name of his wife! Joaquin at once sued Mrs. Rankin and, because of the similarity between the drama and his novel, *First Fam'lies of the Sierras*, was only too apparent, the Rankins' case collapsed and Joaquin established clear title to the play.

Joaquin took no chances with the Rankins when the play was staged abroad. Every night during its entire run in England he appeared at the box office and had his royalty payments counted out to him.

The Danites was just as successful in England as it had been in America. On opening night the applause from the pit was so deafening that the cast was called many times before the curtain, and soon Joaquin came elbowing his way through the actors and insisted on taking bows. He explained later he thought he had heard the cry, "Author! Author!" but that he had been mistaken.

The drama played eight straight weeks at Sadler's Wells Theatre, three weeks at the Standard, and then toured the provinces for a month—and yet apparently Joaquin enjoyed no personal prestige, or even notoriety. He has left no record of this sojourn in England, and his contemporaries have not mentioned his presence there. Toward the end of 1881 he quietly returned to New York. He had caused a tremendous furore during his first two visits to London, and an equally impressive silence on the following two trips. He never was to see England again.

Back in New York, Joaquin dabbled frantically in play-writing. The success of *The Danites* had been so instantaneous, and so easily achieved, that he felt confident he could duplicate it. He never did. Joaquin took a short story he had written for OVERLAND MONTHLY and turned it into a play called *Forty-Nine*. Its heroine was Carrots—"20 karots fine and all pure gold"—an Indian maiden who, peculiarly enough, was a redhead, but, although Mr. and Mrs. McKee Rankin appeared in the leading roles, it was a box office flop. Still later, Joaquin wrote *Tally Ho!* and *An Oregon Idyll*, but he could find no producer to stage either play.

Amidst all this activity he did churn out another novel. *Shadows of Shasta*, dedicated to Whitelaw Reid, was written in protest against the Government's proposal to move the Shasta Indians to a reservation. Certainly Joaquin was not alone in condemning this arbitrary action; and yet one might think from the reaction of the reviewers that he had eaten his grandmother.

How could Miller "commit such enormities as this?" the CRITIC wanted to know. The magazine took Joaquin to task for being an "erratic, untamed, irresponsible poet" and declared that "this last story which he has put forth is to the full as bad as anything he has ever written, which is saying a good deal." Again his personal conduct was attacked—he was labeled a horse thief, a faker, a poseur, an impostor—but these epithets had been used so often that they began to lose their weight.

Joaquin seriously considered retiring as "Poet of the Sierras," or as poet of anything else, for that matter. He could have done so, as he did not have to write for a living. He did not have to support his wife, who was independently wealthy. He had a fat bank account, thanks to the steady flow of royalties from *The Danites*. (Joaquin said he had $90,000 on hand at the time; other reports mention a sum of $22,000.) Luck had been with him, and he was in a reckless mood. The poet decided to turn business man. He would go into Wall Street with his $90,000 and make a fortune in the stock market, just as so many other people were doing. A man could buy on margin, and, if he were smart. . . .

But before Joaquin decided to plunge he thought it wise to consult an expert on stocks, a man who was his friend, and who had the reputation of knowing all the ins and outs of stock speculation. This friend was Jay Gould. Gould told Joaquin that he never, *never* gave advice on market operations, but that, in tribute to their friendship and in deference to Joaquin's poetic genius, he would break his iron-clad rule.

It so happened, Gould smoothly said, that he could give Joaquin the greatest tip that ever had been disclosed to an outsider. "Buy Vandalia railroad stock, and sell Western Union," Gould confided. The wily operator said he was putting every dollar he owned and could borrow into this "sure thing," and he swore Joaquin to secrecy.

Joaquin followed Gould's advice and sat back, waiting to become rich. But unfortunately for the naive poet, he had consulted one of the most unscrupulous market manipulators of the age. Jay Gould—of whom it was said he would cheat his father out of a dollar to make an honest penny—did exactly the opposite of what he advised Joaquin to do. Gould was a bear on Vandalia, and a bull on Western Union.

The Vandalia railroad soon went into the hands of a receiver, and its stock was worthless. With this catastrophe, most of Joaquin's fortune disappeared. The rest of his money vanished in the Western Union deal. If he had *bought* Western Union, instead of selling short, he would have become a millionaire, for its stock went sky-high. In short, the poet had been taken for a sucker.

This was neither the first nor the last time that Jay Gould flimflammed a "friend" and emerged the winner. We do not know exactly whether Joaquin gambled with $90,000 or $22,000 or some amount in between, but we do know exactly how much money he had left afterwards: the sum was $128.

Enraged over the perfidy of stock market operators, Joaquin wrote a novel, *The Destruction of Gotham*, which exposed the iniquities of Wall Street. The book caused little stir. This may have been because Joaquin was ahead of his times—the public reaction against Wall Street finagling that was to become so intense and widespread did not occur until a few years later. In 1906, when President Theodore Roosevelt coined the name "muckrakers" to describe those writers who made a habit of exposing the activities of corporations and men in public office, Joaquin claimed that, with the publication of *The Destruction of Gotham* a quarter-century before, he had been the first muckraker in the country.

I I

Joaquin would always remember the death of James A. Garfield, not because the assassination of the President sent him into mourning, but because of the "wonderful adventure" that subsequently befell him.

Joaquin was at the time in Boston visiting John Boyle O'Reilly, a man after his own heart. (O'Reilly, an Irish-born poet, had made his way to the United States after escaping from an Australian prison camp where he had been incarcerated for being a Fenian subversive.) When Garfield died on July 2, 1881, eulogies in his honor were solicited from Whitman, Longfellow and Joaquin. Whitman liked Garfield no better dead than alive, and declined. Joaquin pointed out to Whitman that he could use the $100 that was offered for a threnody that could be written in a few hours. He and O'Reilly took Whitman to the Revere House saloon and filled him with champagne, but the Camden poet was adamant.

Longfellow hastily wrote his encomium and read it to Joaquin. Joaquin pronounced it a masterpiece, a work of genius. Joaquin then read his own ode to Longfellow. Its tenor was: "Brave heart, farewell . . ." etc. Longfellow pronounced it a masterpiece, a work of genius. Joaquin then returned to his hotel and was about to retire when, as he later told the story to his friend, Harr Wagner, a calling card was sent to his room by a woman, who was not further identified. As Joaquin remembered it:

I had written to order, "The Sioux Chief's Daughter" for the lady who sent the card. She had sent me $50, and I had expected about $20. When I met her in the lobby of the hotel she invited me immediately to her house.

When we arrived at the door, she said, "This is to be no formal meeting. I have loved and admired you, your poetry, and your photographs." She invited me upstairs and introduced me to two young lady friends. * * *

The asterisks are thoughtfully provided by Wagner.

"I thanked the Lord that I was a lion in strength that day," Joaquin told Wagner.

On reflection, Joaquin added, in what decidedly was an understatement: "It was a most unusual and interesting experience."

12

In January, 1882 Oscar Wilde "discovered America." Joaquin had not met Wilde in London, but the Rossetti brothers had written him and commended the flamboyant esthete to his care. Before Wilde arrived, Joaquin commanded his fellow citizens to treat their guest civilly, evidently anticipating that the visitor would be regarded as a queer duck indeed.

Soon after he landed (when the customs official asked what he had to declare, Wilde made his celebrated remark: "Nothing but my genius.") Wilde visited Joaquin, assured him of his immortality as a bard, and asked for advice as to how to conquer America. Joaquin liked Oscar at once, as did most people who met him. He found that Wilde was not at all womanish, no lily-carrier or roseleaf-eater as his pose indicated, but instead a robust six-footer, a valiant toper after Joaquin's own heart—a three-bottle man.

The two became fast friends. (While Joaquin needs no special pleading in this realm, it might be noted in passing that, despite his attitudinizing as a swishy effeminate esthete, Wilde did not begin to experiment with the charms of sodomy until four years later.) Oscar was entertained by Joaquin in his home, and the visitor left behind an inscribed copy of the poem "Charmides," his only literary production up to that time.

Joaquin did all he could to make Wilde's first lecture in Chickering Hall a success. He begged his friends to buy tickets, and he publicly announced that America now had on its shores a writer of supreme talent. This was more of an accurate prophecy than a statement of fact, for Wilde at the time was twenty-six, known merely for his studied eccentricities, his conversational wittiness and for his championship of estheticism, but not as a literary figure.

It is a wonder that Joaquin was so generous, for, when it came to attracting attention through garish dress, he had met for the first time not only his match but his master in Oscar Fingal O'Flahertie Wills Wilde. When the two met in the home of Mrs. Marion Fortesque, where Wilde touted the "intensity" of estheticism, they were, as one of the guests remarked, sights to behold.

Joaquin wore a high-peaked green hat, red kerchief, a fringed buckskin coat, and his bright blue trousers were stuffed in jackboots.

Alas, in comparison to the dazzling Wilde, Joaquin was dressed like a drab. Wilde minced about with a gigantic sunflower in his hand, his long hair cascading over his shoulders. When he had taken off his bottle-green frogged fur coat, it was found he was wearing a black velvet jacket, knee breeches and black silk stockings, a flowing tie with a *lavallière* knot as big as a sweet potato, low shoes with shining silver buckles. The crowd gathered around Oscar; Joaquin was all but ignored.

Wilde was received with amusement and tolerance when he lectured in New York, and in general his reception was favorable. But when he visited less sophisticated sections of the country he found that the stout citizens were suspicious of estheticism and loath to hear of its beauties. There was a tendency to regard Oscar as considerably less than a red-blooded he-man, and there were dark whispers that he had something of "the Greek" in his makeup.

So it was that in a few towns Wilde was greeted not hilariously or raucously, as might have been expected, but with violence. In Rochester, for instance, the lecture on "cultchah" by "Miss Nancy" was broken up when rowdies in the audience rioted and drove him from the stage.

There was the danger that this disorderly behavior might prove contagious when Oscar visited other cities, and to counteract such a possibility Joaquin hastily penned an open letter to Wilde, apologizing for the loutish conduct of his fellow Americans. "I read with shame about the behavior of those ruffians at Rochester at your lecture there," he wrote. "I have read the coarse comments of the Philistine Press. . . . I feel like thanking God that my home lies three thousand miles further on, in what is called the wilderness. . . . I remember how kind your country was to me, and at your age I had not done one-tenth your work." He signed the letter, "Thine for the Beautiful and True—Joaquin Miller."

The New York WORLD and other newspapers printed this missive. Wilde answered "My Dear Joaquin" while lecturing in St. Louis. "I thank you for your chivalrous and courteous letter," he wrote. "I look forward to spend another delightful evening with you in New York." Oscar then went into a long dissertation on the ecstasies of estheticism, for this letter too was aimed at publication.

Wilde continued his tour (strangely enough, the farther the precious esthete traveled into the Wild West, where presumably the he-men abounded, the more cordially he was received; he was accepted unreservedly by San Franciscans when he drank a roomful of topers under the table—and remained sober), and when he reached Salt Lake City he returned the compliment. Wilde lauded Joaquin Miller and Walt Whitman (who also had spoken in his favor) as the only two worthwhile poets in America, and inferentially he placed Joaquin as the superior genius of the two.

Months later, when Wilde returned to New York, he publicly praised Joaquin's incredible poetic brilliance, and when the two were together it was noted that Oscar was ever quick to defer to Joaquin as The Master. In December, 1882, a few days before Wilde sailed for England, Joaquin held a reception in his honor. The two were never to meet again.

It is to be presumed that Joaquin followed the subsequent bizarre career of Oscar Wilde with amazement; but he left no written record of his reactions. We do know that he did not follow the herd thirteen years later, when Wilde was exposed as a pederast. Joaquin then spearheaded a drive to collect money for his convict friend in Reading Gaol. It is significant that few writers and poets in the United States other than Joaquin Miller publicly supported Wilde in 1882, and that even fewer came to his defense when his career was blasted by scandal.

In this same year of 1882 Joaquin entertained, defended, but did not at the time meet, another visitor from England. She was the fabulous Lillie Langtry. No longer the darling of royalty, the Jersey Lily was in need of money and had become an actress. She came to the United States, but right at the outset the success of her tour was endangered by public criticism of her private life. In puritanical Boston it was charged that she slept with men who were not her husbands. It was said that one of her many "hangers-on" was far too intimate with her, and that the fellow was taking and spending all of her money.

"Treat her well," Joaquin admonished Bostonians in a letter to the GLOBE. "She is altogether worthy of your best considerations and esteem; good, truthful, frank, sincere; pure as the snow and very brave. Treat her well." Here, Joaquin used "pure as the snow," but not "pure as the *driven* snow."

Joaquin also sent to the GLOBE the poem he had once written in tribute to Miss Langtry—the one in which he fancied himself to be a bee in the Lily's garden—and thus it was printed for the first time. In letters to other newspapers, Joaquin denied rather vehemently that he had named Miss Langtry the Jersey Lily. He admitted he would have liked to have had the honor, but simply did not deserve it. This the editors found an amusing line of argument, as no one in the country, with the possible exception of Joaquin Miller, had ever claimed that it was he who had bestowed the sobriquet on the great beauty.

13

In the spring of 1882 Joaquin, for the first time in thirteen years, saw "that strange, unhappy woman"—his first wife, Minnie Myrtle. His once fiery and vindictive spouse was a piteous sight, for her spirit was crushed, her health was ruined, and she had no money. Minnie Myrtle had come to New York to seek out Joaquin. She needed more than financial help—she needed a friend. Now that all the bitterness between them was a thing of the past, she could be genuinely glad over his fame and successful marriage. She probably remembered that he had never said a mean word about her. And she trusted him and asked him to stand by her.

Joaquin did all he could. He summoned the doctors, who soon pronounced their verdict: Minnie Myrtle was dying. He spent long hours with her, reading his poetry, and he sent for their three children to come to New York and see their mother for the last time. The boys, George and Harold, long estranged from their father because he had never supported them, could not be located. The daughter Maud, now nineteen, who had attained a measure of success as an actress in San Francisco's Grand Opera House, telegraphed that she was on her way.

But in the first week of May, before Maud arrived, Minnie Myrtle died. "She passed away in my arms," Joaquin said.

The burial was held in Evergreen Cemetery, and the tears streamed down Joaquin's face as the coffin was lowered into the grave. The second Mrs. Miller held up better under the ordeal.

In an open letter to the San Francisco CHRONICLE Joaquin announced he had forgiven Minnie Myrtle for the public attacks she had made on him in her lectures, and he paid tribute to her poetic talents. As if to make amends to the dead woman, he invited Maud, whom he found to be a beautiful girl, to live with him and his new family in West 33rd Street. Maud declined rather coldly, evidently regarding the invitation as being somewhat belated. She went on to Paris, where she became a mild success on the stage.

Joaquin's conscience was at last getting the better of him, and he made efforts to find his two sons, who were believed to be somewhere in the Pacific Northwest. He was informed that a few years before the youngsters, then aged about twelve and thirteen, had been seen roaming about the streets of Portland, but that their present whereabouts were not known.

The prolific poet by now had published a dozen books of prose, poetry and plays. But, after the death of Minnie Myrtle, after his failure to locate his sons, Joaquin found himself unable to write. Perpetually restless and irritated, he traveled to Liberty, Indiana, hoping that a nostalgic visit to his birthplace would dissipate his black moods and restore his poetic voice. There were many old settlers in the town who remembered him as the tow-headed kid who had gone West with Hulings and Margaret Miller in 1852. Embarrassingly enough, there also were many who remembered that the poet now was a mature forty-four in this summer of 1882, and not the thirty-nine he claimed.

Joaquin seriously considered isolating himself in a shabby log cabin outside Liberty, to live a lonely monastic life devoted solely to the sacred muse, but at the last moment he wisely decided that the prophet-in-his-hometown tradition would apply to him too. He returned to New York, but when he still found himself unable to compose poetry—he faced the terrible possibility that he was "all written out"— he concluded that he could stand the city no longer.

Joaquin insisted that his family should leave the sterile metropolis. He talked vaguely to Abbie about moving to the wilderness, any wilderness, of building a rude hut or log cabin, and of communing with nature. The fastidious Mrs. Miller, accustomed to living in the most luxurious of the Leland hotels, was horrified. Besides, her original love for poetry seems to have diminished as the years passed, and whatever romantic cravings she may have had were amply satisfied. She made it plain to her husband that she would not permit their daughter Juanita to grow up in a dirty lean-to, and she would not consider living like an aborigine herself.

The poet-husband was adamant. His poetic genius would wither away, he declared, if he stayed in New York. He threatened to break up the marriage and go West alone. At last his wife surrendered, but the farthest she would consent to penetrate the hinterland was to go to Washington, and then only with the stipulation that they live in a decent house, in style, and not in a tepee or shack or any of the makeshift domiciles that had become an obsession with her husband.

The move of the Miller menage to the capital was made late in 1883. Joaquin did not know it, but he was slowly inching his way back to where he belonged, the Far West.

14

After living in Washington for a few weeks Joaquin concluded that the surroundings were not conducive to recapturing his muse. Instead of living in a log cabin where he could commune with nature, he found himself installed at Florence Court on fashionable California Street. The monastic silence, which he felt would inspire him poetically, was missing too, for either his wife, or his daughter, or the nurse or the cook or the maid always seemed underfoot. Joaquin grimly declared he would not put up with the situation.

For the second time in his life his marriage was breaking up. The second Mrs. Miller was in no conciliatory mood, either. Abbie, who had played a leading role in the society of New York, visualized herself in an equally glamorous position in the capital, and to further her ambition she had spent a considerable sum in redecorating and refurnishing their Florence Court quarters. Now she found, discouragingly enough, that Joaquin professed to be weary of all social doings, and that he frowned on the idea of another member of his family stepping into the spotlight.

Abbie furthermore discovered that Joaquin was actually a social handicap. A stodgy Republican, Chester A. Arthur, was President. Abbie's illustrious husband, treated so respectfully (by all but critics) in New York, was regarded in Washington not only as a Democrat, but as a despised ex-Copperhead. No invitations came to dine at the White House. Instead of presiding over a social salon and having distinguished Senators and Supreme Court Justices drop in for calls, Mrs. Miller was compelled to entertain literary Bohemians who were her husband's cronies, such as the dirty nobody, Walt Whitman, a poet or something. It was most depressing.

No one filed for divorce. No one went to court for separation papers. But the marriage was for all practical purposes at an end. Abbie and Joaquin never again lived together under one roof for any considerable length of time. "As a husband he always was a failure," noted Martin S. Peterson, a student of the poet's career. The breakup was made in a civilized manner, however. Joaquin often went to New York or to Saratoga to visit his daughter Juanita, and Abbie and Joaquin were friendly toward each other and to any outsider kept up the illusion that they were man and wife. He did not contribute to the expense of rearing his child, as Abbie had a large fortune; but on the other hand there is no evidence to show that Joaquin ever spent any of her money on himself.

As soon as Abbie had shut up house and removed the furniture to New York, Joaquin began to scout about for a secluded place where he could live the life of a hermit, where he could write poetry in peace. He found an ideal site in the Arlington Heights section of Washington. There he purchased a few acres of land, hired some laborers and worked with them to build a log cabin to his own specifications. It was, he claimed, the exact duplicate of the cabin belonging to his Shasta county days in California.

Today the cabin would stand (it has been removed) on 16th Street, between Crescent Place and Meridian Hill. Joaquin could enjoy a fine view of the Potomac and the glistening white dome of the capitol. The district was then remote and unsettled, the nearest street car line being two miles distant, and Joaquin found the retreat to be, as he so quaintly described it, "a little edge of God's rest."

The cabin nestled in a circle of huge oak trees, whose branches interlaced over the roof, and it stood far back from the road. There was no path leading to the door, as Joaquin preferred to let the grass grow wild everywhere. In the side yard, the long awkward arm of an old-fashioned sweep dipped picturesquely down into a deep, dark well.

The logs of the cabin were peeled of bark and unadorned with paint or whitewash. On the outside walls Joaquin hung elk skins and bows and arrows. Inside, there were two small rooms, both unplastered, with gaping chinks showing between the logs. There were no furnishings from the Leland hotels in the cabin. The front room contained a writing table, a few chairs, a stove in the corner, a bearskin on the floor, a vase always filled with wild flowers, but little else. The room in the rear was barely large enough to hold a bed. For a blanket, Joaquin used the hides of wild animals, not stitched together, but thrown on the bed in crazy-quilt fashion. Some people thought the new home was on the primitive side. The poet pronounced it perfect.

Joaquin had attracted attention in London by his weird costume. He attracted attention in Washington by living in a log cabin. Log cabins were not a rarity in 1883, but it seldom happened that a person built one himself and voluntarily lived in it. Now the poet, who said he yearned for solitude, found that his home was not quite "a little edge of God's rest." A steady stream of visitors came to examine his cabin, and to examine Joaquin Miller.

Many of the callers were Congressmen who brought their constituents to see the poet Miller. The people would start trooping to the cabin early in the afternoon, and many of them would bring slabs of ham or flitches of bacon to present to the bard. Those who were better acquainted with Joaquin's tastes would bring a jug of whiskey, and usually they were the ones who were invited to stay for potluck. Joaquin grumbled that the visitors were driven his way by curiosity and not because they loved (and bought) his poems. Of course, he could have refused to see the constant stream of intruders, but he did not, and he was always suitably garbed in his frontier outfit when the callers came.

When Joaquin saw the visitors making their way through the tall grass in his yard he usually would take the bearskin from the dirty floor, sling it over his shoulder, and stand statuesque in the doorway. The callers were fascinated by the bearskin and liked to finger it, for, as Joaquin assured them, it was the identical bearskin he had worn during the days of his London triumphs, the same bearskin that had been handled and admired by Queen Victoria, the Princess Alexandra, the Shah of Persia, and a host of others. One day an awed visitor was so impressed that he offered a large sum for the historic trophy. Joaquin reluctantly parted with the combination rug-robe. A few days later, a new bearskin was on the floor. The market held up well, and it is said the poet disposed of no less than nine of the "authentic" London bear-skins.

The poet also appeared frequently in Washington. Elbert Hubbard recalled seeing Joaquin "wearing Indian leggings, deerskin coat, high top boots, hatless, parading down Pennsylvania Avenue, followed by admiring and wondering crowds, of whom he was beautifully oblivious." At this time Joaquin also took to wearing a red skull cap, a type of headgear he was to find indispensable for the rest of his life. (He experimented with wearing a coonskin cap but found it did not flatter his features.) Some people thought that Joaquin wearing a skull cap looked like a Cardinal Richelieu, 2nd class.

Joaquin scandalized many people in Washington by appearing often in the company of Colonel Robert Ingersoll, despised as an "atheist." Ingersoll was nothing of the sort, being an agnostic, a formidable orator who was the terror of religious-minded citizens, and the poet liked his views.

At the time, the streets of the capital were in a continual state of repair, and it was often difficult to make one's way about. Joaquin and Ingersoll were out riding one day, and, as the poet told the story:

> We came to a street torn up, and Colonel Ingersoll said: "I wonder if I shall ever get to a city that is made."
> I glanced up toward the sky and replied: "I'm afraid not, Colonel."

Ingersoll liked the reply so much that he often told it on himself in lectures.

Such excursions wasted many hours, and further hours were lost by entertaining the visiting crowds at his cabin, but Joaquin assures us that he often toiled after midnight as he sought desperately to become his old self again and turn out poetry. For months he felt stale and mentally tired, and then one day there occurred a miracle. As a refresher course, Joaquin read aloud to himself some of the most splendid verse ever written—the poems of Joaquin Miller. This, he found, was the perfect cure, for suddenly he felt inspired—he had regained his magical poetic powers.

The result of this minor miracle was a new book called *Memorie and Rime*, published in 1884. It consisted of stray verse and a series of entries he reputedly had kept years earlier in various diaries. The reviewers dismissed the poetry as preposterous rubbish, but at first they were inclined to treat the diary entries more respectfully. Many of these "Bits from My Journal" dealt with Joaquin's first visit to London in 1870, with numerous famous names of the day sprinkled in between, and the comments in themselves were interesting and possibly of historical importance.

The more the critics examined these entries, however, the more they were convinced that (a) Joaquin's original diary entries had been cut or expanded or doctored for publication, or, (b) the diary jottings had been entirely manufactured— written shortly before publication time. A close examination of the entries today tends to confirm the reviewers' judgment and makes it seem likely that their first supposition is probably correct; but the evidence is by no means conclusive.

15

In the fall of 1884 Joaquin took a leisurely trip through the South, combining, as he liked to say, "biz with pleasure." He had been given a journalistic assignment, to act as correspondent for a syndicate of Eastern newspapers at the opening of the Exposition in New Orleans.

Joaquin took the train to Louisville, where he stopped off for a few days, and then proceeded to New Orleans. He arrived on October 11, two months before the Exposition got under way, and registered at the famed St. Charles Hotel. Newspapermen wanted to interview him, but Joaquin was in a frivolous mood, and unwilling to be informative. He had, the reporters suspected, been drinking too much whiskey. "This is a mighty fine hotel, but I wouldn't take it if they gave it to me," the poet gravely told the newspapermen. Then he pointed at the elevator. "The idea of getting into that thing, and being shot up and down!"

When last seen, the journalists reported, the poet had entered the elevator and was bowing to them as the cage ascended.

Joaquin had arrived on a Saturday. The next morning he had newspapermen escort him to the French Quarter. There he dabbled in gambling and then talked animatedly to the girls, and from there he went straight to church and listened to a sermon. This is one of the rare recorded instances in which Joaquin Miller attended church services. The reporters noted that he was equally at home in both milieus, and an attention-getter in either place.

The next day, Monday, when Joaquin strolled in the streets he was mistaken for an actor, a bearded man who wore a sombrero and was starring in *The Bandit King*, a play that was a sensation in New Orleans. Joaquin did not disillusion his admirers. He led them to the theatre, bought tickets for a dozen of the crowd, and urged the others to join him inside. During the matinee—all we know of the play today is a critic's comment that it was "reeking with slow music, powder smoke, blood and bad villains"—the actors made loud asides, praising the poetic genius of Joaquin Miller, and each time this was done Joaquin would rise and bow. The audience liked it, and so did Joaquin.

New Orleans welcomed Joaquin as a great celebrity whom the city should be proud of, and installed him in the George Washington Cable house in 8th Street. During his three-month stay he was thoroughly lionized. He was received by Governor Lowry, he read his poems to select groups, and he attended many gay parties given at plantations outside the city. Joaquin scorned the gin the natives drank, but they were astounded at the ease with which he drank one glass of whiskey after another, and they marveled at the stories of his adventures abroad. None of the Orleanians had realized he had traveled so widely. Joaquin gave them a blazing account of the times he fought as the chief lieutenant of Garibaldi in Italy, and he topped this with his experiences in India, where he had "gone all the way to the Ganges to see the worshippers of the waters."

No matter how formal the occasion, Joaquin insisted on wearing his frontier costume. A few stray social leaders resented this. "There are people who object to see Joaquin Miller at a full dress reception, in the presence of ladies, with the legs of his pantaloons tucked into high-top boots," the Times-Democrat reported. The newspaper reproved these sartorial stalwarts. "They are too fastidious. If a lion is on exhibition he must shake his mane, show his teeth and claws, and appear natural, else he might be mistaken for a donkey instead of a lion."

When walking about New Orleans, Joaquin was always tagged by an admiring throng, and, as was his custom, he acted as if he did not know he had company. Once he strolled down to the end of Canal Street and, while the ladies in the crowd averted their eyes, calmly stripped down to the skin and plunged into the Mississippi for a cooling dip. As Joaquin remembered it later on his return to Washington, he had swum to the opposite shore of the river and back, and when the man with the stopwatch announced the time, the Orleanians were dumfounded at such prodigious speed.

When Buffalo Bill's Wild West Show opened in New Orleans, Joaquin mounted a horse and rode in the street parade, and received more cheers than did the renowned "Colonel" Cody, who as a result of this setback went into a profound sulk. It is regrettable that Joaquin did not leave his impression of Buffalo Bill, for the two were certainly brothers under the skin and it would have been amusing to see what one great showman thought of the other. But unfortunately the only comment left by Joaquin was that Buffalo Bill could drink a lot of whiskey, an observation confirmed by many others.

The Exposition opened December 16, and Joaquin sent a series of stories to his newspaper syndicate. They were less than adequate, even by the journalistic standards of seventy years ago. Whatever one may think of Joaquin Miller's poetry, it is generally agreed that his prose was worse. Apparently he was too preoccupied with his social duties to take off time enough to write what could have been interesting stories on the Exposition.

It was while he was visiting New Orleans that Joaquin had another fling with his inamorata, Mrs. Frank Leslie. The beautiful Creole now was the sole owner and editor of all the Leslie magazines. Her husband had died. (Persons familiar with Mrs. Leslie's private life hilariously quoted a sentence from the obituary of her husband: "His love for her was poetical, and her devotion to him always perfect.") At his grave, Mrs. Leslie vowed she never again in her life would dance, or drink, or wear color, but a few days later she decided one should not make hasty pledges. Mrs. Leslie had a valid reason for quickly forgetting her third husband, for outside of his good name he left her debts amounting to an estimated quarter of a million dollars.

Mrs. Leslie had come to New Orleans with Ella Wheeler Wilcox the poetaster, ostensibly to attend the Exposition, and not for a rendezvous with Joaquin. But the two were seen constantly together, and were the sensation at the great ball that opened the Fair. Joaquin and Mrs. Leslie were chosen to lead the grand march. As they ascended the winding stairway of the French Opera House Mrs. Leslie was blazing with diamonds, and Joaquin was blazing with Bowie knives. But, because there was waltzing to be done, he had taken off his jackboots and wore dancing pumps. The spectators agreed that a man in Wild West costume with dancing pumps was an odd sight indeed.

All we know of this reunion is Joaquin's indiscreet remark, printed later in a magazine article, that after the revelry "we breakfasted together at my home . . ."

At this time Joaquin was forty-seven years old. He was posing as forty-two and fooling everyone, including no doubt Mrs. Leslie. The Creole in turn was accepted by everyone, including her lover, as being thirty-three. The irony of it was that she actually was forty-eight, a year older than Joaquin. The fact that she had subtracted no less than fifteen years from her age was revealed only after her death.

16

Joaquin reluctantly left New Orleans early in 1885. For the rest of his life he was to remember the warm hospitality it had afforded him, and was to rank it as America's second city, after San Francisco.

Soon after he returned to his log cabin in Washington, the first administration of Grover Cleveland came to power, and Joaquin began to have political ambitions. Cleveland was the first Democratic president since the Civil War, and everyone knew that Joaquin Miller was a loyal Democrat. He asked to be appointed ambassador to Japan, where incidentally, he said, there was a growing demand for his poetry.

Joaquin admitted privately to friends that his mastery of the Japanese language was not perfect, but that he knew it fairly well. However, he had set his sights far too high. Cleveland refused to assign such an important post to a man who had done nothing to secure his election. According to Joaquin, he was offered instead the office of Superintendent of Indian Affairs, a responsible enough job, and one which he was as well qualified as many others to handle. Joaquin claimed he turned down the post. He was tiring of Washington, he said, and wanted to return to the West Coast.

There are two schools of thought as to why Joaquin suddenly felt prompted to quit Washington. One is that he had considered the advice given him by CRITIC and decided that it was sound. The magazine had declared that Joaquin the Westerner was becoming effete living in the East, and that that was the reason for the steady decline of his poetic powers. There was no hope for him to improve, or even to recapture his former abilities as a rhymer, the magazine thought, unless he returned to his Pacific homeland for fresh inspiration.

Undoubtedly Joaquin was influenced by this well-meant advice. He had prophesied a few years before in a lecture that the future great poet of the nation would not be from "the cold centers of commerce on the Atlantic Coast, but from the wild, free, boundless West," and Joaquin visualized Joaquin Miller as that great poet.

But in all probability there was another reason, a more personal reason, for his decision to leave Washington. All at once, the flow of visitors to his cabin fell off to a trickle. The people climbed up the hill, all right, but they walked on past Joaquin's place.

Now the curious were going to see, not Joaquin Miller, but his neighbor. He was an eccentric who had built himself a hut in a tree. The man would climb a ladder, enter his tree-house, pull up the ladder behind him, and stay in the tree for days on end. Everyone was wild to see the tree-man—it was rumored he was one-fourth ape—and at times there would be hundreds of sightseers clustered around the base of the tree, peering up into the foliage to catch a glimpse of this premature Tarzan.

Joaquin was hurt. He was disgusted. He was outraged. He denounced the tree-man as a poseur, as a publicity-seeker, as a homosexual, as a scoundrel. He tried to explain to people who walked blithely by his cabin that such a spectacle was insulting to their intelligence. His anguish increased as the Senators and their constituents came trudging up the hill, and, seeing him standing dramatically in the doorway, a brand-new bearskin thrown over his shoulder, invariably asked: "Where is the man who lives up in a tree?" Joaquin decided he had had enough of Washington and its doltish citizens.

These two incidents unquestionably helped Joaquin to make up his mind. But the opportunity to leave presented itself when Harr Wagner, editor of GOLDEN ERA, a magazine published in San Francisco, telegraphed him an offer to become associate editor. Wagner, whom Joaquin did not know at the time but who was to become his closest friend, offered him $25 for each 1,000 words contributed to the journal. He urged him to leave the eastern seaboard, which did not appreciate him, and return to the West he loved—to the West that loved him.

Joaquin gladly accepted the offer. He gave away his elk skins, his bows and arrows and other mementos, and he sold his last "authentic" London bearskin. He was also able to sell his ramshackle log cabin for $5,000, making a tremendous profit on the deal. This cabin eventually was removed from Arlington Heights to Rock Creek Park in Washington, where it became (and remains to this day) a memorial to the "Poet of the Sierras."

Early in 1886, Joaquin left the East, where he had never felt at home, and where he had not been saluted with the honors he thought were his due. After the many rootless years since he had set out from San Francisco to conquer England, he was going back to where his heart had always remained—the Far West.

CHAPTER SEVEN

Eagle on The Hights

1886-1891

I

*J*OAQUIN was warmly welcomed in California, and for good reason. Over the years the Golden State had contributed more than its share of writers to the nation, but most of them left California posthaste as soon as they had established a name. Bret Harte never returned to us, nor did Mark Twain, OVERLAND sorrowfully noted, but, the magazine added proudly, Joaquin Miller did.

Joaquin's first article for the GOLDEN ERA appeared in the August, 1886 issue and was an essay on, of all things, bricks. This was not a subject calculated to inspire thousands of readers to rush out and buy the magazine, for it was written in the prose style he had evolved. "There are bricks of gold, silver bricks, bricks without straw, and bricks to be hurled at mad dogs. Ergo, bricks."—But it was well received. For almost two years Joaquin contributed his monthly stint— sometimes a reminiscence of his days of youth in Oregon, or of an experience abroad, sometimes a poem or essay—but, although associate editor, he seldom had to report at the office. His boss Harr Wagner became a great good friend, and, as the man was no taskmaster, Joaquin had time on his hands to devote to outside interests.

Most of his spare hours were spent in exploring the San

Francisco area, in search of a few acres on which he could build another log cabin, live the simple life and enjoy the delights of nature. In this place of solitude he intended to write poetry that would win the battle for recognition in his native land. Joaquin spent many weeks in examining various isolated sites, and at last he found the place where he was determined he would build—over the years, for he took a long-range view—an estate that he could be proud of, where he would live until he died.

The site he selected was ideal—a crag across the bay, high in the hills above Oakland. Joaquin acquired a few acres on the tawny slopes of what was known as Leona Heights, and, the more he fell in love with the place, the more land he bought. Eventually he expanded his holdings to seventy acres. Joaquin named his new home The Hights, and as The Hights it was known. All his life he insisted that anyone who spelled Heights any other way than Hights just did not know the English language.

There was not even a lean-to shack on The Hights when Joaquin purchased the land, and even getting up to the place was difficult. The Hights was about seven miles distant from the village of Fruitdale, an Oakland suburb. The trip entailed riding for miles in an electric car, and then the long climb up a beautiful foothill trail that was overhung with the branches of acacia and eucalyptus trees. Joaquin's land was near the top of the crest, and the first thing he did was to post the inhospitable sign: NOT HERE—FURTHER UP THE ROAD. Visitors who followed this advice were to find, as did Ambrose Bierce, that the road soon "ended in a squirrel trail and ran up a tree." For years, until the day finally came when Joaquin had almost single-handedly transformed The Hights into a green paradise, his "estate" was a dismal patch of ground. Much of it was rocky and treeless, tangled with poisonous shrubs, cut through with deep ravines.

But it was the view that counted with Joaquin. Asked where he lived, the poet replied: "Three miles east, one mile perpendicular."

The view was—and is today—no less than superb. Standing on The Hights, Joaquin could see the incomparable San Francisco Bay, and on beyond the Golden Gate the breakers of the Pacific. Below, the clouds floated gently over Oakland. Farther away, eight miles across the bay, the rising streets of San Francisco loomed in the sea-mist. On clear days he could see fifty miles in the distance—and at his feet lay the great shining cross of Lone Mountain cemetery, Black Point and Fort Alcatraz, and the many estuaries of the gigantic landlocked bay.

It was truly an ideal aerie for a poet. As Joaquin wrote of his new home:

> Steep below me lies the valley,
>   Deep below me lies the town,
> Where great sea-ships ride and rally,
>   And the world walks up and down.

There were several springs, a running brook and a waterfall on the grounds, so Joaquin was able to pipe in his water and establish a crude irrigation system. It was on The Hights, Joaquin maintained, that Frémont his childhood hero had camped decades before, and, looking down, with that glorious flash of inspiration, had named the strait in the distance the Golden Gate. Joaquin may have been right, for, although the exact location of that historical spot is unknown, it is believed to have been somewhere in the vicinity of The

Hights. Besides, Joaquin's claim could not be affirmed or denied by Frémont, for he was dead.

Apart from the fact that it had a scenic view and water, The Hights at first glance was a forbidding place for a home. The site Joaquin selected for his house was a rugged rock, overlaid here and there with soil. He built a narrow foot-bridge across an arroyo to reach it, and then went laboriously to work clearing away the poison sumac and southern-wood.

He did most of the work alone, toiling weekdays when he could find the time, and on weekends. Sometimes his friends came to his aid (although Joaquin complained that when Jack London, Ambrose Bierce, Edwin Markham or other literary acquaintances came to "help" him, there seldom was any work done, for they all regarded an expedition to The Hights as a holiday dedicated to talking and drinking), and when he sold a poem for a good price he would hire a man who was importantly titled "the foreman."

Joaquin had to carry everything up the long trail—all his food, all his tools, the lumber and mortar needed for the building of his home. This was a tremendous chore: the rye or corn whiskey alone which he periodically toted up to The Hights was heavy and cumbersome—for Joaquin bought this all-important liquid in two-gallon jugs. Later he solved the transportation problem by widening the road and buying a horse and buckboard.

As for the drinking of whiskey when there was work to be done, the poet set a strict rule. No matter whether he was laboring alone or had helpers, the work took precedence. The first drink of whiskey could not be taken before noon. He took pride in the fact that this edict—known derisively among his friends as Joaquin's Law—was seldom broken. Of course, after a turbulent night, a person might misjudge the position of the sun in the sky and take the first drink at ten when he thought it was twelve. . . .

2

Joaquin called his new home the Abbey, thus honoring both his wife Abbie and Byron's Newstead Abbey. His Abbey was supposed to be modeled after Newstead Abbey, on a small scale, but no one ever noticed the resemblance.

The Abbey was a frame building, consisting at first of a single small room with a porch. The roof was a high shingled peak, and there was no ceiling, for the rafters supporting the roof had been left bare. Visitors often said that the room looked like an unfinished museum. The walls were made of rough boards, hung with hides, bear claws, sheep horns, antlers, Mexican saddles, bows and arrows and weapons of all sorts. Wherever there was a vacant spot, Joaquin had tacked up photographs of actresses and of himself, magazine and newspaper clippings concerning himself, and some original drawings that had been done as illustrations for his poetry.

The floor was covered with the pelts of mountain lions and the traditional "authentic" London bearskin that served as rug and robe. There was a writing table, usually littered with the scratchy quills that Joaquin affected, alongside the manuscript of the poem he happened to be writing. Underneath the table, within easy reach, was a jug labeled "Radium," which was filled as one might suspect with whiskey— "a beverage he preferred above all others," a visitor noted. The poet often took swigs of whiskey straight from the heavy jug, disdaining to pour the fluid into a tumbler, and he did not like to spoil its taste by diluting it with water.

Near the table was a heavy iron-bound chest on which Joaquin had printed the words "Gold Dust," and which was used as a repository for his manuscripts and books. There were two rickety bureaus, both topped with tall cracked mirrors. The bed was an old-fashioned brass four-poster. It was covered with animal hides sewn loosely together to serve as a quilt, and with a gigantic buffalo robe, for it could become quite cold nights up on The Hights. Underneath the bed was a keg of moonshine whiskey, a gift sent semi-annually by a Kentucky admirer of the poetry of Joaquin Miller.

Literary men who visited Joaquin were quick to note that, amid the helter-skelter of objects in the room, there was never a single book in sight. "Nature is the only book a man needs," Joaquin would explain to them. At other times his reasoning varied. "Books cannot help me," he asserted. "My work concerns the future, not the past." But as everyone knew, the poet never read a book of any kind—except his own works. These volumes he kept locked away in the iron chest, and Joaquin prophesied, boldly if not exactly accurately, that some day his first editions would bring fabulous prices on the rare book market.

Later on, Joaquin added two more high-peaked rooms to make a single unit of the Abbey. And eventually, acting as his own carpenter and mason, he was to build three more structures on The Hights, all facing West. But the Abbey was his pride. "I built a little Abbey for little Abbie," he said, and he often asked his wife to visit him and see his new estate. Mrs. Miller preferred to live in New York and Saratoga and could not be persuaded to go West.

Joaquin, so indolent in some ways (he wrote reams of verse but he seldom rewrote at the time), was a giant of industry when it came to building things on The Hights. By and by he was to complete three monuments on the grounds, in honor of Frémont, Browning and Moses—as peculiar a trinity as there ever was. A stone pillar was erected in memory of Frémont. Browning was honored with a stone tower, and Moses with a pyramid tomb. Joaquin said he considered Moses the greatest of all men. "Greater than Joaquin Miller?" his waggish friends asked each other incredulously. Joaquin was questioned as to how it was that The Hights contained Moses' *tomb*. "I'll tell you," replied Joaquin. "No man knows where he is buried, and why not here as well as anywhere else?"

Surveying his handiwork, the poet found it incomplete and decided The Hights should be further beautified. He dug out a small trout pond, and he built a rock garden. He planted beds of roses, and the time would come when he could snip a hundred roses and strew them before a visiting actress, Ellen Terry, just as he had done years before with Lillie Langtry.

He also hacked out a narrow trail which he pretentiously called "The Sacred Lane," a name that amused his friends, for it led straight to the *chef-d'oeuvre* of The Hights—Joaquin's own funeral pyre. The poet kept mortaring black flint rock on black flint rock until the pyre towered eight feet high, ten feet long and ten feet wide. Nearby was a huge boulder, on which, for some reason, Joaquin chiseled the words: TO THE UNKNOWN. Joaquin often would lead his friends out to his funeral pyre late at night, and they would sit on top of the macabre monument or the boulder, watch the flickering lights of the bay cities below them and talk away as they drank their whiskey.

One would think that the pyre on which Joaquin hoped to be cremated some day would strike the visitors as the most incredible feature of The Hights. Instead, it was the contraption Joaquin installed on the roof of the Abbey. One day he concluded that he was not always sufficiently inspired to write pure poetry. But he noticed that the pitter-patter of rain on the roof never failed to put him in a creative mood. Unfortunately, it often did not rain at the time that suited him most.

So Joaquin had pipes built up on the roof, and, whenever he needed inspiration, he would turn on a watercock and "rain" would sprinkle pleasantly for hours.

Joaquin often used the sprinkler system as a practical joke. Dozens of accounts have been left by visitors who were awed, puzzled, or amused when rain fell on the roof of the Abbey, and nowhere else. The poet turned the farce into a rite. He would gravely explain that as a youth he had been selected by the Modoc Indians as their chief medicine man. In that capacity, he had been the only white man in the country to learn the secret of rain-making.

The two huge bear claws hanging on the wall had been given him by the famous chief, Rain-Bear-of-the-North, Joaquin said, and it was through their power that the Great Spirit would bring water to the earth. He would kneel before the bear claws and start chanting what he assured his listeners were magical Indian phrases (one sharp-eared visitor said these Indian words consisted mostly of "goddamma" and "sunnabitchta"). Then he would rise and with uplifted face and hands held imploringly aloft, wander about the room as if in a trance, until he reached behind a curtain and turned on the watercock. And lo! the "rain" came!

3

Joaquin was extremely serious-minded, however, when it came to trees. Trees, to him, were nature's greatest blessing, and worthy of worship. He was one of the most ardent of conservationists—to many people of the West the name of Joaquin Miller was synonymous with the planting of trees, and not with poetry—and he often served as California's official delegate to National Forestry Councils.

Soon after his arrival in San Francisco Joaquin conceived the idea that California's first Arbor Day, celebrated in 1886, should feature the planting of trees, trees, trees. He went to the wealthy Adolph Sutro and influential Senator George Hearst with a plan to convert Goat Island, a rather barren spot in the bay, into a beautiful forest-covered isle. He also recommended that seedlings should be thickly planted in the bare Presidio (for this suggestion San Franciscans are grateful to him to this day). Sutro and Hearst and other civic leaders were easily persuaded to underwrite the costs of both projects.

Joaquin was the guest of honor and principal speaker at the planting held on Goat Island. Generals Howard and Vallejo, Senator Perkins, Wells Drury and many others of prominence were in the audience to applaud him. Joaquin supervised the setting out of the trees, which were planted in the shape of a gigantic Greek cross. California was so proud of its tree-lover that there was talk of changing the name of Goat Island to Joaquin Miller Island, but the poet quashed the move. "I might commit some overt act that would disgrace the Island," he announced. His friends were astonished at this belated display of modesty. The poet privately confided that he did not fancy the change from Goat to Joaquin

Miller (Joaquin was often described as the Goat by people who thought he possessed an overabundance of lecherous qualities), and besides, he said, the isle was far too small to be honored by his good name.

Unfortunately, a great fire swept over Goat (today Yerba Buena) Island and wiped out almost all the trees, but the seedlings planted in the Presidio have grown into the magnificent trees that give this place its dignified beauty.

Joaquin did not confine himself to urging others to plant trees—he was determined that his shrub-ridden Hights should become covered with timber. One of his first acts after buying The Hights was to lay out a fruit orchard, and over the years he untiringly planted thousands of saplings all over his seventy-acre estate, and on adjoining land too. An idea of the magnitude of this undertaking can be gained from the fact that the seedlings—in time to come—were to surround him like a deep dense forest. This forest—today a public park—consisted of no less than seventy-five thousand cypress, acacia, pine and eucalyptus trees, and almost every one of them was planted by Joaquin.

4

Joaquin liked to immure himself on The Hights, set out his trees, put up his buildings and monuments. Guests were always welcome at his aerie, but he seldom could be induced to visit Oakland or San Francisco, not even the place where he "worked"—the GOLDEN ERA office. Harr Wagner remembered the time when Joaquin appeared at the Bohemian Club. He tipped the bootblack a dollar, the bellboy a dollar, threw down a twenty-dollar bill on the mahogany for a drink and motioned for the bartender to keep the change. "How can you do it, Joaquin?" Wagner asked. "Oh, it's easy," replied the bard. "In the first place I only come down from The Hights about three times a year. In the second place that money I got for a poem—it doesn't count."

Joaquin preferred the role of the host, with its attendant prestige, and he did not care to be just another guest elsewhere. There are many accounts of his hospitality, for, although the poet professed to love the cloistered life of The Hights, where he could be alone, high in the clouds, he actually liked to be surrounded by people. His barbecues were famous—one day he broiled an ox and fed one hundred members of the Sequoia Club. He frequently gave "bandit dinners" on The Hights. He would build a fire outdoors under a big iron kettle filled with venison and onions and a variety of vegetables. During the hours that passed while the stew simmered, Joaquin would talk and recite his poetry and pass around whiskey in tin cups. Later the meal would be served in the same tin cups. He was hospitable even to stray visitors. If one of the guest cabins he had built was vacant he would leave the door open so that tramps could sleep there, and there was always a full jug in the room. The jug contained wine, however, not whiskey.

Sometimes Joaquin would invite what he termed "outsiders"—such as "Borax" Smith, the alkali millionaire of Twenty-Mule fame who lived in the neighborhood—but usually the invitations were given to fellow poets and writers. The roistering Jack London, whose literary renown lay still ahead of him, was a frequent visitor. So was George Sterling, the hard-drinking sonnet writer who was destined, like Joaquin's old friend Prentice Mulford, to commit suicide. Herman Whittaker, then known for his novels and two-fisted drinking, was often around, as were the two

Bierce brothers, Ambrose and Albert. There were other steady guests: Frank Norris, the youth who had an ambition to write realistic novels; Fremont Older, the newspaperman who was to become a famous editor; Edwin Markham, who lived in a cliff house half a mile below Joaquin, and who years later was to achieve a measure of fame for his poem, "The Man With a Hoe"; Joaquin's first literary friend in San Francisco, Stoddard, who was now making a name for himself by his books on Father Damien and the Lolokai lepers.

Many of these men who gathered at The Hights were at the time little known, but on the threshold of brilliant careers —and would outshine their host. They all loved Joaquin Miller, no matter how much they might laugh privately at his idiosyncrasies, and most of them loved to drink whiskey. There were times when Joaquin's cupboard was bare and he could not feed his friends, but there always was a sufficient supply of whiskey on the premises.

Sterling has left accounts of his visit to The Hights during the late 1880's. The attitude of the young poet—then barely out of his teens—toward the older man, then in his early fifties, was a curious mixture of amusement and devotion. Joaquin liked Sterling personally, but he disapproved of his poetry. Sterling wrote sonnets, being influenced by a man named Keats. Joaquin thought sonnets were "bad form."

Sterling told of the time he walked up the trail to The Hights, where he found Ambrose Bierce and S. H. E. Partington the painter hard at work building the pyramid tomb dedicated to Moses. Joaquin was propped up in bed in the Abbey, fully dressed and wearing his knee-high boots. Sterling noted that—as Bierce and Partington were outside sweating away for the greater glory of the estate—Joaquin reclined indolently on the bed, his yellow hair spreading out on the pillow, his eyes of clearest blue peering from under shaggy blond eyebrows at the immortal lines of verse he was scribbling down.

One Sunday, when Sterling arrived, Joaquin was drinking whiskey with Albert Bierce, Ambrose's older brother. After Joaquin had had an "appreciable amount of moonshine under his belt," he insisted on showing his skill at throwing the tomahawk. The poet told the two men that, in his Indian days, he had saved his own life many a time thanks to his dexterity in handling this weapon.

The exhibition that followed caused Bierce and Sterling to double up with laughter. Joaquin threw a hatchet, which he used in lieu of a tomahawk, at a big tree not far from him, and missed. He failed to hit that tree at close range four times in succession, and finally, on the fifth try, he managed to hit it with the butt end of the handle. "Bierce jeered him unmercifully," Sterling reported, "a thing we younger men were too timid to do." Many months passed before Bierce was invited again to The Hights.

Sterling said the liquor Joaquin gulped was 110 proof, drawn from a two-gallon wicker-covered jug, and that drinking it was "like swallowing an oil burner." "I'm always deeply religious when I'm drunk," Joaquin told Sterling, "and when by accident I am deeply religious without being drunk, it's a sign I need a drink."

Sterling to the contrary, there is the testimony of many other of Joaquin's friends who never saw the poet drunk, no matter how much whiskey he had consumed, for his capacity for liquor in hard-drinking San Francisco was as well known as it had been in London. The chances are that Joaquin's ineptness with the tomahawk had nothing to do with drinking: he probably had never thrown a tomahawk before.

Unlike some topers, Joaquin never was a man to hoard a bottle when his friends were around. One day in December, Jack London, Whittaker and Sterling decided to go to The Hights and cut a Christmas tree. The three men hired a grocer's horse and wagon and drove up to Joaquin's home. The poet was working in his rose garden, but he quickly dropped his watering can and invited them in for just one drink. They had one, and another, and, as Sterling said, "and then some, and then some."

As the hours passed the visitors insisted they must cut their Christmas tree, although Joaquin pleaded with them to stay. After they had chopped down one of the bard's fir trees, Joaquin pressed them to have a single saddle-cup for the road—just one. "We had it, and more," Sterling said. "He assured us there wasn't a headache in a gallon of the stuff. . . . It was a wild ride homeward. . . . When we stopped at last to leave our Christmas tree at London's home, we found we had lost it en route!"

Sterling has left an amusing description of an encounter with Joaquin in Oakland. When the poet descended from The Hights he liked to visit a bar run by Charlie Cutter, an ex-newspaperman. Joaquin seldom drank anything but straight whiskey, but while in Cutter's saloon he would sample some ancient bottles of Tokay that, according to Sterling, had "exquisite virtues."

Joaquin and Sterling met one morning a block away from the City Hall, and the younger man suggested they sample Cutter's rare old vintage. As Sterling told the story:

He gazed sorrowfully at me for a moment, then said, evident sincerity in his voice: "My boy, I've promised my dear mother never to take a drink in the morning."

I was disappointed, but remained at his side for some time, as we discussed friends and affairs. Miller was nothing if not entertaining in conversation, and the time slipped by at a faster rate than was well for my own duties. And then, suddenly, he grasped me by the shoulder and swung me around, so that I faced up Washington Street, and pointed to the big clock in the tower of the City Hall. No words were necessary: it was noon, and we strode down the street to Cutter's.

5

It was mentioned earlier that, as far as can be ascertained, Mrs. Abbie Miller could not be persuaded to visit her husband on The Hights. But that does not mean that the poet, deprived of legitimate outlets for his amorous impulses, lived a sex-starved existence. Far from it.

Joaquin had a number of liaisons; he was constantly seeking affairs with other women; he was always intrigued with the presumed innocence of young girls, and more than one of his friends thought that he was dissolute and licentious, and referred to him privately as "the Goat." There almost always was a woman living on The Hights and, in justice to Mrs. Miller, this probably was the reason that, until his last days, she refused to go West.

It has been jocularly asserted that the three loves in Joaquin's life were Women, Whiskey and Whimsy. More correctly, there were four loves—women, whiskey, poetry and trees, and possibly they ranked in that order. George Sterling, a sharp observer, noted that the poet was never entirely at ease with men. He realized that his stories of hairbreadth adventure were accepted skeptically by them and he sensed that behind his back they jeered at his many poses. Women were kinder, more appreciative, more gullible. "With women alone he was entirely serene, and then he blossomed out in his entire and very picturesque individuality," Sterling said.

In male company, Joaquin was willing to share the attention, but when women were around he would stand no rival. Men who dressed as garishly as he did were particularly despised. Once when Joaquin visited Ina Coolbrith he found her with a young handsome man whose hair fell to his shoulders. Ina's companion was wearing a complete cowboy outfit. Joaquin was aghast at the wretched taste of the fellow. He surveyed him contemptuously, shuddered, and shouted: "Hell! Another damn fool!"

Joaquin enjoyed himself most when, surrounded by ladies, the only male around, he could play cock-of-the-walk. "To the Queen!" he would cry, saluting the nearest female with his glass of whiskey. "God bless her!" No matter how often they heard it, the ladies were always delighted. When he was introduced to a woman of small stature he would murmur, kissing her hand, "The sweetest flowers grow nearest to the ground." To a tall lady he would whisper, "Divinely tall, and divinely fair." To a blonde he would confide, "Ah, the one fair woman," and to a brunette, "Beauty walks at midnight." Such pat phrases came easily to him, and his flattery for all women was habitual, although the prettier ones were likely to receive more extravagant praise. It is no wonder that most women liked Joaquin Miller.

George Sterling quickly learned that, when ladies were present, Joaquin was the star actor and would permit no males in supporting roles. The members of the Pacific Coast

Women's Press Association obtained permission to make a pilgrimage to The Hights. One Sunday several scores of the ladies waited outside the Abbey for the poet to appear. When Joaquin stalked out of his home he was wearing nothing but a wildcat skin wrapped loosely around his loins!

Sterling could not help but snicker at the incident. Joaquin was forever alert to detect any lack of deference from the younger set. He thought his dignity had been affronted, and he reacted, as Sterling told it:

> He appeared suddenly from the outer darkness, gazed down on me gloomily and announced: "Sterling, you look like a fool!"
>
> Being already of that conviction, I was not greatly embarrassed, and replied: "That's old news. I was afraid I looked like a poet."
>
> Joaquin glared at me in astonishment for a moment. Here was insurrection for you! Here was *lèse majesté!* Then, drawing himself to his full height, and taking a deep breath, he cried: "Yes, but not like a *great* poet!"

Count Perhacs, a Hungarian artist, discovered that Joaquin could not tolerate competition. Joaquin invited the Count to live on The Hights to finish a huge twenty-by-twenty foot canvas outdoors. On the days when several young girls came to pose in the nude Joaquin would station himself behind the painter and talk to the models. But he noticed with mounting rage that he, Joaquin Miller the Great Poet, was entirely ignored, while Count Perhacs the little artist was the center of attention for the girls. He picked a quarrel and drove the painter from The Hights. To his friends, Joaquin indignantly sputtered that under no circumstances should degenerates be trusted in the presence of naked young girls.

Harr Wagner is the main authority for Joaquin's various liaisons. "I know he would want me to write with extreme frankness," said Wagner, "and above all to tell the truth."

Wagner thought Mrs. Leslie was the great love in the poet's life (a poem originally called "Mrs. Frank Leslie" was retitled "The Queen of my Dreams" by Joaquin when it was put out in book form), and it appears that even when these two lusty individuals reached a great old age they pursued their intimacies and had their assignations, and that for decades on end she paid him generous sums—for his poetry, of course.

Joaquin swore to Mrs. Leslie that if she ever married again he would leave the country. In 1891 Mrs. Leslie married for the fourth time. She was dubbed "Mrs. Bluebeard" by the press. The groom was William Charles Kingsbury Wills Wilde, better known as Oscar Wilde's brother Willie, young enough to be her son and a person who has been unkindly described as an "unabashed scallawag, a drunken sponger, who wrote pornography . . ."

Hearing of the marriage, Joaquin remembered his solemn promise. He wrote to Wagner in San Diego, enclosing a letter to be sent on to Mrs. Leslie. Wagner crossed into Mexico at Tia Juana and mailed it there. This letter, when it reached Mrs. Leslie with its foreign postmark, informed her that Joaquin had been true to his vow.

According to Wagner, "Mrs. John Vance Cheney, a musician of rare talent, beautiful, had in Joaquin a romantic and devoted lover," but it is more likely that this friendship was platonic. The lady's husband, a postal clerk when Joaquin knew him, later became a well known poet and the head of a great library.

On the other hand, Joaquin's romance with Alice Oliver

was anything but platonic. It was an affair that lasted for many years. Joaquin was entering his fifties when he met Alice, a girl of sixteen, at Luna's restaurant, a place frequented by San Francisco's Bohemians. The girl was quite beautiful and, despite her youth, possessed an exceptionally mature body. She was believed to be half Mexican, with perhaps a trace of Negro blood.

Joaquin took Alice to stay with him on The Hights, referring to her as his protégée. Alice lived in the Abbey, and her room was connected to the poet's by what he liked to call a "secret passage." Not that it was much of a secret, for Joaquin, like a boy, delighted in showing it to his friends. The girl became pregnant and gave birth to a baby boy who died a short time later. Joaquin buried the child near his funeral pyre, but it was apparent that he cared even less for any illegitimate offspring than for his lawful brood. He made it plain he wanted no more children. "At this period many of his friends practically deserted him," Harr Wagner, Joaquin's most loyal intimate, was forced to concede. "Their sympathy was for the poor forlorn girl with fine instincts and a great longing to be respected, admired, and to have a home and children."

Alice Oliver soon became pregnant again. Joaquin hustled her off The Hights and sent her to Phoenix, Arizona. There she gave birth to another son, and then returned to her lover. The poet never showed any interest in the child, although for a while he sent money for his upkeep. A year or so later when Alice became pregnant once more, he sent her to Hawaii, where still another son was born.

Alice Oliver dropped out of sight and is believed to have died around 1910 in South America. Nothing is known of the fate of her two children. The boy in Phoenix was raised by a compassionate member of the Salvation Army for a while. After Joaquin's death, the newspapers attempted to locate this nameless offspring, and failed.

Wagner said Joaquin was fifty-six years old when he met May Foster Carey, then twenty-five, a divorcee who was described as attractive—not beautiful—but extremely sensuous. The poet was attracted to May when she walked by The Hights one day. With a flourish he presented her with a rose, saying, "This is for the only pair of eyes that can match its beauty. Where do you live?"

May lived near The Hights. Joaquin asked her to become a permanent guest at The Hights. She declined the honor, but she would often spend a few days and nights there with him. "I was his Empress, and The Hights was our Empire," Mrs. Carey proudly wrote. May was the lady whom Joaquin glorified in his poems as having "midnight in her hair" and "perilous Spanish eyes."

Joaquin was extremely jealous of Mrs. Carey, who had other admirers, including even her divorced husband. This man wrote the poet, threatening to shoot him in the back some lonely night (according to Wagner), and Joaquin for some time kept a loaded shotgun by his bed. There were other rivals, too—such as one Lord Redman, a man evidently as hot-blooded as Joaquin.

Lord Redman (we do not know who this man was) appeared unannounced at The Hights one day and demanded that the poet give up all claims to Mrs. Carey. Joaquin was able to convince the Englishman that the lady did not live there, and had never stayed overnight.

A few days later, the poet was out driving with May in a phaeton when Lord Redman appeared, pulled the horse to a stop, brushed Joaquin aside and yanked Mrs. Carey from the carriage. "Drive on!" the noble Lord then ordered Joaquin, but this the poet could not do because, during the fracas, one of the carriage wheels had come off. Instead of retreating Joaquin squared away in a boxer's stance, frightened off Lord Redman, and took his beloved away to The Hights.

Lord Redman soon appeared again, as was expected. Joaquin flourished an unloaded gun and drove him from the premises. He then stood guard all night over one of the guest cabins where Mrs. Carey stayed. The divorcee appears to have been enchanted with the cloak-and-dagger romantics of the situation; but Joaquin did not share her feelings. He served a warrant on the Englishman, charging molestation and his friends among the Oakland city authorities saw to it that Lord Redman relinquished the field and skipped town.

"Our sweet friendship continued for twelve years, until Joaquin passed on," Mrs. Carey informed the readers of the San Francisco CHRONICLE. "I have such wonderful love letters from him. . . . Joaquin was such a wonderful lover."

Wagner revealed that there were also a number of young actresses in Joaquin's life, but their names are not known. One, a svelte "Miss D," spent an entire summer near The Hights, and the pair turned the Abbey into a love nest. But eventually she tried to borrow $500 from Joaquin, who later said he "drove her from my cabin in utter disgust."

Another lady, a "Miss X," sent Joaquin her photograph, which consisted mostly of breasts laid invitingly bare, and added that she adored his poetry. The bard invited her to visit him for a few weeks, and again the secret passage in the Abbey was put to use. After their "honeymoon" had ended Joaquin secured a stage job for "Miss X." Later the actress attempted to blackmail him. Unless she were paid $250 a week, she informed the poet, she would publish the true story of his scandalous life, and would see to it that sermons were preached on his sexual depravity. Joaquin was forced to make at least a gesture: he bought a railroad ticket to Chicago and gave it to the lady, and that was the last that was ever heard of "Miss X."

If the reader is surprised to learn that so many of Joaquin's love affairs appeared to be public property, it must be remembered that none were conducted furtively. Joaquin was an outspoken advocate and practitioner of free-love, and the Californians looked upon this vice with indulgence, for, after all, Joaquin Miller was "different"—an eccentric, a genius.

"Bitter" Bierce was bitter when Joaquin's liking for young girls was brought to his attention. "If that woolly wolf, Joaquin Miller, doesn't keep outside the fold I *shall* come down and club him soundly," he wrote his niece. And if George Sterling's testimony can be believed, the poet had a fondness for girls of an extremely tender age.

Sterling (who is not an entirely dependable authority, for he would exaggerate for the sake of a good story; and the tale he tells here was printed in the American Mercury of the 1920's, and may have been touched up in Mencken's office) remembered the time he camped with Jack London near The Hights, and of being visited there by two of his sisters. "Miller no sooner set eyes on the younger of the two, a blonde pretty girl, than his heart was lost forever," said Sterling. "He would wait for her to pass his home, then appear soon after, and stare at her in almost abject adoration."

The girl was flattered, but at the same time uneasy, for she was only fourteen years old.

"Joaquin's blue eyes blazed on her with unmistakable

meaning," Sterling declared. The poet would cry to her, "Go comb the sunshine from your hair!" and shower the girl with the usual rose petals. Sterling, however, evidently was not worried about a situation which he regarded as both "embarrassing and comic."

Joaquin was then wearing a buckskin coat given him by admirers, and its five buttons were nuggets the size of a man's thumb. "He had parted with all but the top button to other feminine objects of devotion and now insisted on giving my sister the last one," Sterling reported. "She accepted it and subsequently sold it!"

The one-sided romance came to an end when Joaquin (who incidentally was a married man) made clear that his intentions were honorable and serious. He appeared at the Sterling home on several successive Sundays as a suitor, clad somberly in a long black coat. "She was somewhat embarrassed," said Sterling, "but never shrank away from the meeting. It may be that she saw other nuggets as a possibility."

The suit ended, according to Sterling:

> When, however, Joaquin finally came to the point and asked for her hand, addressing her mother, he was met with the objection that there was too great a discrepancy in ages. He took his medicine bravely. He bowed himself out, with regrets, and came no more."

6

As a member of the GOLDEN ERA staff Joaquin Miller brought the magazine prestige, but as editor Harr Wagner sadly noted, few additional subscribers. Competition in San Francisco was strenuous, for no less than six literary journals were published in the city, and so in May, 1887, Wagner decided to move his magazine to less saturated territory. He selected the town of San Diego in Southern California.

Wagner persuaded Joaquin to leave The Hights and temporarily join him there. After San Francisco, Joaquin found San Diego with its 14,000 inhabitants a mere village, but he liked its dry climate and its even temperatures. The San Diegans bowed respectfully to the town's new celebrity and soon it was a common sight to see the poet, wearing a purple pongee shirt, silk neck-scarf, red skullcap and jackboots, striding around the town or regaling the patrons in the saloons with tall tales. A curious San Diegan asked Joaquin why he wore knee-high boots. The poet solemnly explained that he could not afford to buy shoes.

Joaquin held open court during the few months he lived in San Diego. He usually could be found in a bar, or in a rocking chair in front of the GOLDEN ERA office. His behavior might be described as informal. A literary club in nearby Pacific Beach commissioned Joaquin to write and read to them an original poem, paying $200 for the privilege. Joaquin composed the stanzas sitting out in the street in front of his office, while people milled about and peered over his shoulder. Not that this made them any wiser, for the poet's scrawl was altogether illegible. Joaquin wrote on sheets of assorted colors. He would scribble away on a green sheet and let it flutter to the sidewalk, and as the hours passed the street was littered with red, green, purple and blue pieces of paper. The San Diego citizens thought Joaquin Miller a rather queer individual.

Joaquin shuttled back and forth between San Diego and The Hights, but as he found that the commuting tired him, he decided to resign as associate editor of the magazine. It was during one of his absences that Mrs. Frank Leslie came to visit him in San Diego, only to find he was at The Hights. A few weeks later she visited The Hights, all eager for a bout, but he was in San Diego. It is to be presumed that the poet and the flashy lady (who had quickly divorced Willie Wilde, confessing she had committed "a blunder") later did arrange for another of their many rendezvous.

Joaquin celebrated his sweetheart with a three-page article in GOLDEN ERA. In this cautiously phrased tribute (although he mentioned her "spirit that would tire even the strongest man," evidently unaware of the implications), Joaquin lauded the virtues of "this child-woman"—Mrs. Leslie was then fifty-one. As an example of his prose style, with many an old-fashioned "nay" and "wherein," and with his predilection for commas—all of which infuriated the critics—the first two paragraphs of this article are reprinted here verbatim:

> The history of Mrs. Frank Leslie is the history of illustrated journalism, nay, more, it is the history of all that is best and bravest in the last two decades of our literature.
>
> When I first visited New Orleans, that ancient and battle-torn city had two places of interest to me. The first of these was the curious, old, red, tile court house, where General Jackson was fined $1,000 for violating a city ordinance, in order to win the battle of New Orleans. The second place of singular pride and interest, was the quaint, old, house in the aristocratic creole quarter, wherein, Mrs. Frank Leslie was born.

In 1891 Harr Wagner gave up his efforts to make GOLDEN ERA a success, and Joaquin promptly appointed him his business manager. As there was no business to manage, the energetic Wagner manufactured some. He arranged for

Joaquin to write a series of articles on the Indians for the New York INDEPENDENT, and he secured a high fee. Wagner also persuaded the poet to have another try at lecturing.

Joaquin at first shied away from platform speaking, remembering his failure some years before in Philadelphia. But now he found that, if sufficiently loaded beforehand with his indispensable whiskey, he could be a ringing success. He seldom fooled his audiences, however, as most of them were convinced that the lecturing poet was stimulated by more than his own ideas.

When he was a student at Stanford University, Herbert C. Thompson attended a lecture Joaquin gave on "Education in China" at the campus. Thompson said Joaquin rambled on, discussing all kinds of subjects, excepting Education and China. "But it was quite amusing, especially as he was tight," Thompson remembered. "He used to explain that he had to prime himself on liquor for lectures so as to overcome his natural shyness."

It is hard to believe that this fantastic observation was meant to be taken seriously.

There was one lecture given by Joaquin that struck the fancy of all his listeners. It was called "Lessons Not Found in Books," and consisted mostly of his tribute to outdoor life and of the impassioned reading of his own poems. (Joaquin never publicly or privately read any poetry but his own, feeling that the verse of others lacked what he called "character.")

"Lessons Not Found in Books" was first given in the autumn of 1891 in San Diego, and as a result Joaquin was acclaimed as nature's own philosopher. As word spread about the merits of the talk, lecture offers from many other cities began to pour into the offices of manager Harr Wagner, and it appeared that Joaquin's financial future was secure once and for all.

At this juncture the newspapers started to feature a story causing the poet to announce that he was retiring from public life. He issued a statement to the effect that he had decided to shave off his hair and beard, to wear sackcloth and ashes, to eat stale bread and water the rest of his days, and to live the life of a hermit somewhere—where this somewhere was, he did not know, but the world would never again hear from Joaquin Miller.

7

Joaquin Miller was by nature a friendly and congenial man. He needed, and loved, people. He had virtually no enemies. He was comparatively free from violent antagonisms. He was helpful and generous toward his friends.

It is all the more incongruous that, of all the human beings in the world, his own children were apparently excluded from his affections. He simply was not interested in them, gave them no love and no support. His children—legitimate and otherwise—were a nuisance to him, and he must have considered them as intruders who, he was afraid, would interfere with his chosen way of living.

It is in the sphere of family life that Joaquin's supreme egotism assumes truly overwhelming proportions and blots out his inherent kindness and generosity. It is hard to explain his resentment of them on rational grounds, and all we can do—in the absence of a more plausible explanation—is to accept it as such, namely as the least admirable part of his otherwise extremely likeable and warm personality.

8

Joaquin's daughter Maud became an actress through her own perseverance and talent. Joaquin once swore that all his life he had contributed $50 a month to the upbringing of his two sons; but the testimony of too many others conclusively proves that he gave them nothing. Furthermore, until Minnie Myrtle died, he made no effort whatsoever to find out where they lived, or what they were doing.

In this year of 1891 his children were children no longer. Maud was twenty-eight, George B. was twenty-six, and Harold, known as Harry, twenty-two. Maud had made a name for herself, but her brothers, who had not been given any formal education and who had no profession, were drifters.

In October, 1891 a young man who introduced himself as one Joseph McKay appeared on The Hights and asked to speak to Joaquin Miller. The caretaker said the poet was out of town on a lecture tour. The youth then revealed himself to be Harry Miller, the famous man's youngest son, and he was given lodging for the night.

The next morning, Harry had disappeared, and so had Joaquin's horse. This animal, most impressively named "Black Warrior" and called a "charger" by the poet, was a decrepit nag used not ordinarily as a saddle-horse but to draw a buckboard. No alarm was spread to apprehend the horse thief, because evidently the caretaker was aware that the boy was Joaquin's son.

Early in November, Harry rode into Hopland, a town in Mendocino county, about one hundred and forty miles north of San Francisco by the road. Having no money, he sought employment. The only job offered him was cutting wood for a man named Willard, but Harry found he could not live on the pittance received. A few days later, Sheriff Stanley of Ukiah was informed that a farmhouse near Willett's village had been entered and robbed of a rifle.

On November 16, the Eureka and Ukiah stagecoach was held up by a masked man with a rifle eighteen miles outside Ukiah. The highwayman commanded Charles Lambert, the driver, to throw out the express box, and the man hastily complied. But when Lambert was instructed to hand over the mail bags he delayed, explaining they were inside the coach. "Well, get down and get them out!" the bandit yelled.

Lambert made an apparent attempt to drag out the sacks, but the coach was headed upgrade and kept slipping back. The driver explained that he would have to drive to level ground. The highwayman agreed to this, and followed the coach on foot. Lambert drove to the crest of the slope, known as "Robber's Hill," a name well suited to the circumstances. But instead of stopping, he lashed his horses and quickly drew away from the bandit, who stood stupefied.

When the excited driver told Sheriff Stanley the details of this clumsy holdup, the officer at first thought it was the work of a twelve-year-old boy. Then he began to reason that the highwayman must be an amateur, an outsider. The only "city man" in the neighborhood was Joseph McKay, and it was found that he had decamped. The Sheriff tracked the itinerant woodchopper to Santa Rosa, where he arrested him in a hotel.

Joseph McKay at first denied the crime, and the fact that no money could be found on his person was in his favor. But, "after considerable persuasion," as the Sheriff termed it, the youth confessed to the robbery and took Stanley to where he had buried his rifle.

A few days later when he was being closely questioned about his background, Harry was forced to admit he was the son of Joaquin Miller, the celebrated Poet of the Sierras. Once this became known, what had been a minor and futile attempt at larceny became overnight a headline story for newspapers throughout the United States.

Asked why he had become a bandit, Harry said that there was no money in cutting wood, and that he had been "hard up." But it turned out that robbing stagecoaches, the way the bungling Harry Miller did it, was not lucrative either, for the youth had not made a single penny from the hold-up. A wag declared, as if no one would believe him, that Harry Miller—as a stickup man—must be classed as even worse than his father—as a poet. Someone else remarked that here was the case of the Millers "going from horse thief to horse thief, in one generation."

Harry Miller was taken to San Francisco and on December 10 held in $10,000 bail on the charge of attempted robbery of the United States mails. Newspapermen clamored to talk to the son of the famous bard. Young Harry agreed to submit to a mass interview. Declaring that hunger had driven him to crime, Harry told his pathetic story:

Up to the age of ten years I lived with my mother, Minnie Myrtle Miller, in Portland. She gave me in keeping to an aunt at Goose Bay, and went East after my sister, who was being educated in a convent. A year after she left they told me she was dead.

The next seven years of my life was spent on my aunt's farm. While going to school I wrote my father at Oakland, telling him of my desire to go there, and he sent for me to work on his ranch. I was satisfied to do this, because I thought with the money he promised me for my labor I could educate myself in the higher branches. When he declined to pay me anything, anger and disappointment overcame me and I left him.

I traveled about the state doing odd jobs. Then I drifted back to Oregon and, hungry and desperate, I joined a stranger in breaking into a house. But we were caught, and I was sent to the penitentiary in Portland. I managed to escape, and I assumed the name of Joseph McKay. Then followed many wanderings, and I never had any money. I found a house unguarded in Mendocino county. I was famished and ate my fill—and I stole a gun and cartridges and a few articles.

The next day, I suddenly came upon a stagecoach toiling up a hill. The idea of robbing it came to me as an inspiration, and I stepped behind a tree and ordered him to stop. Had he showed any fight I should probably have run away, because I was frightened and shaking like a leaf. When the stage disappeared and I had opened the treasure box the driver threw me, I found in it a pair of baby shoes, a couple of waybills, but not one cent of money.

Sheriff Stanley arrested me in Santa Rosa and I shall plead guilty and suffer the penalty. I bear my father no ill-will, and all that I ask is that he keep away from me.

This interview was front page news everywhere. As one, the press blamed the plight of the son on the sins of the father. "Everyone who saw the lad in this city felt pity for him, as he had none of the traits of a criminal," wrote the San Francisco correspondent of the New York TRIBUNE, "and only showed bitterness when he spoke of his father's neglect and refusal to give him an education."

The reporters repeatedly sought to interview Joaquin, to get his side of the story, but the poet was not at The Hights, which was surrounded each day by sightseers. Finally he was located hiding out in San Diego, but he would not speak to newspapermen. Through Harr Wagner it was announced that "The poet has renounced the world and sought a lodge in the mountains back of the city, where he will not be disturbed. He never wants to see human kind again. He arrived in San Diego recently in a great depression."

The newspapers noted that son Harry Miller, languishing in jail, also was in a state of "depression." Wagner was prompted to issue another communique to the press: "Mr. Miller has cut his hair and he declares he will never again write over the name which he says has been disgraced."

The journalists continued their efforts to interview the poet. One night Joaquin traded clothes with Harr Wagner and, disguised in a drab outfit, managed to slip out of town unnoticed. The next morning Wagner announced that Joaquin was on his way to Japan, where he would become a Buddhist monk. The world would hear no more of Joaquin Miller.

The newspapers became irritated. They were hearing too much about the alleged fact that they would hear no more from Joaquin Miller.

Joaquin later claimed that he had traveled as far as British Columbia on his way to Japan (a rather roundabout route), but that he decided it would be unwise to abandon his native America and to desert his native religion for Buddhism. But the evidence shows that he went straight to his home on The Hights, where for many months he remained incommunicado.

Harry Miller was tried by a jury, convicted, and sentenced to San Quentin penitentiary. Public sympathy was entirely on the side of the incompetent highwayman, and, considering that his crime was a serious offense in the West, he was given an extremely light sentence. By one of those unbelievable coincidences, which will happen at times, Judge W. W. Morrow of the United States District Court, who presided over the case, was the same Private W. W. Morrow who had served in Oregon under Captain Joaquin Miller in the battle against the Indians at Harney Lake. Joaquin's old friend sentenced Harry to a mere three years' imprisonment.

Harry's only wish had been that his father "keep away from him." Joaquin scrupulously observed the instruction. He did not come to his son's defense before, or during, or after the trial. As Joaquin saw it, *his* life was being ruined, and not that of his youngest child.

But Joaquin was able to extricate himself from the embarrassing dilemma. After several months had passed and the furore had died down, he issued a statement declaring that, after an honest and impartial investigation of the case, it had been proven that Joseph McKay was not his son. Perhaps the young man's name actually was Miller—this fact could not be satisfactorily established—but Miller was a common enough name, Joaquin said, and as far as he could determine the fellow was not even a remote relation.

In addition to this incredibly shabby disavowal of his own son, Joaquin made the assertion that this was not the first time he had "been the victim of a strange passion among young desperadoes for claiming him as their parent," and he deplored the awful abuse of his "family name" which was "thus being constantly dragged in the dust."

We do not know what happened to the young convict Harry Miller when he emerged from San Quentin. It is to be presumed that he took another name, and it is not beyond the realm of possibility that he is alive today, an octogenarian. But we do know what happened to Joaquin Miller. His life and career were not ruined as he had feared. He retained his proud title of Poet of the Sierras, and he went on to greater "glory."

CHAPTER EIGHT

Sailing On!

1892-1900

I

Mrs. Frank Leslie commissioned Joaquin to write a commemorative poem suitable for recitation during the Columbian year of 1892. Joaquin quickly turned out the verses and called them "Columbus"—a title not conspicuous for its originality. He surely must have regarded this as a routine assignment, as an easy way to make the $50 Mrs. Leslie offered him. It is doubtful that, though he rated all his poetic efforts as magnificent, he had any premonition whatever that "Columbus" would become one of the most popular poems ever written by an American.

Few read "Columbus" today, but for decades it was acclaimed by adults who wanted their poetry simple and understandable. "Columbus" was all of that. Its first and last stanzas, quoted here, were memorized and chanted by countless schoolchildren:

> Behind him lay the gray Azores,
>   Behind the Gates of Hercules;
> Before him not the ghost of shores;
>   Before him only shoreless seas.
> The good mate said: "Now must we pray
>   For lo! the very stars are gone,

Brave Adm'r'l, speak; what shall I say?"
"Why, say: 'Sail on! Sail on! And on!' "

. . . .

Then, pale and worn, he kept his deck,
  And peered through darkness. Ah, that night
Of all dark nights! And then a speck—
  A light! A light! A light! A light!
It grew, a starlit flag unfurled!
  It grew to be Time's burst of dawn.
He gained a world; he gave that world
  Its grandest lesson: "On! Sail on!"

Joaquin's poetic saga of Columbus the Adm'r'l was received with what can only be described as universal rapture.
In one of the most sweeping statements ever made, the London ATHENAEUM declared that when workmanship, feeling
and power were considered "Columbus" must be ranked as
the best poem ever written by an American. "A masterpiece,"
Tennyson avowed. "The greatest poem expressive of a nation's destiny ever written."

Even the bilious critics in the United States, who could
always be counted upon to assail any product by Joaquin
Miller, conceded that his poem of the Adm'r'l was a supreme
work of art. The applause was overwhelming. There have
been editions printed of this short poem—it consists of only
five stanzas, or forty lines in all—in which the poem itself
occupied two pages, while the rest of the text consisted of
thirty solid pages of enthusiastic critical comment. Indeed,
the acclaim was so unanimous that Joaquin, never the man
to back away from adulation, called it "overgenerous."

Tastes change. Today "Columbus" is regarded a pseudo-
heroic and bombastic.

The popularity of "Columbus" as a vehicle for recitations

has been rivaled only by Whitman's "O Captain! My Captain!" Because of this, and because of the structural similarity of the two poems (Joaquin was accused of what might be termed unconscious plagiarism), and perhaps because both poets wore beards, there grew a tendency among some unlettered Americans to confuse Joaquin Miller with Walt Whitman. But with "Columbus" the superficial resemblance between the two poets begins and ends. Whitman passed serenely through his "O Captain!" period and went on to write poetry for the ages, while Joaquin, outside of one or two exceptions, remained on the unsubtle level of his fustian Adm'r'l composition. "It is not wholly unjust to say," the poet-critic Horace Gregory has perhaps harshly declared, "that 'O Captain!' and 'Columbus' had contributed their share in spreading an active dislike and a false conception of poetry to many young Americans who outgrew and fled from the elocution classes of the public schools."

Joaquin at first was bewildered by the accolades his Adm'r'l poem received, for he felt that these hastily scribbled lines were inferior to many of his other efforts. But in time he explicitly accepted the verdict of the public and the critics, and acknowledged it to be the greatest poem ever written in any language.

For years the question was to be put to Joaquin as to how he came to write "Columbus." The poet gave a variety of answers, but eventually he tired of hearing the inevitable query and was apt to be facetious. One day on The Hights he was closely questioned by a stalwart member of the Women's Christian Temperance Union as to what had inspired him.

"Whiskey, ma'am," Joaquin replied, flourishing aloft a glass of the precious fluid and then draining it. "It was with whiskey Columbus got his crew to sail on and on, and I did the same. But I couldn't mention it in the poem, ma'am, 'cause they need it in the schools, ma'am."

2

As had been predicted, Joaquin's literary output increased once he had left the confining shores of the East for the wide open West, and, gratifyingly enough, some critics began to detect an improvement in the quality of his work.

In 1887 the poet published *Songs of the Mexican Seas*, which he said had been composed during a long residence south of the border—a residence that Joaquin, through an oversight, forgot to mention had never taken place. In 1890, *In Classic Shades, and Other Poems* was issued. In these books of poetry Joaquin inserted many prosy footnotes, all of which dwelt on his thrilling experiences in the past. For instance, as he now remembered it, during the Castle Crags battle against the Indians (in which he had not participated), he had been wounded twice—in the head with an arrow, in the body with a silver bullet. His addiction to footnotes seemed to increase in direct proportion to their declining veracity as the years passed.

In 1890 Joaquin also revised the autobiographical work he had published eighteen years earlier. What had been *Life Amongst the Modocs: Unwritten History* in London and *Paquita, the Indian Heroine* in the United States, now had a new title: *My Own Story*. This revision was also issued as a paperback dime novel under still another name, *My Life Among the Indians*.

Joaquin actually confessed there had been "follies and fictions" in the original story, but he assured his readers that the rewritten version contained nothing but the cold and sober truth. What happened, however, was that some of the follies and fictions of the original were eliminated, while other follies and fictions were added. The episode of his Indian baby daughter was glossed over. His life among the aborigines was considerably toned down, while his battle against the Modocs received greater attention, and with many a stirring detail. The fact that he was jailed for being a horse thief, and pursued by a civilian posse, was deleted. Instead, in the new version, Joaquin escaped from an entire army—from what he described as "The Army of California"!

Songs of the Summer Lands, a lengthy volume of 254 pages, was published in 1893 and consisted of a few new poems together with many older ones. In that same year Joaquin wrote an account of his friendship with Edward John Trelawney, whom he had met in London, but this did not appear until 1922. Joaquin revealed that Trelawney had sent him his books and many flattering letters to The Hights. Here is another example of the poet's incredibly short memory, as Trelawney died in 1881, five years before Joaquin moved to The Hights.

All these books were received graciously—the author of the famed "Columbus" was now regarded almost with respect. One critic discovered that Joaquin had "the witchery of the true bard," while another felt his mind was "touched by the wand of Genius." It suddenly developed that the Poet of the Sierras, once belabored so unmercifully, now possessed "the mystic's insight and the open ear of the true philosopher." The tastes of critics change, too.

At last Joaquin was recognized in his own country—underneath all the posturing and clowning, the publicity-seeking and the frantic eccentricities—this was what he had striven for, this was what he had in a measure achieved. If his artistic conscience often failed him, if he consistently confused vigor with genius—at least he had *tried* to grow, at least he had made a bid for immortality even if in the end it eluded him.

Now there was an influx of distinguished visitors to The Hights. Ellen Terry and Henry Irving, the two shining lights of the English stage, trudged up the steep path to the Abbey. Joaquin strewed a few bushels of rose petals before the actress, and, as usual, the performance was a great success, although Irving felt he too should have deserved some floral attention. Hamlin Garland, the indefatigable literary biographer, came to see the poet, and after him a string of lesser known interviewers. There was a monotonous sameness about their stories: Joaquin Miller had his breakfast coffee at eleven, his first drink of whiskey at noon, he wrote in bed until one, he had dinner served at three, he had been an idolized hero in London, he was a devout Christian, he had a number of personal idiosyncrasies . . .

Joaquin, when told that he was the first poet in the land, now could afford to disavow the honor. He classed himself as the second greatest, ranking Walt Whitman first, and when the sage of Camden died he penned the lines that at the time were often quoted:

> He heard his "Drum Taps," and God drew
> His great soul through the shining pass.

Always generous, Joaquin now tried to draw the attention of the interviewers to a rival poet who lived below The Hights—Edwin Markham, then completely unknown. It was not until later, when Markham wrote his Man-with-Hoe poem that he was able to attract the public's fancy. "A man ever hospitable to all the clients of Apollo, jealous of none," Markham described Joaquin. "In all the years I knew him I never heard him say a bitter word of any human being. He always leaned to mercy, and always lent a hand."

With his rise in reputation, there was a corresponding rise in his income, for business manager Harr Wagner now secured good prices for his poems and books. Joaquin was able to hire as fulltime workers A. W. Darling, a Civil War veteran, to act as overseer, and his wife Isabel, who copied his manuscripts so that the printers could read them, and both lived as tenants on The Hights. Joaquin had enough money to buy more acres to add to his estate and to invest in a publishing company with Ambrose Bierce and others as partners. The house put out a number of volumes, but the venture was a failure. Joaquin lost about $50. Bierce, the self-admitted cynic, was not cynical enough. He was the chief stockholder and dropped $400.

Bierce at this time wrote a long and hilarious parody of a typical Joaquin Miller poem. The poet, although ordinarily sensitive to the lampooning of his work, accepted this one with smiles, and indeed would quote himself the opening lines:

> And I rose in the strongest strength of my strength,
> With my breast of brass and my hair's full length,
> And I shook myself out of my clothes in the land
> Of the Mormons, and stood there and kissed my hand.

Bierce in his lifetime said and wrote many harsh things about Joaquin, but he also was quick to acknowledge that "Nobody has been more delighted than I in pointing out the greatness of Joaquin's work"—meaning his poetry, not his prose.

3

In 1893, a Japanese youth came to The Hights and begged to have a few words with "The Philosopher." When Joaquin was informed of this wonderful appellation he sprang from his bed and appeared instantly. The visitor was Yone Noguchi, then penniless and eighteen, but who later became renowned as a poet and Professor of English Literature at the University of Japan. He bore a letter of introduction from Sir Edwin Arnold, and this made him doubly welcome, for Arnold was the critic who had prophesied Joaquin Miller's words would be immortal in world literary annals. Noguchi hoped to be invited to stay overnight. He was another "Man Who Came to Dinner"—he was to stay for four full years.

Noguchi became Joaquin's part-time helper, and proved to be a real bargain. The Sierra poet gave him his food and a cottage room to sleep in, but paid him no salary. The Japanese earned his bed and board by brewing the breakfast coffee, by cooking dinner, and by acting as general factotum. One of his duties was to turn on the tap to start the water sprinkler whenever Joaquin began to chant for rain in front of visitors.

Whenever he could find the time, Noguchi attended the University of California, graduating with high honors. In his autobiography, published in 1914, he remembered Joaquin with genuine affection and also with good-natured irreverence. When the two were alone together on The Hights, the master reminded the Japanese "of my imaginary picture of childhood days for a certain *Tengu* or Mountain Elf with a red long nose." But when there was company about, Joaquin was more impressive. Then, Noguchi noted, he would drape the bearskin over his shoulders even when eating, would wear a red crepe sash around his waist, and would gesticulate violently to show off the large diamond ring sparkling on his right hand. And Noguchi was amused at Joaquin's solemn habit of calling his workroom the "Holy Grotto."

Joaquin always maintained he "discovered" the Japanese in America, and it is true that he was one of the first public figures to accept them without condescension as his fellow men, not as "Japs" or some variety of "Chinks." Noguchi said Joaquin was the first man in America to call him "Mister," and that he strictly adhered to this form of address. In 1905 Noguchi the student and Joaquin the master were to collaborate on a book of poems, *The Japan of Sword and Love,* which was published in Tokyo in the Japanese language.

At this time Joaquin adopted another Japanese protégé, Takeshi Kanno, who later became well known as a poet and philosopher. Kanno stayed on The Hights for several years, acting as handy man. When Kanno married Gertrude Boyle, a sculptress, Joaquin gave them a cottage to live in, rent free, and he called Miss Boyle his "adopted daughter." Joaquin, so notorious for being close-fisted when it came to supporting his own children, with the passing of the years became increasingly generous to comparative strangers.

With the two Japanese, the foreman and his wife, with Harr Wagner and with the inevitable current sweetheart of Joaquin, the population on The Hights numbered seven. Now the poet added an eighth member to his colony—his mother Margaret. He had all but ignored his mother for twenty years, and now he made up for the neglect. Joaquin found, when his mother arrived from Oregon, that the old lady was senile and given to incomprehensible babbling. The tall, thin woman was a familiar figure to those who lived on The Hights, but she was shunted out of sight whenever company arrived.

The poet treated his mother with affectionate irritation. "Mother, you talk too much," Noguchi remembered him admonishing her. "Silence! Silence helps our digestion." And then, turning to the others at the table: "Eat slowly, all of you —think of something higher, and be content!" Needless to say, Joaquin did not feel himself bound by such injunctions.

4

In the meantime, manager Harr Wagner was busy securing lucrative assignments for the poet. He persuaded the San Francisco EXAMINER to send Joaquin to the Sierra Mountains to interview Chris Evans, a train robber then much in the news, who was hiding out there. Joaquin dived deep into his old haunts and obtained the interview—or at least he said he did, for he quoted Evans on a variety of subjects—and the stories were front page copy. But because of his reputation for playing lightly with the truth, the authenticity of his newspaper articles was doubted in some quarters. The chances are he did talk to the desperado, for later on, after Evans was captured and had served a term in Folsom penitentiary, we know that he visited Joaquin at The Hights.

Wagner obtained another journalistic assignment for the poet—to visit Hawaii as correspondent for OVERLAND magazine and for various West Coast newspapers that were demanding annexation of the islands. Joaquin was eager to make the trip for, during the third of Alice Oliver's pregnancies he had hurried her off The Hights to Honolulu for her accouchement. Now, being temporarily without female companionship, he found he missed his young sweetheart.

Joaquin liked the climate and scenery of Hawaii, and high-flown phrases were a dime a dozen in the dispatches he sent back to the States. He loved the "argent, opal sea" and the "cloud-capped peaks where thunders slept" in that "Sweet Arcadia." And when he descended into an active volcano and saw the swirling molten lava, he came up with a memorable description: "There it was, working, working there, the dough of hell."

Joaquin was welcomed as a celebrity in Hawaii, and it is likely that he would have remained on Oahu for some time had he not been forced to cut short his stay. He was accorded a prized honor, an invitation to the Governor's house. The poet arrived at the executive mansion in the company of Alice Oliver, whom he introduced as the wife of his plumber, a lonely lady whom he had happened to encounter in Honolulu.

Mrs. Dole, the Governor's wife, later learned he was living in adjoining hotel rooms with the pregnant girl. Mrs. Dole was rather strict about such matters. Joaquin was advised—officially and in no uncertain terms—to leave town, at once. According to Harr Wagner, Joaquin at the moment was without funds and had to pawn his diamond ring to raise his passage money. Miss Oliver followed later, with a baby boy.

Some time after he had returned to The Hights, Harr Wagner booked the poet for a series of lectures in the Southern and Midwestern states. Joaquin was never at any time a polished speaker on the platform, but his bearing had become assured, his voice was loud and he was given to dramatic gesticulations that were appreciated. The tour was a huge success, and it was estimated that he netted more than $5,000 in less than two months.

The tour opened in January, 1897 at New Orleans, where Joaquin had been welcomed so whole-heartedly twelve years before. Again he captured the city, and every move he made was considered news. When he walked down the street, clad in his Wild West costume, waving aloft a bouquet that had been given him by schoolchildren, he was cheered by the crowd that followed him. Joaquin bowed graciously and, in the middle of the street, recited "Columbus."

Joaquin's repertory consisted of two lectures. "Lessons Not Learned in Books" was sure-fire. The other talk centered on the glories of the Sierras and the West. Each lecture was illustrated by stereopticon slides, with Harr Wagner operating the mechanism. The poet also sang Methodist hymns in what he claimed was an obscure Indian dialect, one that no other white man had mastered. He would weep and sob, then break down altogether as he chanted these "Indians songs my mother taught me in the cradle," and the audiences loved it.

The enthusiasm ran so high in New Orleans that Joaquin lectured five times. On his departure, he announced that, after fulfilling similar commitments in England, he would return and spend the rest of his days in the Crescent City. He also revealed that never again would he write a word of poetry or prose. He would devote all of his time to meditation.

In nearby Mobile, four hundred lovers of Nature, Art and the Beautiful rioted while trying to get into the hall to hear Joaquin Miller. The rest of the tour (he did not get to England) was a triumphal march North, borne on the tidal wave of local patriotism.

In Louisville, Joaquin assured his listeners that as a youth he had lived in many places, but that he remembered his days in Kentucky as being the happiest of all. The poet talked so much to his admirers at the depot that he missed three trains.

In Cincinnati, Dean Philip Van Ness Myers of the University of Cincinnati introduced him to an overflow audience. Here Joaquin appropriately remembered that his parents had named him Cincinnatus, in honor of the great city to which he was so devoted. He then informed the student body that he, too, was a college man. He had graduated *summa cum laude* from Columbia College in Oregon, and had studied at Oxford, Bonn and Heidelberg. He sat for a portrait by the artist Webber, and the oil was hung in the halls of the university.

In Canton, Joaquin was entertained by President McKinley in his home, where he recited "Columbus" not once but twice. As the crowds gathered outside the President's house Joaquin told them of his many visits to beautiful Canton when he was a boy.

In Cleveland, the poet rode down the streets on a white horse, and while attempting to bow to the people was in continual danger of falling from the saddle. He prophesied that, within thirty years' time, Cleveland would be the greatest city in the world.

In Indianapolis, James Whitcomb Riley greeted him at the train and took him to his hotel. These bards, who met for the first time, found they had two bonds in common: they liked good whiskey and they liked each other. They immediately formed a mutual-admiration society. Joaquin pronounced Riley "Indiana's Homer." Riley thought that Joaquin was "saint-like," a "master," and "all-divine." More privately, the Hoosier Poet marveled at the ease with which this saint-like creature put away incredible amounts of hard liquor. The next day, Joaquin was introduced to the Indiana legislature.

He talked to the assembly about his childhood days in the state—an unprecedented excursion from the fanciful into the realm of truth.

There is no doubt that Joaquin could have continued his tour indefinitely, but he cut it short. Gold had been discovered in Alaska and in the Yukon Territory, causing a stampede of fortune-seekers to that bleak land. Joaquin—remembering the experiences during his Gold Rush days in California—announced that he could not sit idly by. He was off for the Klondike.

5

Joaquin's Yukon adventure was a most distressing fiasco. The trip was to take a year out of his life—a life that he all but forfeited in that near-Arctic country. He also came close to losing a reputation that he had been carefully nursing along since the year 1886 when he went West to The Hights.

The New York WORLD and the Hearst papers bid for Joaquin's services to act as their correspondent, the former offering him more money, the latter more publicity. Joaquin accepted the Hearst offer. The New York JOURNAL and San Francisco EXAMINER, kingpins of the chain, advertised he was going to the Yukon as an "Ambassador"—just for whom he was going to be Ambassador was not revealed. Soon, the Hearst advertisements screamed, the public would be reading a half-page of news each week from the Klondike, written by America's Greatest and Most Beloved Poet.

Hearst had chartered a boat to take his reporters to Alaska, but Joaquin was too impatient to wait for it to be fitted out. He sailed for Victoria in British Columbia. He informed his readers that, armed with pick and pan and pack, he was heading north on July 26, 1897, steamer-bound for Juneau.

It appears that Joaquin, in an effort to rush the stories of the gold stampede to the Hearst papers, committed an unpardonable sin: he wrote dispatches about the land and its conditions on the boat, before he even reached Alaska.

This made for good newspaper copy, but tended to make it inaccurate. Joaquin implicitly believed what others told him of the gold fields ahead, and what he was not told he manufactured. The result was a rosy picture of the Yukon, presenting an ice-bound and terrible country as a wonderful Eden (admittedly a trifle coolish), that was accessible to anyone with small capital, and where a person could live comfortably on little money until the inevitable day came when he struck it rich and made millions.

As the widely read paper of the Yukon, the KLONDYKE NUGGET, wryly commented on Joaquin's newspaper yarns:

> His glowing words were eagerly devoured by millions of readers, many of whom rested neither night nor day until they traveled and saw for themselves. . . . But what an awakening! Where, oh where, are the gorgeous blossoms changing the complexion of the hills from base to crest like the blushes of a maiden? Where are the endless varieties of nature's jewels which gladden the eyes of our traveler, and the mighty game on every hand, and the trout in every stream, and the gold glittering in every gravel bed?

From Juneau, Joaquin traveled by boat to Skagway, then crossed the snow-filled Chilkoot Pass to get to the headwaters of the Yukon.

> Have you, too, banged at Chilkoot,
> That rock-lined gate to the golden door?

Joaquin asked, and to his American readers the crossing at Chilkoot seemed like a gay walk over a verdant hill. Joaquin declared in one dispatch that he crossed the Chilkoot with a bouquet of freshly-picked violets in his hand—and when this became known in the Yukon the miners rolled in the snowdrifts, hysterical with laughter.

Actually, for a man who admitted to being fifty-five, but who was a few days removed from his sixtieth birthday, it was a perilous journey. And instead of carrying a bunch of violets, Joaquin was loaded down with a forty-pound pack on his back containing food, a notebook and pencils. For once he had to be without his quill.

After a twelve-day trip down the river in Yukon boats, the poet arrived at Dawson, the capital of Yukon Territory in Canada, on August 16. The trip from Skagway to Dawson had been a tiring and a trying five hundred and seventy miles. And yet, in another outlandish dispatch to the Hearst papers, Joaquin declared that the entire journey from the States to Dawson could be made alone, and for less than $100. A few weeks later he reduced this estimate to $50. By the charitably inclined, this bit of "news" can only be described as utterly misleading, but, more truthfully, it was an invitation to disaster, for it was to lure many a poorly-equipped and penniless gold-hunter to the Yukon.

Dawson, today a town of a few hundred, was then a city of 20,000 gold-mad citizens. Joaquin found to his dismay that a bottle of whiskey sold anywhere from $12 to $20, that a drink alone retailed for the unheard-of price of fifty cents, and that indeed a person could buy nothing for less than half a dollar. But he stayed for six weeks in Dawson, sending on stories that described in glowing terms the wondrous Klondike—the gold region that actually was several hundred miles to the North of him.

Joaquin lived in Dawson with an old miner, H. E. Canavan,

in a comfortable cabin. When a fellow correspondent arrived in town—he was Tappan Adney of HARPER'S WEEKLY —Joaquin offered to provide him with temporary accommodations. Adney supposedly stayed on a month, cadging drinks and food (this story comes to us second-hand, via Harr Wagner, who heard it from Joaquin), and at last he asked Canavan to move out so there would be more privacy for the working journalists.

According to Joaquin, he refused to countenance such an act of incivility and helped throw out Adney. These may be the facts—we cannot be sure—but it is a matter of record that Adney suddenly became a bitter enemy who slurred, and even libeled, the poet in HARPER'S.

On October 26 Joaquin arrived in Circle City, a collection of cabins just below the Arctic circle, where people supposedly stumbled over nuggets wherever they went. Joaquin, who had told his readers back in the States about the gold that glittered everywhere, staked out a number of claims. Not a one produced an ounce of the shining metal.

Later on, after he had become a Congressman from California, E. J. Livernash told President Roosevelt how he had lived with Joaquin in the Yukon. There was no coffee strainer in the cabin and Livernash, cook for the week, did not relish tramping over twenty miles of ice to buy one. He fashioned a workable sieve by taking a tin cup and punching holes in the bottom with an awl.

There was in the cabin a single gill of whiskey, which Joaquin had been hoarding for a special occasion. One day a lady came by. She was young and passably pretty and appealed to the poet, who had not seen a woman in weeks, and so he decided to salute her with his last drink. He filled the tin cup and eyed the visitor with admiration before pronouncing a poetic toast to her charms, and in the meantime all the precious whiskey dripped away. Livernash said Joaquin displayed on that occasion a "remarkable capacity for marshalling startling expletives."

The Arctic storms zoomed down and Joaquin was forced to winter in Circle City, but when he heard that men were starved and dying in a blizzard on the trail between Dawson and Circle City, he hastily packed a few provisions on a sled he would have to pull by hand—Eskimo dogs were not available—and set out to cover the story for the Hearst papers. It was a courageous but extremely foolhardy venture for an elderly man who knew little of the hazards of the Yukon trail in wintertime.

He was starting out on a trip of two hundred and thirty agonizing miles, in temperatures that would drop treacherously as low as forty below zero. All the seasoned sourdoughs of the Klondike advised Joaquin not to brave the dangers of winter travel. They warned him explicitly of the hardships ahead, they prophesied he was deliberately inviting misfortune and risking his life.

The sixty-year-old poet ignored them—"You seem to forget that I am an old hand in the rough country," he told those who remonstrated—the story came first!—and, in the company of Canavan, an even older man, started out. The journey was to take thirty-five days and they were to arrive in Dawson more dead than alive.

"It was just the sort of thing Miller has been doing ever since he started to come here with $50 in his pocket," Tappan Adney wrote in HARPER'S WEEKLY (though this was a rather vicious distortion in every respect), "and is characteristic of the man who in his reports is still advising more men with $50 in their pockets to come in to the Yukon."

Canavan and Joaquin slept on the trail much of the time. They spent one night in a tiny log cabin, eleven feet square, in the company of no less than eleven other Klondikers. Against the counsel of their new friends, they set out on the trail the next morning. The inevitable happened. When they reached Charley's River—only eighty miles out of Circle City, and one hundred fifty miles from their goal—they were marooned by a king-sized blizzard and could proceed no further.

The two men found shelter in a lean-to. There was no choice but to face the prospect of spending the winter there, unless, as was unlikely, someone happened by and rescued them. And, for a four-or-five-month stay in a ramshackle hut, with below-zero temperatures outside and one blizzard after another sweeping down from the Arctic, their supplies consisted only of two and one-half pounds of sausage, six pounds of bacon, six pounds of pilot-bread, ten pounds of beans, and some moose meat. The chances were they would freeze and certainly starve to death, for they could not forage for game in the deep snows.

Luckily enough, after a few days of incarceration in the buried lean-to, Al Thayer, an experienced Klondiker, drove by on a dog-sled, across the river. They waved at him and at last attracted his attention. The ordeal was partially over. Thayer took the ice-bitten men to Dawson. Joaquin arrived with frozen cheeks, frozen beard, frozen nose and feet, and was taken to a hospital run by nuns. He stayed there for weeks and was finally nursed back to health. He lost—not his life—but both little toes.

Tappan Adney, who suppressed any mention of Joaquin's serious condition and of the perils he had met on the trail, sternly wrote:

Miller is advising people about this country, using the prestige of his name as a writer of fiction and poetry. He is not fitted to advise those who come into this ill-provided country without an outfit, and who has been from the start, and is now, dependent wholly upon the bounty and foresight of others.

It must be admitted that we know little of what actually happened to Joaquin in the Yukon, for the available information is colored by prejudice for or against the poet. Though ordinarily voluble about his adventures, he was always reticent about his stay in the Northland, and one might presume that the stories about him were true. On the other hand, it is known that other correspondents in the Yukon—none of whom had much of a name in the United States, and certainly did not approach the poet's national reputation—were jealous of what most Klondikers regarded as their illustrious visitor.

There was, for instance, the story of Howard V. Sutherland, a journalist. Some years before Sutherland had written hostile articles about Joaquin in WASP and NEWS-LETTER, the two San Francisco weeklies. Now, the way Sutherland was to remember it, he took the penniless poet (who certainly was not that, having just made $5,000 on a short lecture tour) into his tent in Dawson, and in good Samaritan style fed and clothed the poor fellow.

Then, one day, according to Sutherland, Colonel Steele of the Canadian Mounted Police happened by and, on learning that Joaquin Miller—the famous poet, who had depicted the Yukon as a paradise—was there, he could not restrain his wrath. What followed, according to Sutherland's story as recorded in Kathryn Winslow's eminently readable "Big Pan-Out" was this:

He pulled back the tent flap and gave the old man a tongue lashing. "You're responsible for the death of many fine men and the ruin of thousands!" he cried at Miller, who lowered his head and held it meekly over his plate. When Sutherland felt Steele had bellowed long enough he reminded him that Miller was a guest at his table. . . . Steele backed away, with a last shot warning to Miller about not writing any more poetry about the Yukon.

Sutherland further averred that after this scene Joaquin immediately decamped from Dawson, in deep shame. "He was not liked there," Sutherland declared. "No one but my-self came to wish him godspeed on his journey."

This incident could very well have happened. But we do not know that it did. The chances are it did not, for it must be kept in mind that Sutherland was certainly no trustworthy witness. We know from many other sources that Joaquin was highly popular with Klondikers, who found him a jolly and formidable drinking companion, and who liked the way he spun his tall tales and recited his poetry.

Sutherland is also the lone authority for the statement that on his arrival in Dawson he carried with him a letter entrusted to him by Joaquin's aged and dying mother. "When Miller saw the familiar handwriting he wept audibly," Sutherland asserted. "Inside was money to buy a steamer ticket. 'But I know I'll never see her alive,' Miller said. 'It's too late.' It was. She died while he was on his way home."

If a witness lies in one instance, he is apt to lie in another. The facts are that the poet's mother at that time was quite feebleminded, incapable of writing letters, and had no money except for the bounty of her son. And she did not die until nine years later, in 1907 and not 1898, under the care of her son on The Hights. So much for Mr. Sutherland.

But we do know that the Yukon trip was a sorry adventure —one that Joaquin never boasted about to his friends, hoping that his inglorious role would eventually be forgotten—and that he left for the States in June, 1898.

6

Joaquin had scarcely settled himself on The Hights when the July 9, 1898 issue of HARPER's WEEKLY was handed him by reporters. In a dispatch dated March 12 from the Klondike, Tappan Adney declared that the destitute Joaquin Miller was subsisting on the charity of miners in Dawson.

The poet informed the newspapermen that he had been paid $6,000 above expenses to act as correspondent in the Yukon. He asked his visitors to look around his spacious estate on The Hights, with its seventy acres and four buildings and many tenants, and to see for themselves how poverty-stricken he was. The poet said he had been offered $66,000 in cash for his aerie, and that in addition he had a steady income from play and book royalties.

The reporters wanted to know what he planned to do about the HARPER's canard. Joaquin said he would sue the magazine for libel, asking $100,000 damages. He would not accept any money himself—when the sum was levied by the court it would be handed over to charity. The chances are the poet could have won such a libel suit, but he never filed charges. It is more likely that, instead, a "deal" was made, for from then on HARPER's began to treat him respectfully.

Joaquin intended to capitalize on his year-long Yukon adventure—a bold undertaking indeed, considering its dismal outcome—and to go on a lecture tour, but the impresarios of the Keith vaudeville circuit convinced him that he could make more money, at less personal inconvenience, if he went on the stage. Harr Wagner wisely cautioned him against taking such a step: the role of just another vaudevillian would be incompatible with his dignity. But Joaquin never worried much about his dignity, and he could not resist the lure of the stage and the adulation that went with it. He signed a $500-a-week contract with the Keith circuit. So far as is known, he was the first poet ever to appear in vaudeville.

Joaquin Miller, Actor, went to Chicago to open his tour. He was entertained by the town's literati and widely interviewed. The Actor denied he had "lured" people to the Yukon or had inaccurately portrayed conditions there. Throughout the festivities Joaquin wore the buckskin coat that was mentioned earlier, with buttons which were fashioned of nuggets. He was sculpted by Lorado Taft, then much in vogue, and painted by the fashionable Ralph Clarkson. Both artists commented on the fact that for a robust man standing six feet high, Joaquin had exceptionally small hands and feet.

Joaquin's vaudeville debut took place on December 6. He appeared onstage in full Yukon costume—parka, furry pants and sealskin boots, drawing a sled behind him—and spoke on "My Impressions of the Klondike." He also delivered some poetry in the Chinook idiom:

> El ker na sa ka clatter wah nannish
> Sa yah copa Boston ille hé!

Joaquin said that the Chinook was a language that for decades had defied the linguists, but that he had mastered the dialect during his first month in Alaska, and that he was hard at work on compiling a Chinook dictionary. (The Chinooks were Indians from Oregon and Washington.) When he was asked what "Boston" meant in Chinook, Joaquin explained that the word was untranslatable.

In this and subsequent performances, Joaquin the vaudeville star was only a mild success. He was regarded more with curiosity than with interest. The reviewers seemed to consider it symptomatic that he made his debut in the Windy City. As for the press at large, many echoed the thought of the editor of CRITIC: "There are those, who recalling Mr. Miller's first visit East . . . will say that this is not the poet's first appearance as a vaudeville artist."

His heavy Alaskan costume caused him to perspire profusely onstage, the "five-a-day" turn proved strenuous, and he realized that he was cheapening his reputation, for the public tended to regard him not as a great poet but as a sideshow freak. Early in 1899 in New York Joaquin asked that his contract be canceled, and the Keith people obliged. Publicly, Joaquin treated the situation in humorous fashion. He said that his performance had followed an act featuring alligators, that he was always stepping on their tails, and that the reptiles had resented the familiarity.

Before returning to The Hights, Joaquin renewed old friendships in New York. He visited his wife Abbie (their marriage can be best described as a long casual acquaintance) and his daughter Juanita, both of whom he had not seen in thirteen years. Juanita now was an extremely beautiful girl of about eighteen who was taking elocution lessons and planning to be a singer.

While in New York Joaquin traveled upstate to East Aurora to visit the Roycroft artist colony run by Elbert Hubbard. Hubbard was then regarded as a subversive Bohemian; but his status was soon to change, for later in the year he wrote "A Message to Garcia," which industrial tycoons were to reprint by the millions and give to their employees to promote greater efficiency. "Everybody took a holiday," Hubbard said on the occasion of Joaquin's visit. "We laughed and played and picknicked until night came on apace. Then we built bonfires and told ghost stories until midnight."

Hubbard wanted the poet to become a member of his colony and contribute to his inspirational magazine, the PHILISTINE. But Joaquin preferred to return to The Hights, where he could rule over a circle of devout disciples of his own, and where he, not Elbert Hubbard, was lord and master.

7

Back on The Hights, Joaquin went to work assembling material for new books and preparing an edition of all his poems. Then he returned to the lecture platform. Harr Wagner had booked a tour of forty consecutive nights in forty towns in Texas. This tour netted $4,000, and in 1900, when Joaquin was in the town of Alice near the Mexican border, he used some of his profits in land speculation. The name Alice brought memories of his Alice Oliver, and on a hunch he bought seven hundred acres of land in the town.

Joaquin later said that oil had been discovered on the property and that he had been offered $100,000 for his holdings. Once again his erratic short memory failed him; but the gamble did pay off. He had purchased the land for $2 an acre, and he sold out for three times that figure, making a profit of $2,800, an excellent return on an impulsive, hazardous investment.

Joaquin returned to The Hights and continued to lecture in and out of San Francisco, where he always drew good audiences. The poet was no conventional platform speaker. If he did not feel inspired to talk on the topic that had been announced he would discuss a subject that pleased him more, or he would drop the talk altogether and simply recite his poetry—in the most reverent manner imaginable.

One of his friends, Colonel John P. Irish, recalled the time he was late in arriving at one of Joaquin's lectures. The poet stopped declaiming as Irish tiptoed down the aisle. He then stepped down from the rostrum, took his friend by the hand and pumped it up and down. "James, Irish!" he shouted. "Irish, James!" He mounted the platform again and blithely resumed his talk. Such a scene never bothered Irish, whose name incidentally was John and not James—he was a hard-drinking editor who was an eccentric himself, and who boasted that he had never in his life worn a tie—but the audience was bewildered by such goings-on.

The poet then visited Portland, where he was affectionately hailed as "Oregon's Own" by a large audience when he lectured on March 13, 1900. Joaquin soon became a familiar sight in the city's streets. He had discarded his frontier costume, but was still weirdly attired. He wore one trouser leg stuffed inside his boots and the other outside—an affectation copied from Horace Greeley—and his long-tailed coat was provided with oversized pockets to hold an ample supply of tobacco and a big flask of whiskey.

He made an especial hit with children, who were fascinated by the long beard he was cultivating and which made him resemble a prophet out of the Old Testament. When some of these children had grown up, they wrote their memoirs. One of them remembered Joaquin taking him on his knee to tell him a bear story—and the way the little boy heard it *Joaquin* was the bear. A woman recalled years later the impressive bearded giant, his face flushed crimson, who kissed her so "aromatically" when she was a child.

In 1952, Mrs. Camellia Edith Perry, an Oregon pioneer, recaptured Joaquin Miller's charm which had delighted his audiences a half-century before. When approached by a small girl with a bouquet, he "with all the grace and courtesy of a French cavalier" would kiss the back of her hand. The poet's response when he was applauded at the lecture's end or when honored in any other fashion, seldom varied, but was always appreciated. "I have traveled widely," Mrs. Perry remembered the patter after he had been visited by a group of schoolchildren, "I have been wined and dined and met the great in the capitals of foreign lands, but I have never been more pleased at any reception than I am this evening. . . ." —and so on, and so on.

8

Around the turn of the century Joaquin was probably at the peak of his popularity, both as a poet and as a personality.

His poetry had become the subject of parodies (a sure sign of recognition), he was in demand as a speaker, the cranks came to The Hights in droves to harass him, and the more serious-minded devotees wanted him to reveal his "philosophy of life." The embryonic poets throughout the nation began to shower him with their verse, pleading with the famous Joaquin Miller to give them an opinion on their work. His rule was never to offend any bard, no matter how inept he or she might be. "As to Joaquin Miller, it is his detestable habit, as it was Longfellow's, to praise all poetry submitted to him," Ambrose Bierce remarked disgustedly.

Joaquin's popularity was at high tide, but this did not prevent him from speaking freely. If anything, his unorthodox sympathies became more pronounced. Any cause of a minority was his own cause, particularly if it was opposed by the plutocrats. The persecuted Chinese, the Japanese, Armenians, Cubans and Indians always found his voice on their side. He wrote poems in praise of the Boers in their fight against mighty England, he condemned the Russian massacre of the Jews in Kishinev and subsequent pogroms. "Miller's heart went ever out to the under-dog," as Sterling noted.

Joaquin was as prolific as ever with his quill. Between 1894 and 1900, when he reached his sixty-third birthday, he published seven books, four of them works of poetry. Almost all the critics saluted these volumes with heavy praise.

In 1894, Joaquin put out a novel, *The Building of the City Beautiful*, and its "tall, dark lady" was easily recognizable as Mrs. Leslie. The book was attacked for being Communistic— the poet proposed that literally everything in the world should belong to the people, who lived in a classless society —and yet it was received well, perhaps because a depression was on the land and capitalism was temporarily in disrepute. The book was so popular that eleven years later Joaquin rewrote and expanded it, with renewed success in sales.

That same year, Joaquin's name was on the title page of *An Illustrated History of the State of Montana*, a ponderous volume aimed at the old pioneers of the Northwest. Some of the text was written by Joaquin, but what the publishers wanted primarily was his "name." This was the first and last appearance of the poet-novelist as historian.

Songs of the Soul appeared in 1896 and its poems were thought to be "Whitmanesque." This epithet had once been a sneer; but now that Whitman was dead, it was a compliment.

Joaquin's *Complete Poetical Works* was published in Lon-

don in 1897. It was issued in the United States in 1900, and
in a revised edition two years later. It was a fairly large
volume of 330 pages printed in double columns, selling at
$2.50 and $4.50 for trade and deluxe copies, with autographed copies priced at $7.50.

The *Complete Works*—he had reached the goal of all
writers, to have a collection of all his poems put out in his
own lifetime—was commended by all critics except those
living in California. For some reason, Joaquin, who was always hostile to the ruthless tycoons, dedicated the volume to
Collis P. Huntington. Without exception, all of Joaquin's
literary friends in the state considered the railroad magnate
as an unscrupulous old monster, a debaucher of legislatures,
and they were aghast at Joaquin's tribute to the man who
had "done the Greater West and South more enduring good
than any other man." We do not know what prompted Joaquin to act as he did. There is no record of his friendship with
Huntington, or of any subsidies received from him.

In his *Collected Works*, as in most of his other books, Joaquin permitted himself a profusion of autobiographical footnotes. Years later, Stuart P. Sherman was to describe them as
"shredded memoirs." Ambrose Bierce was more outspoken.
"It is hardly too much to say that every line of prose in this
book is both needless and foolish," he declared. Bierce
thought Joaquin as a poet was sometimes great, but as an
autobiographer he bluntly described him as "the greatest
liar this country has ever produced."

"In impugning Mr. Miller's veracity, or rather in plainly
declaring that he has none," Bierce savagely wrote in a full
page article in the San Francisco EXAMINER, "I should be
sorry to be understood as attributing a graver moral de-

linquency than he really has. He cannot, or will not tell the truth." But even Bierce was forced to concede that the poet "never tells a malicious or thrifty falsehood."

Instead of ignoring or shrugging off this attack, Joaquin took it seriously. "I am not a liar," he told reporters. "I simply exaggerate the truth." The newspapermen thought that this minor *mot* was a fair enough answer. And as a friend of his who came to his defense put it, "Joaquin Miller tells the truth *as he sees it*."

Many people have testified that the poet was never heard to speak a harsh word against any man. But in this instance his patience was exhausted. "I've always wondered why God made Bierce," he confided with surprising bitterness to George Sterling.

In 1899 Joaquin published *A Song of Creation*, his longest poem. The next year he issued *Chants for the Boers*, in which he attacked his old friends, the imperialistic British. These poems were immensely popular and the book ran through six editions. In that same year there appeared his *True Bear Stories*, with an introduction by David Starr Jordan, president of Stanford University. The reader learned that Joaquin had many an encounter with grizzlies, and the facts must be faced: he was a mighty courageous fellow. Forty-nine years later this book was reissued, but this time the "True" stories were plainly labeled *For Children*.

All these books constituted quite an output, but Joaquin was at work on a more ambitious project. Belford, Clarke & Co., a Chicago publishing house, advanced him $2,000 to edit a twenty-volume set of his writings, but the company went bankrupt and the books were never issued.

Joaquin's fame was at its peak. At this juncture Edmund

Clarence Stedman published his *An American Anthology—1787–1900*. Five fat pages were devoted to ten of Joaquin's poems, and he was treated reverently as a master.

In the present day, when the anthologizers get to work, they either ignore the Poet of the Sierras altogether or print a single poem (usually "Columbus") to point to the extraordinary poetical taste that once prevailed in the country.

9

In 1900 Joaquin Miller made his last trip outside the United States, sang his swan song as a newspaperman, tasted his last adventure. He went to China to report on the Boxer Rebellion.

The members of a secret society called "Order of Literary Patriotic Harmonious Fists" (hence the distantly derived name of Boxers) had stirred the Chinese people into a crusade to drive out the foreigners. The foreigners soon found themselves besieged in Peking, and the six great Powers sent an international army of American, British, French, German, Japanese and Russian troops to their rescue.

Joaquin was impatient to be off to the war. He felt cramped on The Hights. "I need room!" cried the poet. He was to find Asia a roomy place.

Joaquin was chosen to be the correspondent of the San Francisco EXAMINER, which was to feed his copy to other Hearst papers. Remembering the accusation that he had arrived in the Klondike with only $50, he stuffed several $500 bills in his shoes before he left. Harr Wagner and May Foster Carey saw him off at the pier, and the poet told his friend that, if May needed money, to draw it from the salary he would let accumulate at the EXAMINER.

From the standpoint of both Joaquin and the Hearst

executives, his trip to China was a waste of time, if not a total loss. The war did not last long, and he arrived too late to see much action. The EXAMINER used but a small amount of the material he sent back, and he was being paid on space rates. Perhaps the editors were wary of his dispatches, recalling his blithe account of the Klondike; but it is more likely that they thought his stories did not depict the enemy in the fashion of the day—as bloodthirsty heathen running wild and trying to kill off good white people.

Joaquin arrived just in time to accompany the American troops in the drive to lift the siege of Peking, and, according to his stories, he was of invaluable assistance in helping the Red Cross to care for the wounded. But he did score a "beat" when he secured an exclusive interview with Li Hung Chang, then much in the news because he had been appointed to dicker with the Allies over the peace terms.

At the outset of the interview, Li Hung Chang was inscrutable, in keeping with the hoary tradition of the East, but his sphinxlike calm was shattered when Joaquin took off his shoes and proudly showed him the $500 bills he had been walking on through China. In his dispatches Joaquin predicted the emissary as a wily old Oriental who would be more than the match for the naive Westerners when it came to skillful negotiation. This prophecy could scarcely have been less accurate: China was forced to pay $320,000,000 as indemnity and make many economic concessions.

The interview with Li Hung Chang took place on August 28, and shortly thereafter Joaquin returned to the States, having been in China only a little more than a month. When he discovered that the Hearst papers had used only a few of his dispatches (and, what hurt him more, had not gone to the trouble of publicizing their poet-correspondent), he wrote several magazine pieces based on the unused material. One of the articles was about a people on whom he considered himself an authority—the Japanese—and this proved to be a rash undertaking.

His "Little Brown Men of Nippon" piece in ARENA was typical for its absurdities. The poet said that when he was fighting the Boxers he often came into contact with "our Allies," the Japanese, who were so poorly clad that he personally collected American uniforms to clothe the "suffering little brown soldiers." And then, when it suddenly dawned on him they did not have enough to eat, and were even starving to death, he frantically cabled everywhere for food. According to Joaquin, the King of Korea responded to his plea by sending ten thousand sacks of flour "that came with incredible swiftness," and the day was saved for the starving Japanese army.

Ever since that historic moment, Joaquin solemnly declared, the Japanese have scorned their traditional staple food, rice, and turned to eating good nutritious white bread, just like Americans. This bit of foolishness almost cost him the friendship of his dear protégés, Yone Noguchi and Takeshi Kanno.

The short Oriental adventure was Joaquin's last plunge into the outer world. He had been living a strenuous life, from the time he was a boy and crossed the Great Plains, until his return from China at sixty-three. The Eagle on The Hights was aging. From now on he would settle back and enjoy the quiet life, and play the part of the revered patriarch and sage.

CHAPTER NINE

The Patriarch

1900-1913

I

FROM the turn of the century until he died, Joaquin Miller was a Very Important Person. He was especially important in California, where he was regarded as a state jewel, a landmark, a combination of Homer, Shakespeare, Keats and Edwin Markham. Joaquin was a professional Californian, and this endeared him to the climate-conscious people of the state, for he pronounced California "A Grander Greece"—a turgid epithet that may well be resurrected any moment by some enterprising chamber of commerce.

Now that he had assumed the role of the bearded sage, Joaquin became more serious, more grave, more philosophical. He hinted that perhaps he was older than was generally believed—for as everyone knew, with old age came deep wisdom. "The snow of age is on my brow, but spring is in my heart," Joaquin often told his visitors at The Hights, and the apt phrase was widely quoted, even though one alert editor pointed out that it not only resembled Victor Hugo's comment before his death, but was exactly the same, word for word.

Once upon a time the critics would rather have kissed a leper than tossed a kind word Joaquin Miller's way, but now they came trudging up the slope to beg for interviews, for a chance to sit at the master's feet. When he regaled them with the incredible tales of his "old adventurous days," his words were now solemnly written down. The poet even began to display a vein of modesty. "I never did a stroke of work which amounted to anything, or had a thought worth recording," Joaquin informed one interviewer. The man stood transfixed, his mouth agape, and as he said later, he thought the wax in his ears had impaired his hearing. "That is—after the sun went down," Joaquin added hastily.

The poet's habits were carefully copied down for posterity. He rose with the sun. He sipped his breakfast coffee on the porch of the Abbey. He then returned to his bed where, fully clad, he reclined on a couch of cured skins, his head with its long golden-gray hair propped on pillows, and wrote poetry until noon. There was no mention now of the fact that the celebrated poet periodically resorted to drinking whiskey. No. The afternoons were spent in his rose garden, or in meditation. Usually, it was meditation.

No idiosyncrasy of his was ignored. It was faithfully recorded that at the three-o'clock dinner he served plates full of food to his guests, then collected all the tureens on the table and ate directly from them. This effectively restrained anyone from asking for a second helping. The poet did not like conversation at the table, unless he himself initiated it, and he could not bear being interrupted. It was noticed that, with his flowing white beard and high boots, he began to resemble Tolstoy, whom he so much admired, and when the poet was informed he was looking more and more like the simple but infinitely wise old Muzhik philosopher, he nodded and agreed that the description was a fitting one.

The famous visited Joaquin—Roosevelt, Taft, Darrow,

Sarah Bernhardt and others—but most of those who jour-
neyed to The Hights were the usual hangers-on, the celeb-
rity-chasers, the sightseers, the idlers who had nothing better
to do, and then of course there were the lovers of poetry who
considered a trip to The Hights as a low-priced pilgrimage to
Parnassus.

And instead of being turned away as the busybodies that
they were, they found themselves heartily welcomed by the
poet. He was gracious to everyone, no matter who he or she
might be. At first he did not fancy giving out the many auto-
graphs he was asked for, fearing that this would depress the
market, but eventually he gave his signature to anyone who
requested it, and when they begged him to recite poetry he
cheerfully acquiesced—provided the poetry was by Joaquin
Miller. Even the children came to see the patriarch—on
Arbor Day of 1877 school children from Oakland came to
plant 3,000 trees on The Hights. Joaquin wrote his own
funeral elegy and invited the schoolchildren to come and hear
him read it on his pyre. There were many cheers and hand-
claps when he finished.

Stray visitors would wait patiently outside the Abbey for
the poet to come out, talking in low tones so as not to disturb
the genius. Often someone would reverently snip a rose from
the bushes that twined around the porch, and later the flower
would be pressed into a book of Joaquin Miller's verse. A
familiar refrain of these visitors has come down to us today—
"I still have that rose . . ."

Eventually, whenever Joaquin felt like it, he would make
his appearance and bow grandly to the throng. Now he was
dressed in a khaki shirt and trousers—he had discarded his
buckskin shirt because it irritated his skin—a red-fringed

sash around his middle, wearing tasseled jackboots and what usually was described as a red Turkish fez, but in reality was his skullcap.

Joaquin would sit in a rocking chair on the porch and give his silent audiences a chance to see Genius at Work, at work writing poetry, *pure* poetry. The cutting of his pen alone was a dedicated ceremony. Joaquin would carefully inspect a bundle of goose-quills and, after eliminating those that had flaws, would impressively take out his knife. Then, slowly, fastidiously, he would cut the pen. The quill had to be sliced just right, or he would throw it impatiently aside—and then there would be a scramble for the possession of the precious souvenir.

His autograph remained totally unreadable, but at least it now became more distinctive. Above his scrawling signature he would draw a pictograph which he explained was the name the Indians had bestowed on him: Chief Cut-Arrow. This was an arrow broken in two, showing the barb and the feathered shaft. The name Cut-Arrow had been given him, Joaquin would say, after his fight against the Modocs, when an arrow had pierced his head. He had been forced to break off the shaft, pull the flinty head from the back of his neck and the feathered shaft from the front of his jaw. It had hurt.

Joaquin was often asked why he wrote poetry. He had always hated writing, the poet answered, but he felt driven to it by some terrible intangible urge. "My ambition has always been to build a little home and make a modest living by raising something in a garden, and also by practicing law in a quiet way," he confided to more than one person. But he could not help himself—this overwhelming cosmic force out of nowhere drove him to creating poetry.

As visitors had noticed through the years, there were no

newspapers, no magazines, no books in sight on The Hights. However, the favored few who were asked to stay overnight in a cabin always found a volume by Joaquin Miller placed by their bed. The poet professed to have no interest in what was going on in the outside world. "I'm just a hill man," he confessed humbly. But when he walked down the trail to Fruitdale to buy liquor and provisions, he read all the newspapers and magazines he could buy, although he never took them back to The Hights.

If there was no reading material around, there were plenty of pictures to look at. Joaquin would often escort his visitors around the estate and show them the photographs of people he most admired. Many of them were autographed. First of all, there were numerous portraits of Joaquin Miller, Poet of the Sierras. But there were others too—of Whitman, Lord Houghton, Browning, the Rossetti brothers, Millet, Hugo, Andrew Carnegie, Elbert Hubbard, and a caricature drawn by James Swinburne, showing Joaquin—with his hat on—dining with Queen Victoria, the Prince of Wales and Gladstone. There was also a portrait of his idol, Frémont, which Joaquin said was worth a fortune. This masterpiece had been painted on a tablecloth taken from one of the Panama steamers by an artist named Jewett.

Of course, the poet could not be serious, grave and philosophical all the time. He still delighted in praying for rain, and would roar at the astonishment of his guests when they heard the tinkling noise on the roof of the Abbey. He would squeeze the juice from an orange, inflate the skin, and then offer it to a visitor, and he would double over with laughter when the unsuspecting individual tried to peel the fruit. The poet began to find joy in small things.

Joaquin had once referred to his workroom in the Abbey

as the "Holy Grotto," and he had meant it seriously, but now he could afford to be less pretentious. "And now I am going to take you to the Holy of Holies, the place where I go daily to worship, yes, often two and three times a day," he would say solemnly. "No pagan worshipper values his sacred shrine more than I . . ." The poet then would sweep aside the curtains hiding his greasy iron stove where his simple meals were cooked, and stand aside modestly with lowered eyes.

However, there were some people who thought Joaquin did not exactly fit the role of Old Testament Prophet when it came to drinking whiskey. It was felt that he drank far more than was good for a wise old Patriarch, for this propensity, which he had developed so masterfully at an early age, was never to desert him. Harr Wagner defended him and said Joaquin drank like a gentleman. "He was not a periodic drinker like Edgar Allan Poe or James Whitcomb Riley," said Wagner. "He could not be persuaded to take a drink before noon."

The thirsty George Sterling could match bottles with Jack London and all the other hard-drinking young bloods, but, although he was twenty-one years younger than the sage, he had to confess that he was awed by Joaquin's capacity for putting away liquor without being any the worse for it. There was the time—it happened during a lecture tour—when Joaquin outdrank Stoddard, no mean drinker himself, who thought he was about the same age as the poet but actually was five years his junior. Finding his companion under the table, Joaquin sent a message summoning Sterling to take up where Stoddard left off.

Sterling hurried to El Adobe, a dude saloon in Monterey, arriving in the early afternoon. Joaquin insisted that he keep him company at the bar. A few hours later they took the helpless Stoddard to Sterling's cabin in nearby Carmel and deposited him on the bed. Joaquin was in splendid condition and wanted to see the sights, but, as Sterling noted, Stoddard "kept feebly moaning he wanted 'his baby,' whatever that meant."

The poet decided they must look over the Mission in Carmel. "The old Portuguese sexton's daughter accompanied us with a great key," Sterling recorded. "Joaquin devoted his entire attention in trying to get her off guard, but she was too alert . . ."

Later on the two remembered Stoddard and returned to Sterling's cabin, where they found the man dead asleep. "Leave him there," Joaquin commanded. "And you'd better stand by with a drink when he wakes up." The poet then departed, possibly for his home on The Hights, more likely for the nearest doggery.

2

Joaquin may have been a sage, but he was no seer.

His brother George Melvin, who was living in Oregon, wrote him excitedly about the glorious future of aviation. He explained that two people named Wright had made the first flight in a power-driven airplane. George Melvin's imagination was fired. He visualized the day would come when flying a hundred miles or even more in an airplane would be as commonplace as riding to market in a horse and buggy.

The brother told Joaquin that he had taken out a patent on a flying device which, after an experimental try-out, had risen in the air a hundred feet. True, no one had ridden in the contraption, but that would come later. First things had to come first. He asked if Joaquin would invest his spare capital in the venture and become his partner—they would get in on the ground floor together and make a killing.

Joaquin sat down, sharpened his quill, and sternly wrote a big-brother letter of advice.

"Let the flying machine and all flying and flying machines alone!" he commanded. "Keep your feet on the solid ground. It's unnatural to fly: therefore, it will not do. It is only a damn craze."

George Melvin obediently followed the instructions of his famous brother and abandoned the preposterous scheme. There were others, however, who continued the hopeless experiment . . .

3

In five years' time, Joaquin lost through death three people who were dear to him—all of them tenants on The Hights.

His daughter Maud, known as Maud Miller on the stage and as Mrs. Maud MacCormack in private life, had been a fair success on the stage—but no more than that. She abandoned her career and came to live on The Hights, the victim, as Harr Wagner put it, "of many matrimonial escapades."

On Christmas Eve of 1901, Maud died unexpectedly of heart trouble. She was buried near Joaquin's funeral pyre. Her son, Aloysius, was to marry the daughter of Henry Meade Bland, a poet, and the couple had a child—London Bland MacCormack—Joaquin's great-grandson.

(The poet's daughter by his second marriage, Juanita, never married—that is, not in the sense that an ordinary mortal would conceive it. Some time after her father's death she was wedded to the Sun, in rites unrivaled for their content and character. As a newspaper story of this notable event started off: "In a sweetly solemn ceremony, Juanita Miller, daughter of Joaquin, Poet of the Sierras, was married to the sun yesterday . . ." Understandably enough, this mystical union produced no offspring. And as to Joaquin's two obscure sons, George and Harold, we do not know whether they married or left any children.)

Cali-Shasta was the next to go. Ina Coolbrith had cared for the half-Indian girl for seven years and had given her a good education. This beautiful maiden had then left public school to marry a young man connected with the Wells Fargo Express in San Francisco, but, because of "her uncontrollable appetite for liquor," the union was not a success. The Shasta Lily came to live with her father on The Hights. Joaquin treated her tenderly and acknowledged her as his daughter, but their life together was full of reproaches and strife. "What have you given me?" Ina Coolbrith remembered the Shasta Lily crying bitterly as she berated her father. "Your name and this blood! For both of them, I curse you!"

Drowning her sorrows deeper and deeper in the firewater of the white man, Cali-Shasta died a wasted creature, from "over-excess," as a newspaper bluntly put it. She was buried on a hillside near her father's pyre.

Joaquin's mother, Margaret De Witt Miller, was often pictured by visitors on The Hights as a simple-minded woman, now in a state of senility. And yet one wonders. "He is greater than Shakespeare," the old lady once confided to Elbert Hubbard during one of his visits. "Only, do you know, he is such a fool that he is going to write his poems over, but he never does." Evidently the mother was not so foolish in her old age as people would like to think, for the observation shows some insight even if she expressed herself awkwardly. If Joaquin Miller had been more concerned with quality than quantity, his poetry might well rank considerably higher than it does today.

The old lady lived in what was known as the Grandma Miller Cottage on The Hights, a high-peaked frame house, its interior shaped like a tent and lined with canvas. Each week Joaquin placed a bottle of whiskey in her cupboard. People remembered her as a mind-wandering old soul, who would timidly ask a question and then withdraw before a reply could be made. Joaquin treated her tenderly, but obviously regarded her as utterly daft.

Mother Miller died in 1907 at the great age of ninety-two. She too was buried near the pyre. Later, Joaquin presented a bronze bust of this pioneer of the Northwest to the University of Oregon, and today it rests in the school's library.

As if these three deaths were not enough, newspaper dispatches noted on May 11, 1903 from Saratoga that "Mrs. Joaquin Miller and daughter Juanita were prostrated today, after being told by reporters that Joaquin Miller was dead at his home in Oakland." The wife and daughter, who had not seen the poet for years, were described as sorely stricken, but it finally was revealed that the report was false.

4

Joaquin long remembered the "warm sweet spring morning" of April 18, 1906.

He was awakened from sleep at 5:12 a.m. by a slight bump, as if someone had jarred his bed. However, there was no one in the room. He dressed and went out on the porch to have his breakfast coffee. He was greeted by his Oriental gentleman's gentleman with "Ohioa"—according to Joaquin this was pure Japanese. "Ohioa," the poet replied. "Earthquake," then said the Oriental, being a man of few words.

Forty minutes later, from his aerie on The Hights, Joaquin saw wisps of smoke starting to curl over the city. The poet felt a premonition of disaster. He had a feeling he would never see again some "precious manuscripts" that he had cached in the Bohemian Club.

His agitation increased as he "looked down at the dense black smoke" that now began to spiral into the air, and occasionally he could see darts of flames. There on The Hights —a perfect grandstand seat—he was witnessing the great San Francisco fire and earthquake, below him eight miles away, as the crow flies.

Forty-five minutes after the first tremor, the poet could see smoke in sixteen separate places, now rising in ominous columns, and some of the flames were beginning to soar high into the air. Clearly the fire was out of control, for even on his distant cliff he could hear explosions. "My place is on the firing line!" Joaquin later remembered saying. He was speaking to himself, as he was alone.

Joaquin called to the Japanese to hitch his "charger" to the buckboard, and he drove down the hill to Alameda on the waterfront. He ferried across the bay, taking along the horse and buggy, and made a "hard landing" in San Francisco, amidst a mass of half-clad refugees. He drove slowly through the streets, pushing his way through the throng that was headed the other way, to the waterfront, in an effort to reach the Bohemian Club. There was a continual roar of explosions, as the Army was blowing up buildings in the path of the spreading flames. The air became hotter and closer, the crowds denser, until finally the milling mass barred his way.

He was forced to abandon his manuscripts to the fire. He put some women and three children into the buggy, turned around and drove to the ferry. He managed to cram his homeless charges into the boat and take them across to Alameda.

The rest of the day, and far into the night, Joaquin watched the terrible catastrophe from The Hights. The next morning, he made another attempt to get at his private papers in the Bohemian Club. He reached the premises but was unable to enter, for the place was full of drunken soldiers waving bottles. Joaquin was disgusted, for he never had any use for people who could not hold their liquor. He then tried to make his way to Ina Coolbrith's home, intending to take her to the safety of The Hights, but soldiers were patrolling the streets, on watch for looters, and they would not permit him to pass. He went back to The Hights and watched the fire at last burn itself out late in the night of the third day, feeling most disconsolate.

Joaquin lost not only his "precious manuscripts" in the fire—San Franciscans suffered too, for the fire gutted four hundred and ninety city blocks, causing a damage of half a billion dollars—but, indirectly, some other valuable papers as well. In a broken-hearted note, May Foster Carey informed him that almost all the love letters he had written her had been consumed by the holocaust. The news hit the poet hard, until he realized that Mrs. Carey had experienced an even greater loss.

"So my many letters to you were destroyed," he wrote to May. "Too bad, too bad! They would have made you famous."

5

In November, 1906 Joaquin made his last trip East, visiting his wife and daughter at Saratoga. He did not stay with them long, for, as he explained, he had an important appointment to keep with President Theodore Roosevelt at the White House.

While in Washington, Joaquin was introduced to Allan Benson, editor of the TIMES. Benson said his eyes were blinded by the tremendous diamond ring the poet wore and which he described as being big as a carbuncle and gleaming like a star. "A gunman would go crazy now to see such a ring," Benson recalled later.

The editor was equally blinded by the charm of the poet who told him about his many wondrous experiences. He was so overcome that he signed a contract with Joaquin for the story of his life, giving him a $300 advance for publication rights in the Munsey newspapers. The result was, as Van Wyck Brooks put it, "His fabulous autobiography, which contains, one is told, not a syllable of truth!"

Actually, it was not an autobiography, but only the story —as Joaquin remembered it—of his early days on the frontier in Indiana and Oregon. The poet intended to write the entire story of his life, but he soon tired of the task because— this was his excuse—Benson kept harassing him from the moment he turned in his first batch of copy.

"I was dumfounded to see that I could not read a word of it," Benson said. "It was the worst writing I ever saw." The editor insisted that Joaquin read off the manuscript to a stenographer and have it typed. This Joaquin found wearisome —for deciphering his own handwriting was quite a chore— and therefore he left his adventures in later life untold.

The story was widely syndicated in newspapers, and was highly popular. It was not published in book form until 1930, under the title of *Overland in a Covered Wagon*. Mr. Brooks' statement to the contrary, the volume is one of the most believable of all of Joaquin's prose work.

Joaquin visited the White House and was received by President Roosevelt. It is not known what they conferred about, for Joaquin left no mention of the visit, nor did he discuss it at length with anyone as far as is known. We only know that, according to Harr Wagner, Roosevelt "received him coldly." This is surprising for, although Joaquin was a Democrat and Roosevelt a Republican, the President had a special fondness for Westerners, for colorful characters, and for forest conservationists.

Joaquin was not the hero in Washington that he was on the West Coast, and he was more or less ignored by the nation's lawmakers. However, whenever he appeared in the streets he made the usual sensation with children. One day he was out walking and found he was being trailed by a dozen youngsters. "It's Santa Claus!" they whispered to each other in awed tones, for the Christmas holiday was at hand.

Joaquin did not deny he was Santa. But his actions did. He gave the smallest child in the group a penny.

6

In the last decade of his life, Joaquin devoted his time to writing poetry and preaching forest conservation. "He was one of the few genuine American nature-lovers," Percy H. Boynton thought, "but his experiences quite surpassed those of Thoreau or Burroughs or Whitman or even Mark Twain in their elemental vigor." Joaquin exhorted the people of the West to plant more and more trees, and he continued to set the example by putting out thousands of saplings each spring on The Hights.

Joaquin wrote some new verse, but much of his time was spent in working over poems published many years before. It was generally agreed that his verse was greatly improved after being rewritten and polished, but there was no improvement in his prose. He would not, or perhaps could not, resist inserting autobiographical absurdities as footnotes into his books which, as Martin S. Perterson put it, sought "with characteristic lack of taste to glorify an already overglorified life." Bierce continued to condemn "his vanity and general humbuggery that makes his prose so insupportable." "Joaquin is a good fellow, all the same," Bierce wrote Sterling, "and you should not demand of him impossible virtues and a reach of reasonableness that is alien to him."

Joaquin could not be convinced that his footnotes were making him the laughingstock of the more discriminate readers, no matter how often he was warned; and as far as his poetry was concerned, he had no qualms: he knew it was superb. Once he was introduced as the greatest poet in California. "That title belongs to Bret Harte," Joaquin declared, bristling. "I do not represent California, but a little hill called 'The Earth.'" This prompted Edmund Clarence Stedman to remark caustically: "I am surprised that Joaquin did not say 'The Universe.'"

Joaquin started to write the life of Andrew Carnegie, but after he had finished a few chapters, a full-length biography of the steel magnate was published, killing his own project. But other books with his name on the title page kept rolling off the presses.

In 1903 *As It Was in the Beginning* was published, a long poem of ninety-nine outsized pages. "It's great! It's great!" Jack London wrote Joaquin. "You know what you are singing about."

In 1907 Joaquin visited his old home in Canyon City, Oregon. At the behest of the old-timers he wrote a belligerent article about the muddy "six-foot Indian trail" that served as a road between Canyon City and Burns. This protest by the famous writer brought results, for the state soon built a wide road into the town—today it is known as Joaquin Miller Highway. Twenty-five years later this particular essay was published as *A Royal Highway of the World* in a limited edition.

In the same year Joaquin published a long narrative poem of one hundred and fifty-one pages called *Light,* and, although the bard was now seventy, it was saluted as being as fine a poem as he ever had written. This, his last major work, was believed by the *Dictionary of American Biography* to "represent his closest approach to full maturity as a poet."

In 1909 the "Bear Edition" of his works was issued—seven volumes containing all of his poetry and prose that pleased him. Some poems he had discarded altogether, some he had trimmed, and others he had expanded. His vogue now was on the wane, however, for the collected edition sold poorly, with royalties never amounting to more than $260 a year.

Joaquin published his last poem in 1912. It was called "Berkeley"—a tribute to the city and written to order—but the poet, then approaching his seventy-fifth birthday, knew that his imaginative powers were exhausted. "Berkeley" was closely modeled on a poem he had penned years before, "San Diego."

7

The poet was in the winter of his life. He reluctantly gave up his friendships with women now that he had become a septuagenarian, and for the first time in years there was no sweetheart living with him on The Hights; but he did not give up whiskey.

It depressed him that each year he would hear of the death of an old literary friend, even though the feeling was gratifying that he was still alive. Oscar Wilde died as the dissipated Sebastian Melmouth in Paris in 1910. Joaquin's intimates in England—Lord Houghton, Browning, William M. Rossetti—had preceded Wilde to the grave, while Swinburne and Savage-Armstrong soon followed him. Death came to Bret Harte in 1902, and Joaquin with characteristic generosity pronounced his old enemy as "the brightest genius that ever set foot on American soil." Stoddard, the first man Joaquin had known who had a literary reputation, died in 1909.

It seemed as if all "the old crowd" were dead, or dying. It was, as Mark Twain wrote gloomily in July, 1907 on remembering a dinner in London given in honor of Joaquin by Anthony Trollope:

> Trollope is dead, Hughes is dead, Leveson-Gower is dead. Joaquin Miller is white-headed and mute and quiet in his dear mountains.

Twain himself was to go three years later.

For many years Joaquin had pleaded with his daughter Juanita, who was living in New York and Saratoga, to live permanently with him on The Hights. He wrote a pathetic poem—in the form of an open letter—to his daughter, which was widely printed at the time:

> You will come, my bird, Bonita?
> Come! For I, by steep and stone,
> Have built such nest for you, Juanita,
> As not eagle bird hath known.

Juanita, however, refused to be lured West. She appears to have prepared herself for an artistic career, for by 1912 she had spent ten full years in studying singing and composition.

Apparently her only appearance on the stage was at the Empire Theatre in New York, when the students of the Sargent Dramatic School put on a performance for their parents.

In February, 1911 Joaquin was stricken on The Hights by paralysis, and it was believed he was mortally ill. He was taken to Fabiola Hospital in Oakland, and for a while his death seemed imminent. Newspapermen throughout the land prepared his obituary and set it in type with the notation: "Hold."

But Joaquin Miller was not prepared to die, not at this time. He rallied and regained his health, and he demanded to be sent home to The Hights. The poet railed bitterly against the nurses—the "damned starches," as he called them—because they had cut down his whiskey consumption to a single glass a day. This, Joaquin found, was intolerable.

Sterling visited him in the hospital and listened to the poet's outraged complaints about the lack of whiskey. "Without it, all is vanity, and I but a broken reed," he confessed to Sterling. His understanding friend smuggled some brandy into the sickroom, which produced a noticeable improvement in Joaquin's health. He was permitted to return to The Hights.

It was during this stay in the hospital that, in response to a telegram from Joaquin, his wife Abbie and his daughter Juanita finally traveled West. They both took up residence on The Hights to take care of the convalescent.

8

A few months later, Joaquin had recovered. To all appearances he had completely regained his health in 1912. "He was then seventy years old [sic], but his boyishness and zest for living were still with him, and it was difficult to think of him as old," a visitor noted. The poet resumed his life where he had left off before going to the hospital. He seemed to be the same robust individual as before, he worked on his poems, he drank his whiskey and he entertained his guests, although it was noticed that now and then he was apt to doze off in the midst of company. This prompted Ambrose Bierce to dub him "The Drowsy Demon."

At this time Joaquin was ostensibly laboring over a poem. He said it was to be the most momentous work of his literary career, and he guarded the manuscript so jealously that even his wife and daughter knew nothing of the subject. It is probable that this was Joaquin's last joke, his last exaggeration, for no such manuscript was found after his death.

And, strangely enough, in the last years of his life he seemed at last to tire of the over-heavy praise accorded to his work. He now took the attitude that inasmuch as his poems were the product of genius their merits were self-evident and needed no further eulogizing. One day, when a lady was gushing away about the thrills she experienced from reading his verse, Joaquin interrupted her. "Madam," he said coldly, "don't you know that liars go to hell?" This was one of the extremely rare instances when he was unchivalrous toward a woman—providing they were not "damned starches."

Joaquin was honored with several banquets in 1912, and he would always recite "Columbus" in a strong, resonant voice. The poet still was tall and erect, but now he had what was described as "a round duffy face," and his once yellow long hair and beard were almost completely white.

There were other honors. The cabin he had built on the Potomac was purchased by Henry White, former Ambassador to France, and presented to the California State Association of Washington. As mentioned earlier, it was removed to Rock Creek Park in Washington (where it stands on exhibition today) and dedicated as a permanent memorial to the bard. Joaquin wrote a poem that was read at the ceremony: "To My Log Cabin Lovers."

Toward the end of 1912, the poet was interviewed by a newspaperman on The Hights. Joaquin somberly said he knew he could not live forever, but that, when the moment came to depart, at least he would be happy in the knowledge that he would leave behind a name that would shine in the annals of poetry. For some reason, the reporter steered the conversation to Prohibition, which was then the subject of wide agitation.

"I believe in Prohibition," Joaquin said, looking the fellow squarely in the eye. "It is a great cause. I wish it every success."

Joaquin's belated advocacy of Prohibition was printed in many newspapers, but the editors on the West Coast, who knew their man, deleted the statement. And privately, to friends, the poet said that when a person asked a silly question, well, he deserved a silly answer.

9

In the autumn of 1912, shortly before the Presidential election, Joaquin and Gertrude Atherton spoke at a Democratic rally in Oakland. The poet said he had never voted anything but the straight Democratic ticket all his life, and that of course he intended to cast his ballot for Woodrow Wilson. On election day he appeared at the polls and voted. Newspapermen were alarmed at his enfeebled condition. That was his last public appearance.

In December, the poet received Dr. Frederick Cook, the explorer who claimed he had discovered the North Pole but could not prove it. Joaquin complained that he was not permitted to eat any meat but had been put on an ignominious diet of honey and hominy; furthermore, once again his whiskey had been rationed to one glass a day.

In January, 1913 two of his old friends, George Sterling and Herbert C. Thompson, visited him, separately and each for the last time. Sterling found the poet confined to his bed, "a superb and yet pathetic sight." "Truly he looked as we like to imagine that one of the Hebrew patriarchs should have looked," Sterling said.

Sterling, the drinking man, was sympathetic as he listened to Joaquin's laments about his enforced abstinence. His heart went out to the poet when the daily ration of whiskey was doled out to him in the sickroom. Joaquin held the glass aloft, sneered at its size, and growled:

"There, Sterling—what do you think of that? What sort of a drink is that to give a sick man—and only once a day?"

Sterling, a kindred spirit, tried to intervene on behalf of his friend. "I assured Mrs. Miller that if they wished to keep him alive they would better increase, and that handsomely, his daily allotment," Sterling declared. "My advice was not followed, and as I feared . . ."

Thompson said that Joaquin was a completely changed man, without any of his usual poses and postures, and that he resembled "a sweet old farmer." The poet was wrapped in a heavy quilt, his long beard spread out on the bed, and was wearing a golf cap set cockily on his head. Joaquin gloomily complained that his legs were always cold—that he was getting old, and that a person never knew. . . .

Lillie Langtry was appearing on the stage in Oakland, and

early in February of this year of 1913 she asked Harr Wagner to take her to The Hights to see her old friend.

The always gallant Joaquin apologized for being unable to rise from his couch to greet the lady, and he said he was greatly honored by the visit. The Jersey Lily would not hear of that: *she* was being honored, and she hoped to make many another pilgrimage to the aerie of the poet in the years to come. Joaquin seemed to doubt that the actress would ever again walk up to The Hights to visit him. And then, with his courtesy of old, he declared that the lady was as lovely as when he first had met her in London—and he was tactful enough not to remind her that this had been forty long years before. "Ah, beauty and health always remain with the good," he said, beaming on Miss Langtry.

"My greatest thrill," the Jersey Lily told Joaquin, "was to walk up the steps of Lord Houghton's palace on the rose leaves you scattered there for me." The remark greatly pleased Joaquin, and he began to reminisce animatedly about the old London days, but he was gripped with coughing spasms and the visit had to be cut short.

Walking down from The Hights, the actress told Harr Wagner that she feared the pale and wan poet was on his deathbed.

10

Perhaps Joaquin did not know it then, but he was dying. Six weeks before, his physician, Dr. J. H. Stout, had told Abbie and Joaquin that the poet was suffering from diabetes, arteriosclerosis, uremic poisoning and organic complications, and that there was no hope for his life.

"When I die," the poet once had confided to Harr Wagner, "I want to fall prostrate like the giant Sequoia which

I have loved." Unhappily, he was to be bedridden for more than three months.

On Sunday, February 9, Joaquin looked through the windows of the Abbey and admired the glories of the sunset. He seemed in cheerful spirits, and his wife read to him from Tennyson—Joaquin always thought that Tennyson was the second greatest poet in the world. Later, Abbie sang her husband to sleep.

In the middle of the night the poet began to twist on his bed and moan, calling for his dead brother John and for his "Pappy"—his dead father.

"Abbie," he said the next morning, according to his wife, "these are my last hours." And yet he protested violently when it was suggested that Dr. Stout be called for another consultation. In his eyes, the physician had committed a crime in decreeing the whiskey ration, and he wanted to have nothing to do with him. Instead, he permitted Dr. Stark to see him, not as a physician, but as an old friend.

Dr. Stark insisted that he take some medicine, but Joaquin flatly refused.

"Doctor, I am a poet," he said. "It is not poetic to take pills."

Joaquin Miller was determined to keep up the pose, to the end.

Tuesday, the poet was only partly conscious, and so Dr. Stout could be summoned. Again he reiterated that there was no hope. The family notified Joaquin's younger brother, George Melvin, who lived in Eugene, to come to The Hights at once.

On Wednesday, the sick man seemed to improve, but on Thursday morning, February 17, he was found totally unconscious in his bed. Again he rallied, emerged from the coma, and for a while conversed in a clear-headed fashion.

In the afternoon, however, he appeared to be sinking. Juanita drove down the hill—for there was no telephone on The Hights—to ask Colonel Irish to take her father to the hospital. But, by the time they returned, shortly before three o'clock in the afternoon, the poet had closed his eyes forever.

"Just before he died," his wife told the reporters, "he called to the Angels: 'I love you, Abbie, I love you, Abbie.' " And then, she said, the poet's face became relaxed and peaceful, and all was quiet in the room filled with the scent of violet and acacia blooms from his garden.

A few days later, however, Abbie revised her recollection of his final goodbye. The Poet of the Sierras, she said, had cried: "Take me away! Take me away!" and these were accepted and recorded as his last words.

I I

The death of the seventy-five-year-old poet was mourned throughout the nation. In the press, Joaquin Miller often was referred to as the country's greatest bard, or, sometimes more conservatively, as "the most *picturesque* poet in America— perhaps in all the world." The obituaries were impressively long and prominently displayed, and the accounts of his life and death invariably were preceded by an appropriate excerpt from one of his poems. As, for instance, in the New York HERALD:

> Rest, as the harvester rich from his soil,
> Rest you, and rest you for ever and ever.

The day after the poet died, it was announced that for years he had wished to be cremated, and that his ashes were to be scattered over the Sierras. He wanted no religious ceremony to be performed, and he did not want to lie in state in a church. He particularly did not want to be embalmed in an undertaker's parlor. He wanted his body to be taken straight to his funeral pyre, to be burned there by his friends.

His wishes were, in the main, ignored. The undertakers' association howled that the cremation could not be conducted by friends, because this would be a violation of municipal law. And Abbie thought it would be more fitting to have a preacher conduct a regular church service over the body. Later on, she said, after the poet had been embalmed and the undertakers were paid their fee, she would permit the cremation rites.

At ten o'clock on the morning of February 19, Joaquin's body was on display to his friends on The Hights. The friends all appeared, and, unexpectedly, so did thousands of the morbidly curious who had never met, or read a line of, Joaquin Miller, but who had heard that a celebrity had died.

The crowd was restive as The Reverend William Day Simonds, a Unitarian minister, lauded the poet, ranking him ahead of Tennyson, Byron and Whitman. And then, when the time came for the people to file by the coffin for a last glimpse of the poet, the great American public rioted in mob style. The revolting multitude pawed at the face of the bard and even attempted to cut pieces of clothing from his body. What began as a solemn procession degenerated into a mad stampede. Everything on The Hights that was movable was taken away by the souvenir-hunters. The mob broke into the Abbey and gutted the place, carrying away bits of wood and bricks from the chimney, curtains and sheets and whatever was handy.

The mass hysteria prevailed until the police managed to

make their way to the coffin and rescue the corpse of Joaquin Miller. The officers guarded the body as the funeral cortege drove down the winding road to Oakland. There Rupert Schmid, the sculptor who had done busts of Pope Leo XIII, Grant, Rockefeller and Edison, made a death mask.

Public memorial services were held on Sunday, February 20, at the First Unitarian Church in Oakland. Thousands were turned away, but this time there was no mob hysteria—perhaps because it was the Sabbath Day.

The verses of Joaquin Miller were read, and there was a recital of "River of Rest." Colonel Irish was the speaker of the occasion. He declared California should be the first state in the Union to place a man of letters—Joaquin Miller—in the Hall of Fame in Washington. This did not come to pass. The Reverend Simonds announced he was starting a public subscription to erect a life-sized monument of the poet in Oakland. This did not come to pass. Professor William Darmes of the University of California presented a critical estimate of Joaquin's poetry. He prophesied that future generations would conclude that Byron, at his best, was never the equal of Joaquin Miller. This did not come to pass, either.

12

On May 25, 1913, on a beautiful sunny day, a hundred people and more walked up the road to The Hights to the square funeral pyre of Joaquin Miller. It was an orderly crowd, consisting mostly of members of the Bohemian Club of San Francisco and the Press Club, all of whom had known Joaquin. They had come to scatter the ashes of the poet to the winds.

No one was solemn or gloomy; if anything, the people

were gay, as they knew Joaquin would have wanted them to be.

An urn bearing the bard's ashes was placed on the pyre he had built with his own hands. Colonel Irish lighted a torch and mounted the steps of the tomb. He reminded those gathered on The Hights that their "beloved savage was at last truly chained to a star." He applied the torch to the oil-soaked faggots surrounding the urn. The friends of Joaquin Miller watched silently, but not reverently, as the flames shot up, and the urn disintegrated and the soft winds bore away the ashes.

13

The poet had left no will. When his widow took an oath to that effect, she was appointed administrator of the estate. In the absence of a will, the wife automatically received one-half of the estate—estimated at $100,000. Joaquin's daughter Juanita received the other half. Maud and Cali-Shasta were dead. The whereabouts of his two sons by Minnie Myrtle, and of his children by Alice Oliver, were unknown, and they received nothing.

In filing the papers, Abbie wrote on the documents that the matter pertained to the property left by:

"Cincinnatus Heine Miller, frequently known as Joaquin Miller."

Afterword

I

To Ambrose Bierce, Joaquin Miller was "a great soul," praise indeed from the bitter cynic. To Ina Coolbrith, who lived on until 1928, dying in her eighty-sixth year, he was the most "vibrant" man she ever knew. To Herbert C. Thompson, "No man ever called him commonplace." To Mrs. Leslie, who wept when she heard her seventy-five-year-old lover was dead, he "was supreme in whatever role he essayed." To May Foster Carey, he was "just a big boy, a sweet child." "He did pose, I know," she added, "but I think that most great men assume a pose toward the world."

To George Sterling, of course the man posed and fibbed, but: "All were indeed harmless. Whatever pretenses and exaggerations as to his early life he promulgated or allowed to persist as colorful legends, never could he have lied to inflict harm or pain." To Andrew Carnegie (who, as was not revealed until after Joaquin's death, had given the poet an annual pension of $900 for many years) his was "a noble voice." "One thing about Joaquin was that he was never a pretender," stated Fremont Older. "He never pretended he didn't like whiskey." To Walt Whitman: "Miller is big, wholesome, does things his own way, has lived in the open, stands alone—is a real critter: I rate him highly."

To Edwin Markham, as wretched a poetaster as ever lived,

284

and who was to step into Joaquin's shoes and become California's Bard:

> Poet once I saw you hoeing
> While a song in you was growing. . . .

a rhyme which surely must have caused even Joaquin Miller to wince in his grave.

And to his daughter Juanita, as she remarked to Stuart P. Sherman: "Did you ever hear of anyone like Joaquin Miller in all the world? Wasn't he unique?"

2

Briefly, in bringing to an end the story of the imaginary and real adventures in the life of Joaquin Miller, it should be remembered that he is considered here (as he should have been, and usually was, considered in his lifetime) as a *personality*, not as a poet. A person of meager poetic talents, he made his mark and won world-wide recognition—but because he was the man he was.

As a poet, he is generally ignored today, but not entirely so.

The authoritative *Cambridge History of American Literature* thought his debt to Byron was quite obvious, but that he was by no means purely the sedulous ape. Its editors disparaged him as a poet of ideas, but concluded "he could use to the full his immense energy—this was his chief excellence." Years after the poet's death the LITERARY DIGEST thought it was his life that mattered—and the magazine described this life as a combination of Lincoln and Byron and Tom Mix.

To the critic Ernest Sutherland Bates, it was the man who counted, not the poet. Bates conceived Joaquin Miller as being an authentic part of the old West, his aim being "to celebrate on an heroic scale the freedom and beauty" of its pioneer days.

To C. C. Goodwin in his *As I Remember Them:*

> A head of gold, breast and arms of silver, but all the rest potters' clay. A half-savage chained to a star. Had he learned a little discipline in his youth who knows what he might not have achieved!

To the *Dictionary of American Biography* he was "the splendid poseur all his life." This work is both harsh and kind in its appraisal of the Poet of the Sierras:

> Banal, half literate, and imitative, as much of his writing was, he told the simple truth when he said to acquaintances that he wrote neither for fame or money, "but because I can't help it." His novels and plays are now dead, and most of his poetry, but he himself will long remain a living tradition in the annals of Western literature.

It is true that today most of his poetry is dead, but not all of it. In the sixth edition of the *Oxford Anthology of American Literature*, published as recently as 1945, there are printed four poems by Joaquin Miller: "Columbus," "Kit Carson's Ride," "Crossing the Plains," and "Songs of Creation."

"What one should remember," Percy H. Boynton declared in his *American Poetry*, "is that his poetry is an eloquent and often beautiful evidence of an abounding American youth, manhood and old age. But people cannot know this unless they read Miller."

"When 'Joaquin' Miller died two or three years ago," Professor Boynton wrote elsewhere, "very few people paid any attention to the fact, and some of these were a little

amused that the Pacific Coast took his loss so seriously, setting this down to characteristic 'native son' enthusiasm. . . .
Yet Miller had really grown up with the country, and in both
his career and his work had recorded the stirring melodrama
of frontier life."

Bruce Weirick in his *From Whitman to Sandburg in
American Poetry* compared Joaquin Miller to the American
poet Sidney Lanier, inasmuch as "both lived in a dream
world." But, Professor Weirick concluded, "Miller was more
vital, perhaps, more inclusive, less a prig, less afraid of life,
and more desirous of really accepting the universe." Weirick
found Joaquin by no means as subtle, as elevated, as polished
a poet as Lanier, but "a looser, a more natural writer . . .
more gorgeous, more exotic."

Perhaps the fairest estimate of Joaquin Miller the Poet was
made in the *Literary History of the United States*, published
in 1948:

> Except for his influence, which was not lasting, and his
> reputation, always slightly tainted with ridicule, Miller
> seems of little account today. His long verse dramas, his
> panoramic and tempestuous narratives of the Indian coun-
> try, Nicaragua, the mountains, and the deserts, are mainly
> sound and fury. The poet's own posturing, his bald self-
> aggrandizement, made him a character, though he was only
> in flashes a true poet. He wrote through a long life many
> books, but a large proportion of what he wrote is chaff.

3

In the early 1920's, there was a momentary revival of interest in the poetry of Joaquin Miller. Stuart P. Sherman, then
a Professor at the University of Illinois, was approached by
the editor George H. Putnam to edit and write an introduc-

tion for a one-volume edition of the poet's works. Putnam made it clear that "the literary worker accepting the editorial task should be one who had a full measure of appreciation for Miller's work and who was able to commend his productions to the public today."

Sherman replied diffidently. He thought the poet "a striking and picturesque figure in our Western literature," but he cautiously declared that "I don't know Miller's work as a whole quite well enough to say just how I rank him."

Professor Sherman received a $300 advance for his services, and he did the job. He found it a chore, however, and complained about "The lack of all kinds of trustworthy biographies . . ." In a private letter to W. C. Brownell he commented that "just now [I] am trying to do something with that unmitigated liar, Joaquin Miller." Sherman's collection was published in 1923, and the reading public was apathetic.

"His adventures," Stuart P. Sherman wrote in his outline of the life of Joaquin Miller, "have never been adequately written." This book is a modest attempt to fill the gap.

4

The Hights with its seventy thousand trees was sold to the city of Oakland in 1919 for $33,000, with the poet's daughter Juanita reserving life tenure. Each year, thousands of people climb Joaquin Miller Road to reach the highland area that is now a memorial Joaquin Miller Park. There are hiking trails, community kitchens and picnic grounds.

The estate is not what it used to be in Joaquin's time, however, as a forest fire in 1933 ravaged some of the extensive grounds. The people who come are not the same either: they love the open air, the trees and the camp fires, but they have no interest in the poetic sentimentalities and heroics of an era with which they have little in common and of which most of them know less.

Miss Juanita Miller, at this writing, still lives on The Hights. As a gracious old lady, widely admired, she is now standing guard over what remains of her father's once famous past. Anyone writing to her for directions how to reach the estate will receive detailed information, deeply moving in its minute descriptiveness, lest one misses the place that still means a good deal to her and to the many who continue to cherish Joaquin Miller's memory.

Once the chance visitor on the trail of the poet has passed a rustic gate, he is requested to call out loudly, "Miss Miller!" several times, and she will join him in his pilgrimage—a poignant attempt to conjure up Joaquin's spirit as it seems to hover over The Hights.

In 1870, when Joaquin Miller set out to conquer England —an ardent "unsophisticate" on a one-man crusade—he stopped by the graves of famous poets and recited odes of his own composition to celebrate their glories, and offered them for sale to amazed bystanders, for a small sum.

Now, some of his own poems are on sale in a similar setting —"Papa's poems," as his daughter calls them—and the price is $2. The wind of oblivion is rustling in the trees that Joaquin Miller planted, and it seems that the cycle has come to a full close, on a full life. But who ever knows which way the wind is blowing?

Selected Bibliography

JOAQUIN MILLER is seldom considered in print today, but in the past an enormous amount of wordage was devoted to him in books, magazines and newspapers. Thus this is a *selected* and not a complete bibliography. Nor is any claim made here that the listing of Joaquin Miller's writings is complete. Just a few of his many magazine articles are noted—only the ones pertinent to the text. And none of the many poems he first published in magazines are listed.

For readers who wish to delve further into the life of Joaquin Miller, the biographies written by Harr Wagner (1929) and Martin S. Peterson (1937) are particularly recommended. The *California Diary*, edited by John S. Richards, and the sketch of Miller's life written by Stuart P. Sherman as an introduction to the one-volume edition of collected poems (1923) are most valuable. The best of the magazine articles are those written by George Sterling and Herbert C. Thompson.

The author has consulted all of the listings below with the exception of the thesis written by Frank R. Reade, which has been unavailable.

There has never been published a volume of Joaquin Miller's letters, possibly because his handwriting is all but unreadable.

BOOKS

Beadle, J. H. *Western Wilds, and the Men Who Redeem Them.* Detroit, 1877.

Bierce, Ambrose. *The Letters of,* ed. by Bertha Clarke Pope. San Francisco, 1922.

Boynton, Percy H., ed. *Anthology of American Poetry.* New York, 1918.

Brooks, Van Wyck. *Sketches in Criticism.* New York, 1932.

————. *The Times of Melville and Whitman.* New York, 1947.

————. *The Confident Years: 1885–1915.* New York, 1952.

Brown, T. Alston. *A History of the New York Stage.* Vols. II, III. New York, 1903.

Bruce, John. *Gaudy Century.* New York, 1948.

California. *American Guide Series.* New York, 1939.

Cambridge History of American Literature. Vol. III. New York and Cambridge, 1921.

Carey, C. H. *History of Oregon.* Portland, 1922.

Castro, Adolphe De. *Portrait of Ambrose Bierce.* New York, 1929.

Clapp, John B., and Edgett, Edwin F. *Players of the Present.* Part III. New York, 1899.

Clemens, Samuel. *Mark Twain in Eruption,* ed. by Bernard DeVoto. New York, 1940.

De Voto, Bernard. *Mark Twain's America.* New York, 1932.

Dictionary of American Biography. Vol. 12. New York, 1933.

Dunham, Sam C. *Men Who Blaze the Trail.* (Introduction by Joaquin Miller.) New York, 1913.

Elliot, Alexander, ed. *Hood in Scotland.* Dundee, 1885.

Fatout, Paul. *Ambrose Bierce.* University of Oklahoma, 1951.

Glaenzer, Richard B. *Decorative Art in America, a Lecture by Oscar Wilde.* New York, 1906.

Goodwin, C. C. *As I Remember Them.* Salt Lake City, 1913.

Goulder, W. A. *Reminiscences: Incidents in the Life of a Pioneer in Oregon and Idaho.* Boise, 1909.

Gregory, Horace, and Zaturenska, Marya. *A History of American Poetry: 1900–46.* New York [c. 1946].

Hale, Edward Everett. *The Letters of* (2 vols.), ed. by Edward E. Hale, Jr. Vol. II. Boston, 1917.

Halline, Allan G., ed. *American Plays.* New York, 1935.

Halsey, Francis W. *American Authors and Their Homes.* New York, 1901.

Hare, Augustus. *Story of My Life* (4 vols.). Vol. IV. New York, 1869–1901.

Harte, Bret. *The Letters of,* ed. by Geoffrey Bret Harte. Boston and New York, 1926.

Hawthorne, Julian. *Shapes That Pass.* New York, 1938.

Hill, Walter M. *A Rare First Edition—The Story of Joaquin Miller's "Pacific Poems."* Chicago, 1915.

Hubbard, Elbert. *A Little Journey to the Home of Joaquin Miller.* East Aurora, N.Y., 1902.

Kanno, Takeshi. *The Passing of Joaquin and Fragments of Creation-Dawn.* Brooklyn [1928].

Keiser, Albert. *The Indian in American Literature.* New York, 1933.

Langtry, Lillie (Lady de Bathe). *The Days I Knew.* New York, 1925.

Leslie, Miriam F. *California.* New York, 1887.

Lewis, Lloyd, and Smith, Henry Justin. *Oscar Wilde Discovers America.* New York [1936].

McWilliams, Carey. *Ambrose Bierce.* New York, 1929.

Markham, Edwin. *California the Wonderful.* New York [1914].

Mason, Mary Murdoch. *Mae Madden.* (Introduction by Joaquin Miller.) Chicago, 1876.

Miller, Joaquin. *Specimens.* Portland, Ore., 1868.

———. *Joaquin, et al.* Portland, Ore., 1869. (Reissued in London, 1872.)

———. *Songs of the Sierras.* London, 1871. (Also Boston, 1871, and Toronto, 1871.) (Reissued in Boston, 1872, 1873, 1877 and Chicago, 1893.)

———. *Life Amongst the Modocs: Unwritten History.* London, 1873. (Also published under titles of *Unwritten History: Life Among the Modocs,* Hartford, 1874; *Paquita, the Indian Heroine,* Hartford, 1881; *My Own Story,* Chicago, 1890; *My Life Among the Indians,* Chicago, 1892.)

———. *Songs of the Sun-Lands.* Boston, 1873.

———. *The Ship in the Desert.* Boston, 1875.

———. *First Fam'lies of the Sierras.* Chicago, 1876.

———. *The One Fair Woman.* New York, 1876.

———. *The Baroness of New York.* New York, 1877.

———. *The Danites, and Other Choice Selections from the Writings of Joaquin Miller,* ed. by A. V. D. Honeyman. New York, 1878.

———. *Songs of Italy.* London, 1878.

———. *Songs of Far-Away Lands.* London, 1878.

————. *Shadows of Shasta.* Chicago, 1881.

————. *The Danites in the Sierras.* (Revised edition of *First Fam'lies of the Sierras.*) Chicago, 1881.

————. *The Danites in the Sierras.* (A Drama in Four Acts.) San Francisco, 1882, and London, 1882.

————. *Forty-Nine.* (Revised and enlarged edition of the story as originally appeared in OVERLAND MONTHLY.) San Francisco, 1882.

————. *Forty-Nine.* (An Idyll Drama of the Sierras.) San Francisco, 1882.

————. *Memorie and Rime.* Philadelphia, 1884.

————. *The Destruction of Gotham.* New York and London, 1886.

————. *The Little Gold Miners of the Sierras, and Other Stories.* Boston, 1886.

————. *Songs of the Mexican Seas.* Boston, 1887.

————. *In Classic Shades, and Other Poems.* Chicago, 1890.

————. *Songs of the Summer Lands.* Chicago [1893].

————. *An Illustrated History of the State of Montana* . . . (2 vols.). Chicago, 1894.

————. *Songs of the Soul,* San Francisco, 1896.

————. *Complete Works of,* in One Volume. London, 1897, and San Francisco, 1900. (Reissued in San Francisco, 1902).

————. *A Song of Creation.* San Francisco, 1899.

————. *Chants for the Boer.* San Francisco, 1900.

————. *True Bear Stories.* Chicago, 1900. (Reissued in Portland, Ore., 1949.)

————. *As It Was in the Beginning.* San Francisco, 1903.

————. *The Building of the City Beautiful.* Philadelphia, 1905. ("Three small editions of parts of this book appeared in 1894" —Joaquin Miller.)

————. *Light: A Narrative Poem.* Boston, 1907.

————. *Complete Poems,* in Seven Volumes. San Francisco, 1908. (Reissued in Six Volumes, San Francisco, 1909.)

————. *Trelawney with Shelley and Byron.* Pompton Lakes, N.J., 1922.

————. *Poetical Works of,* in One Volume, ed. by Stuart P. Sherman. New York, 1923.

———. *Overland in a Covered Wagon,* ed. by Sidney G. Firman. New York and London, 1930.

———. *A Royal Highway of the World,* ed. by Alfred Powers. Portland, Ore., 1932.

———. *Adah Isaacs Menken,* ed. by E. B. Hill. (Reprinted from San Francisco CALL, 1892). Ysleta, Texas, 1934.

Miller, Juanita. *About "The Hights" with Juanita Miller.* Oakland, 1917.

———. *My Father, C. H. Joaquin Miller, Poet.* Oakland, 1941.

Mulford, Prentice. *Prentice Mulford's Story.* London, 1913.

Noel, Joseph. *Footloose in Arcadia.* New York, 1940.

Noguchi, Yone. *The Story of Yone Noguchi, Told by Himself.* London, 1914.

Odell, George C. D. *Annals of the U.S. Stage.* Vols. X, XI. New York, 1939.

Oregon. *American Guide Series.* Portland, 1940.

Oregon Almanac. *Almanac for 1950.* (Sponsored by the Joaquin Miller Associates.)

Paine, Albert Bigelow. *Mark Twain.* Three Volumes. New York, 1912.

Pattee, Fred L. *A History of American Literature.* New York [1915].

Pemberton, Edgar. *Life of Bret Harte.* New York, 1903.

Peterson, Martin Severin. *Joaquin Miller, Literary Frontiersman.* Stanford University and London [1937].

Quinn, Arthur H. *A History of the American Drama* . . . New York, 1927.

Reade, Frank R. *Cincinnatus Hiner Miller: A Critical Biography.* ("Completed at the University of Virginia"), 1926.

Richards, John S., ed. *Joaquin Miller: His California Diary, Beginning in 1855 and Ending in 1857.* Seattle, 1936.

Riley, James Whitcomb. *The Letters of,* ed. by William Lyon Phelps. Indianapolis, 1930.

Sadleir, Michael. *Trollope: A Commentary.* New York, 1947.

San Francisco. *American Guide Series.* New York, 1938.

Spiller, Robert E., ed., and others. *Literary History of the United States.* Three Volumes. New York, 1948.

Stoddard, Charles W. *Exits and Entrances.* Boston, 1903.

Sutherland, Howard V. *Out of the North.* New York, 1913.
Traubel, Horace. *With Walt Whitman in Camden.* Boston, 1906.
Vedder, Henry C. *American Writers of Today.* New York, Boston, Chicago, 1894.
Wagner, Harr. *Joaquin Miller and His Other Self.* San Francisco, 1929.
Walford, Lucy B. *Memories of Victorian England.* New York and London, 1912.
Walker, Franklin. *San Francisco's Literary Frontier.* New York, 1939.
Walterhouse, Roger R. *Bret Harte, Joaquin Miller, and the Western Local Color Story* . . . University of Chicago, 1939.
Washington, D.C. *American Guide Series.* New York, 1942.
Watts-Dunton, Theodore. *The Life and Letters of* (Two Volumes), ed. by Thomas Hake and Arthur Compton-Rickett. London, 1916.
Weirick, Bruce. *From Whitman to Sandburg in American Poetry.* New York, 1928.
Wells, Harry L. *History of Siskiyou County.* Oakland, 1881.
Winslow, Kathryn. *Big Pan-Out.* New York [1951].
Young, Rose. *The Record of the Leslie Woman Suffrage Commission, Inc., 1917–1929.* New York, 1929.
Zeitlin, Jacob, and Woodbridge, Homer. *Life and Letters of Stuart P. Sherman.* Two Volumes. New York, 1929.

MAGAZINES

AMERICAN COLLECTOR. "Joaquin Millerania," by Henry Meade Bland. Vol. 4, 1927.
AMERICAN LITERATURE. "A Note on Joaquin Miller," by Fred W. Lorch. Vol. 3, Jan., 1931.
———. "A Note on Columbia College (Ore.)," by Royal A. Gettman. Vol. 3, Jan., 1932.
AMERICAN MERCURY. "Joaquin Miller," by George Sterling. Vol. 7, 1926.
ARENA. "A Day with Joaquin Miller," by Helen E. Gregory-Flesher. March, 1895.

———. "The Little Brown Men of Nippon," by Joaquin Miller. July, 1904.

———. "The Chinese Exclusion Act," by Joaquin Miller. Oct., 1904.

———. "Joaquin Miller: A Nature-Loving Poet," by B. O. Flower. Dec., 1904.

———. "Looking Backwards from The Hights," by Helen Ellsworth Wright. Dec., 1904.

———. "Rambles in Boston with the Poet of the Sierras." (Unsigned.) Feb., 1907.

———. "A Conversation with Joaquin Miller." (Unsigned.) Feb., 1907.

BOOKMAN. "The Wild Joaquin," by Bailey Millard. Dec., 1908.

———. "Joaquin Miller in England." (Unsigned.) April, 1913.

———. "A Sierra Poet in the Making," by Herbert C. Thompson. July, 1920.

CALIFORNIA MAIL BAG. "California's New Poet." (Unsigned.) Aug., 1871.

CRAFTSMAN. "Joaquin Miller; His Life and His Art," by Henry Meade Bland. Vol. 20, 1911.

CRITIC. "Shadows of the Shasta." (Unsigned.) Vol. 1, 1881.

———. "Joaquin Miller." (Unsigned.) Jan., 1892.

CURRENT OPINION. "The Passing of Joaquin Miller." (Unsigned.) April, 1913.

DARK BLUE. "Mr. Miller's 'Songs of the Sierras,' " by G. F. Armstrong (later known as George Francis Savage-Armstrong). Vol. 2, 1872.

FRASER'S. "Joaquin Miller's 'Songs of the Sierras,' " (Unsigned.) Sept., 1871.

FRONTIER. "The Border Days of Joaquin Miller, 1854–70," by Martin S. Peterson. May, 1931.

———. "Letters of Joaquin Miller," ed. by Beatrice B. Beebe. Jan., 1932.

———. "More Letters of Joaquin Miller," ed. by Beatrice B. Beebe. March, 1932.

———. "Joaquin Miller and His Family," ed. by Beatrice B. Beebe. May, 1932.

FRONTIER AND MIDLAND. "Joaquin Miller's California Diary," by John S. Richards. Vol. 16, Autumn, 1935.

GODEY'S LADY'S BOOK AND MAGAZINE. "Joaquin Miller as a Botanist," by Alfred C. Stokes. Jan., 1877.

GOLDEN ERA. "Mrs. Frank Leslie," by Joaquin Miller. May, 1887.

HEARST'S MAGAZINE. "The Poet of the Sierras," by Elbert Hubbard. April, 1913.

HARPER'S MONTHLY. "Songs of the Sierras." (Unsigned.) Dec., 1871.

HARPER'S WEEKLY. "News from the Klondike," by Tappan Adney. July 9, 1898.

INDIANA MAGAZINE OF HISTORY. "The Indiana Boyhood of the Poet of the Sierras." June, 1934.

INTERNATIONAL BOOK REVIEW. "The Poet of the Sierras as I Knew Him," by Herbert C. Thompson. Nov., 1925.

LAKESIDE. "The Border Life of Joaquin Miller," by Clint Parkhurst. Aug., 1872.

LIPPINCOTT'S. "How I Became a Writer of Books," by Joaquin Miller. July, 1886.

LITERARY DIGEST. "On the Collected Works of Joaquin Miller." (Unsigned.) April 23, 1898.

———. "Close-up of the Poet of the Sierras." (Unsigned.) Nov. 25, 1925.

LITERARY WORLD. "Joaquin Miller in His Cabin," by Faith Wynne. May 30, 1885.

LOUISIANA HISTORICAL QUARTERLY. "Joaquin Miller in New Orleans," by Arlin Turner. Vol. 22, 1939.

MODERN LANGUAGE QUARTERLY. "Some Letters of Joaquin Miller to Lord Houghton," ed. by Clarence Gohdes. June, 1942.

MUNSEY'S. "The Poet of the Sierras," by Henry V. Clarke. June, 1893.

NATION. "Joaquin Miller and Japan," by S. Tsushima. May 29, 1913.

NEW ENGLANDER. "Songs of the Sun-Lands." (Review, unsigned.) Jan., 1874.

———. "The Ship in the Desert." (Review, unsigned.) Jan., 1876.

New Republic. "Joaquin Miller," by Percy H. Boynton. Feb. 24, 1917.

New York History. "Mrs. Frank Leslie: New York's Last Bohemian," by Madeleine B. Sterne. Jan., 1949.

North American. "The Chinese Exclusion Act," by Joaquin Miller. Dec., 1901.

Occult Review. "Some Personal Reminiscences of Prentice Mulford." (Unsigned.) Dec., 1915.

Oregon Historical Society Quarterly. "Reminiscences of Joaquin Miller and Canyon City," by Herbert C. Thompson. Dec., 1944.

———. "Joaquin Miller: Lawyer, Poet, Judge in Canyon City," by Howard McKinley Corning. June, 1946.

Oregon Native Son and Historical Magazine. "Crossing the Plains," by Isaac V. Mossman. Nov.–Dec., 1900, Jan.–Feb., 1901.

Outing. "Poet of the Sierras." (Unsigned.) June, 1905.

Out West. "Joaquin Miller As I Saw Him," by Howard L. Terry. April, 1913.

———. "Joaquin Miller," by Marian Taylor. Feb., 1914.

———. "Some Memories of Joaquin Miller," by John P. Irish. Feb., 1914.

———. "Miller, Friend," by Bessie I. Sloan. Feb., 1914.

Overland. "Sketch of Joaquin Miller," by W. L. Hill. Vol. 8, 1872.

———. "A Ride Through Oregon," by Joaquin Miller. Vol. 8, 1872.

———. "Poet of the Sierras," by Charles W. Stoddard. Vol. 27, 1896.

———. "Greater Texas," by Joaquin Miller. May, 1901.

———. "Joaquin Miller's After Dinner Speech," by Myrtle E. Akin. Sept., 1908.

———. "Joaquin Miller's Cabin," by E. B. Sherburne. Feb., 1913.

———. "Joaquin Miller, Poet," by Marian Taylor. Vol. 63, 1914.

———. "My Memories of Joaquin Miller," by Abbie Miller. Feb., 1920.

————. "A Broad Estimate of the Poet," by W. C. Morrow. Feb., 1920.

————. "The Human Side of Joaquin Miller," by George Wharton Jones. Feb., 1920.

————. "A Last Visit," by John Jury. Feb., 1920.

————. "California's Great Poet," by M. Shipley. Feb., 1920.

————. "Joaquin Miller and His Books," by Henry Meade Bland. Feb., 1920.

————. "Mostly about Joaquin Miller," by Herbert Bashford. Feb., 1920.

————. "Personal Reminiscences of Joaquin Miller," by Harr Wagner. Feb., 1920.

————. "Justice to Joaquin Miller," by Ella Sterling Mighels. July, 1926.

————. "Fighting the Indians with Joaquin Miller," by Beatrice B. Beebe. Feb., 1929.

SOUTHERN MAGAZINE. "An Hour with Joaquin Miller," by C. S. Brown. Vol. 5, 1873.

SUNSET. "Joaquin Miller's Printshop Towel," by Mabel C. Redington, Sept., 1906.

————. "Joaquin Miller," by Hamlin Garland. June, 1913.

TRANSACTIONS OF THE OREGON PIONEERS' ASSOCIATION. "Joaquin Miller." 1899.

Index

		DATE DUE	